Essence of HINDU Religion and Philosophy

Essence of HINDU Religion and Philosophy

D. Jagannatha Rao

Viva Books

New Delhi | Mumbai | Chennai | Kolkata | Bengaluru | Hyderabad | Kochi | Guwahati

Publisher's note

First Published 2012
Reprinted 2013, 2015, 2017, 2018, 2024

Viva Books Private Limited

- 4737/23, Ansari Road, Daryaganj, New Delhi 110 002
  Tel. 42242200, 23258325, 23283121, Email: vivadelhi@vivagroupindia.net
- 76, Service Industries, Shirvane, Sector 1, Nerul, Navi Mumbai 400 706
  Tel. 27721273, 27721274, Email: vivamumbai@vivagroupindia.net
- Megh Tower, Old No. 307, New No. 165, Poonamallee High Road, Maduravoyal, Chennai 600 095, Tel. 23780991, 23780992, E-mail: vivachennai@vivagroupindia.net
- B-103, Jindal Towers, 21/1A/3 Darga Road, Kolkata 700 017
  Tel. 22816713, Email: vivakolkata@vivagroupindia.net
- 7, GF, Sovereign Park Aptts., 56-58, K. R. Road, Basavanagudi, Bengaluru 560 004
  Tel. 26607409, Email: vivabangalore@vivagroupindia.net
- 101-102, Moghal Marc Apartments, 3-4-637 to 641, Narayanguda, Hyderabad 500 029
  Tel. 27564481, Email: vivahyderabad@vivagroupindia.net
- First Floor, Beevi Towers, SRM Road, Kaloor, Kochi 682 018
  Tel. 0484-2403055, 2403056, Email: vivakochi@vivagroupindia.net
- 232, GNB Road, Beside UCO Bank, Silpukhuri, Guwahati 781 003
  Tel. 0361-2666386, Email: vivaguwahati@vivagroupindia.net

www.vivagroupindia.com

ISBN: 978-81-309-1987-4

Published by Vinod Vasishtha for Viva Books Private Limited, 4737/23 Ansari Road, Daryaganj, New Delhi 110 002.

Printed & bound in India by Replika Press, Kundli, Haryana

S0000

Contents

Preface

This book aims to provide a bird's eye view (along with a deeper understanding) of all aspects of Hindu religion and its various philosophies to the general reader. The book also helps the students of Indology, Indian Studies and Ancient Indian History to get a comprehensive perspective about Hindu religion. One important feature of the book is that it discusses the origins of the Vedic religion in the light of latest discoveries and evidences.

While the book deals with all aspects of the Hindu religion, the most important feature of the book however, is the discussion of several prominent Hindu concepts according to their number symbolism (Annexure 4 and 5). This has not been attempted anywhere and in any other book so far.

Literature pertaining to Hindu religion and philosophy is an ocean in itself. One life time is not sufficient for anyone to understand in depth, all aspects pertaining to Hindu religion and its philosophy. While writing this book, I have drawn material from many sources - commentaries by various Acharyas, originals as well as translated editions of various works, books by present day scholars, Puranas, Shastras, and Scriptures and also some internet sources.

Several scholars, friends and acquaintances have guided me in the preparation of this book. They have also patiently read through various chapters of the book, (in draft form), and made valuable comments and suggestions from time to time. This has greatly helped me in presenting balanced views on various aspects of religion as well as philosophy. I thank all of them for their valuable support, guidance, comments and help in writing this book. I also thank the publishers for bringing out this book in record time.

Lastly, it is my sincere duty to thank the 'Divine Grace', whose benevolence has guided me at every step, in writing this book.

Bangalore
3/6/2011

D. Jagannatha Rao
(djrao303@yahoo.com)

1

An Introduction to Hindu Religion

SANATANA DHARMA

Hinduism is the oldest living organized religion in the world (with its roots pre-dating history). It has primarily evolved from the Vedic religion of the Aryans which is often referred to as 'Vaidika Dharma' (Religion of the Vedas) or 'Sanatana Dharma' (Ancient and Eternal religion). The concepts of Dharma, Karma and Brahman (the Supreme Being), form the three pillars of this 'Sanatana Dharma'.

Unlike other world religions (Ex. Christianity, Islam, Buddhism, etc.), Hinduism did not originate from a single person, a single book, a single place or at a single point of time. That is why; Hinduism does not have a unified system of belief, or a doctrinal authority (like the Church), a single philosophy or even a single faith. Over several millennia, many religious sub-sects have evolved within the broad spectrum of the Hindu Religion, as can be seen today by the wide variety of sub-sects, customs, traditions, practices, philosophies, beliefs and modes of worship, all of which form part of Hindu religion.

Reference to the word 'Hindu' (derived from the River Sindhu) was initially made by foreigners to represent a geographical identity and only much later did the word take on a religious connotation. Hindus did not use this name for themselves until about the fourteenth century CE, and even then it was sparingly used.

DEFINING HINDU RELIGION

It is difficult to provide any one single definition for Hindu Religion, as it constitutes a complexity of beliefs, social values, customs, traditions, gods, philosophies, ways of life, ethnic and cultural diversity along with a complex society of followers speaking a wide variety of languages.

Dr. Radhakrishnan explicitly stated that Hinduism cannot be 'defined' but is to be only 'experienced'. The Supreme Court Chief Justice P.B. Gajendragadkar in 1995, in a ruling, described Hinduism as follows:

> *When we think of Hindu religion, unlike other religions of the world, the Hindu religion does not claim any one prophet; it does not worship any one god; it does not subscribe to any one dogma; it does not believe in any one philosophic concept; it does not follow any one set of religious rites and performances; in fact, it does not appear to satisfy the narrow traditional features of any religion or creed. It may be broadly described as a way of life and nothing more.*

The Supreme Court largely concurred with Bal Gangadhar Tilak's defining features of Hinduism in another case: *Acceptance of Vedas with reverence, recognition of the fact that the means or ways to salvation are diverse and the realization of the truth that the number of gods to be worshipped is large, that indeed is the distinguishing feature of Hinduism.*

Hindu Religion can be said to be largely based on the practice of Dharma. It can probably be described as an umbrella of religious beliefs and diverse systems of philosophy and thought, broadly based on Vedic traditions.

UNIQUE CHARACTERISTICS OF HINDU RELIGION

Hindu Religion – its religious doctrines, traditions and practices are inextricably linked to the culture, ethos and demographics of India. Despite its diversity of doctrines, traditions and practices, the Hindu religion exhibits certain unique and easily identifiable common characteristics along with a common core of values and beliefs which distinguish it from other religions of the world. Some of these concepts have become so popular across the world, that they have entered the dictionaries of all most all the major languages of the world. Prominent common Hindu beliefs include:

1. ***Dharma***: The concept of Dharma has a very wide range of meanings. Even though it is normally considered as the righteous way of life, the interpretation of the concept changes with a person's age, class, occupation, gender, etc. For example, the 'Brahmacharya' dharma is different from 'Grihasta' dharma and 'Stree-dharma' is different from 'Purusha dharma'. The concept of Dharma has been separately discussed in detail in Chapter 3.
2. ***Kama***: Kama includes all the natural desires of man, including wealth and all the sensual pleasures. Kama is considered as one of the four 'Purusharthas' (human-ends).
3. ***Samsara***: It is the cycle of life, birth, death and re-birth (Punarjanma, Refer Chapter 12) and is also closely associated with Karma. It is also referred in the context of today's physical world and family.
4. ***Samskara***: This is a process of purification by which good qualities are imbibed and bad qualities are eschewed in an individual. It also signifies cultural heritage and quality of upbringing in an individual. This 'Samskara' is also part of the cycle of birth and re-birth as a good 'Samskara' is believed to help the soul to get a higher level of birth.
5. ***Moksha/Mukti***: means liberation or total freedom. Each Vedantic school defines it differently. It is one of the 'Purusharthas' and means liberation of the soul from the cycle of births and deaths. It may also mean union with God or securing eternal bliss depending on the philosophy one believes in.
6. ***Yoga***: Yoga (Paths/Practices/Methods) is one of the best known words in the world today. *Bhagavad-Gita* describes the different forms of Yoga to attain self-realization or Moksha – Bhakti Yoga,

Jnana Yoga, and Karma Yoga. Patanjali's Yoga sutras also describe 'Astanga Yoga'. (Refer Chapters 3, 5 and 10)

7. ***Guru:*** A Guru is one who has great knowledge, wisdom and authority and guides the disciple in his 'Sadhana' to achieve a particular religious goal. In Hinduism, finding a true Guru is considered a pre-requisite for self-realization. But currently, the term 'Guru' is used more in the context of a teacher.
8. ***Diksha:*** The process of initiation of a disciple, (by a Guru) in undertaking a religious practice. 'Vishnu Yamala Tantra' describes 'Diksha' as the process which bestows 'divya Jnana' (spiritual knowledge) on the concerned person as it destroys his sin and ignorance.
9. ***Karma:*** The concept of Karma requires a little more elaboration. The doctrine of Karma – influenced to a great extent by Jain and Buddhist philosophies – has evolved over centuries. Karma connotes moral justice – *results of good and bad deeds (Punya-Paapa) that follow every soul in this and subsequent births.* According to some Vedantic schools, divine grace is also necessary to enjoy the fruits of one's Karma.

   Krishna explains in the Gita that one should perform one's duty according to his Dharma and at the same time he should not get himself attached to its fruits. He further explains that Karma done without expectations, leads one towards the spiritual path.

   However, scriptures further treated the concept of Karma as an instrument for maintaining social order – Varnashrama Dharma. 'Chandogya Upanishad' describes the result of Karma as follows:

   > *Those whose conduct here has been good, will quickly attain a good birth, the birth of a Brahman, the birth of a Kshatriya, the birth of a Vaishya. But those whose conduct here has been evil, will quickly attain an evil birth, the birth of a dog, the birth of a hog, or the birth of a Chandala. (5.10.7) (tr. Dr. S. Radhakrishnan)*

This means, actions in the present life determine the condition of the next birth. This cannot be construed as fatalism, since one can modify one's destiny by consciously performing one's actions (like good deeds). However, what is termed as fatalistic is whether or not these actions are in accordance with one's Dharma (as prescribed by Dharma Shastras and according to one's Varna).

In contrast, according to Buddhist philosophy, the improvement of one's Karma to ensure a better life (in this and subsequent births), is dependent on observing the code of social ethics based on the eightfold path (enunciated by Buddha), which is unlike the Hindu concept of Karma which is based on Varnashrama Dharma.

The concept of Karma is also explained in different chapters under different contexts.

10. ***Punarjanma***: (Reincarnation): Some philosophers call it transmigration of the soul from one body to another body. This is a part of karmic theory that an individuals soul follows the different stages of birth, death and re-birth in a continuous cycle. This concept is elaborately discussed in Chapter 12.

11. ***Vedanta***: Most Hindus believe that the Soul (Atman/Jiva) is eternal. As per Advaita Vedanta, this Atman is ultimately indistinct from Brahman, the Supreme Being. The 'goal of life' as per this school, is to realize its identity with the Brahman and attain Moksha.

    Dualistic schools (like Dvaita and Bhakti) believe that Brahman as the Supreme Being possesses a personality and worship him as Vishnu, Shiva or Shakti, depending on their respective faiths. According to these schools the Soul (Atman) is distinct from God and Moksha depends on devotion, good deeds and divine grace. The philosophy of each of these schools is discussed separately in Chapters 6, 7, 8 and 9.

12. **Freedom of Belief and Worship:** Another unique feature of Hinduism is that it grants absolute and complete freedom of belief and worship to every follower. Thus, he can follow any one of the schools of Hindu philosophy – Advaita (non-dualism), Dvaita

(dualism), Visisthadvaita (qualified non-dualism), Dvaita-Advaita (dualism with non-dualism), Bheda-abheda (Difference-Non Difference), etc.

He may further choose not to follow any school of philosophy at all. He may also choose to worship any one God as the Supreme Being or any one of the numerous Gods or even remain a Nastika (without any belief).

THE EVOLUTION OF THE CONCEPT OF GOD

Early Vedic Gods

At the beginning of the early Vedic period, when the Vedic people were still leading pastoral lives, the concept of worshipping gods for spiritual enlightenment had not yet developed. The gods worshipped by them included Indra, Varuna and Mitra. These were also considered the monsoon storm gods (maruths) of thunder and rain, who were much feared by the Vedic people, as the monsoon rains brought all sorts of problems – floods, destruction of villages and agricultural crops, diseases, sickness, and death.

Indra, the rain God was considered the most important god. Indra also played the role of warlord and is called in Rig Veda as 'purandara' (breaker of forts). 250 Hymns are devoted to him in Rig Veda. He is also considered as the rain god. The second position was given to Agni, the fire God (with 200 hymns). Agni was also considered as an intermediary between gods and the Aryan people. The oblation offered to different gods was carried by Agni in the form of smoke to the sky and thus transmitted to the gods. Varuna was the water God. He was expected to uphold the natural order. Soma was considered as the God of plants and 'Soma-rasa' an intoxicating drink was named after him.

We also find some female divinities in the form of Aditi and Ushas (associated with dawn and dusk). In addition, Rig Veda also speaks of eight Vasus, eleven Rudras and twelve Adityas being the gods of earth, heaven and space. The Vedic people worshipped these gods for prosperity, wealth, health, etc.

In the later Vedic period, sacrifices gained more importance compared to hymns and prayers of the early Vedic period. As the households became well established, elaborate rituals were devised offering oblations to Agni in 'homa-kundas'. Towards the end of the Vedic period, there appears to be strong objections against cults propagating rituals and sacrifices.

The rise of Jainism and Buddhism also saw some sort of reformation in the earlier Vedic religion. Some of the Vedic gods started losing importance. Varuna and Mitra quietly passed into oblivion. Indra and Agni lost their pre-eminence. Prajapati, the Creator, came to occupy the prime position, as the supreme god ('Brahman'). 'Rudra' the God of animals (known as Pasupati), gained prominence and got a new role as the 'destroyer'. Vishnu came to be recognized as the preserver and protector of the people, as the transition of Vedic people from a pastoral life to a settled life began.

People started giving more importance to Upanishads (philosophical texts) which gave importance to the knowledge of the self (Atman) and its relation to the Brahman. During this period, the doctrine of 'the supreme cosmic spirit (as Brahman) pervading everything' gradually took shape (Ishopanishad).

Evolution of the Concept of 'Brahman' as the Supreme God

Ancient Rishis by systematically observing the regularity of natural phenomena in the world around them concluded that Nature is governed by a mysterious force and called it the *'Universal Truth or Brahman'*. This is the earliest unitary concept of God as depicted in the Rig-Veda. Over a period of time, the concept of 'Brahman' underwent many semantic changes, till its meaning was firmly established as the *'Ultimate Reality'*, and that there is nothing beyond it.

This concept was described fully in later Vedic scriptures thus – *This Truth in its absolute aspect is considered to be without name, form or qualities* (like Anaam, Niraakaar, Nirguna). *It is also described as infinite, eternal, birth-less and death-less* (Ananta, nitya, anaadi, and shaashvat). *This Truth is also considered to be shrouded in what is called* 'Maya'

(Swhetaashwatara Upanishad and later elaborated by Adi Shankara in Advaita Vedanta) *and it is for the seeker to remove this veil and realize the Truth.*

'Taittiriya Upanishad' one of the earliest Upanishads says: *Satyam Jnanam Anantam Brahma* (Truth, Knowledge, and the infinite is Brahman). *Sarvam Khalvidam Brahma* is another popular ancient concept which means 'all of this, including Brahman, is that absolute reality'. Along with this concept of the supreme god, we also sometimes come across the word 'Iswara' in Atharva Veda and Brhadaranyaka Upanishad, to represent this Supreme Being.

Over several centuries, the concept of Brahman was debated and then clearly two groups emerged attributing two different aspects to Brahman – one was termed as 'Nirguna Brahman' and the other was called 'Saguna Brahman' although the two aspects were considered not mutually exclusive. Here the word 'guna' meant a distributing attribute or quality.

The differentiating idea between 'Nirguna' and 'Saguna' was the idea of personality. From ancient times, scholars belonging to different schools have varied views on these two aspects of the Brahman. They are separately discussed in Chapters 6 and 7, when we discuss the Vedantic philosophies.

This earliest unitary concept of God as 'Brahman' later expanded and underwent modifications extensively over a period of centuries. The later scriptures in support of this say: 'The Truth is One, but interpreted variously by the wise' (*Ekam sat vipra bahudhaa vadanti*). Truth is also called by various names – the Universal Self, Brahman, Paramatma, Bhagavan, etc. *(ex. Brahmeti Paramatmeti Bhagavan iti kathyate).*

Subsequently, God as the 'Supreme Being' took on different aspects to perform different functions. This is beautifully put in 'Swhetaashwatara Upanishad' thus:

Eko devah sarvabhuthesu ghoodah |
Sarva-vyapi sarvabhuta-antaraatmaa |
Karmaadhyakshah sarvabhutaadhivaasah |
Sakshii chetaa kevalo nirgunascha ||

'God is one, he is in all things, he envelopes everything, he is the inner soul of all living beings, he is "Karmaadhyaksha" (monitors all our actions), "Sakshi" (he is a witness to all our actions), "Chetana" (provides us life), and "nirguna" (without having any attribute)'.

By the time of the *Mahabharata*, the concept of a single, Supreme and all powerful God (Iswara equated with Vishnu) had taken final shape. Krishna in *Bhagavad Gita* describes himself as that all powerful Brahman. (See Chapter 10)

The Concept of the Trinity (Trimurti)

The 'Truth' according to Upanishads, is that this world constantly undergoes three changes – Creation, Preservation and Destruction. In fact, it is said to be a unitary and continuous process. Without the existence of one aspect, the other two do not exist. It is also impossible to draw a line where Creation stops and Preservation begins or Preservation stops and Destruction begins. (As in Physics, Destruction of one state of matter is creation of its other state).

Hence these three important aspects of the Supreme Brahman, came to be represented by the 'Trinity' of gods – Brahma (the Creator –representing Rajasic Tatva), Vishnu (the Preserver – representing Satvic Tatva) and Shiva (the Destroyer – representing Tamasic Tatva). Each of these gods is associated with an Upanishad – Brahma with Mundaka, Vishnu with Katha and Shiva with Swhetaashwatara.

Brahma also represents the 'Original Word' (in the form of the 4 Vedas), Vishnu – Knowledge (as described in *Bhagavad Gita*), and Shiva as the Destroyer, brings everything to a stand-still when the concepts of Time and Space disappear. Thus the 'Trinity' forms the three different aspects of the same Truth – the Supreme Brahman.

Further, as Krishna says in the Gita, whenever there is decline of Dharma (*Yada yada-hi dharmasya, glanirbhavati bharata)*, he takes on special forms and incarnations to perform his various functions (of the Trinity):

1. Anugraha (Blessing the good – *Paritraanaaya Saadhunaam*)
2. Nigraha (Destroying the Evil – *Vinaashaaya cha dushkrutaam*)
3. Establishing the path of Dharma (*Dharma samsthaapanaart-haaya*)

These are almost similar to the functions of any government which are – to protect its subjects, punish evil doers and establish law and order for the benefit of the community. Vishnu as the preserver successively assumes many forms (Avatara) in order to save this universe from evil forces and establish the path of Dharma – of which ten (Dashavatara) are considered important. From a religious point of view, the most important incarnations are Narasimha, Rama, and Krishna – who are worshipped by a large number of Hindus even today. We also find a number of temples for these deities.

EVOLUTION OF MAJOR SECTS IN HINDUISM

During the early Vedic period, both Vishnu and Shiva (earlier identified as Rudra and later as Pasupati) had relatively minor roles. But by the time of the Brahmanas, both started gaining ascendance. The notion of a trinity of gods (Brahma, Vishnu and Shiva) gained ascendance and among the trinity, Brahma receded into the background over a period of time, whereas, both Vishnu and Shiva gained a vast following.

The Epics, *Ramayana* and *Mahabharata* (originally considered as poetry sung by the bards) were revised and raised to the level of sacred texts. Probably the *Bhagavad Gita* was incorporated into *Mahabharata* at this point of time. The worship of epic heroes – Rama and Krishna as incarnations of Vishnu gained popularity.

By the Puranic period, major sects – *Vaishnava* and *Shaiva* had come into existence in the name of these gods. These sects believed that their god alone was supreme. As with Vedic religion, the Vaishnava and Shaiva sects were not founded by historical personages. However, over the course of time they evolved from a wide variety of cults, beliefs and rituals. The concepts of 'Karma' and 'Samsara' – originally found in Upanishads but later developed elaborately by Jain and Buddhist religions – gained prominence.

Evolution of Sects in South India

In South India, both anti-Vedic and non-Vedic groups evolved and had quite a following in their own right. In Tamil Nadu and Kerala, even at the beginning of the Christian era, the deities worshipped were prominently Shiva and Murugan (Subramanya). Vedic religion was first confined to the upper classes of society and worship of Vishnu gained prominence only at a later stage.

There was also a strong influence of Jainism and Buddhism which later declined over a period of time. 'Kanchi' and 'Sravana Belagola' were centres of Jain religious activities. The Tamil devotional movement was deeply divided in the choice of the worship of the deity. Bhagavata and Pasupata sects preached devotion to Vishnu and Shiva respectively. Their rituals and religious practices were derived from the Agamas of each sect. The Alvar saints popularized the worship of Vishnu. Nayanars rendered a similar service in the worship of Shiva. Ramanujacharya called the sacred texts written by Alvars as 'Dravida Veda'.

Evolution of Secular Concepts in Hinduism

Many scriptures viewed both the gods Shiva and Vishnu as one and the same. In fact, Dattatreya represents all the three gods of the trinity. 'Vishnu Purana' shows Vishnu awakening and becoming both Brahma (the creator) and Shiva (the destroyer). Shiva is also viewed as the manifestation of Vishnu in 'Bhagavata Purana'. The 'Shata-rudriya' says that Shiva is a form of Vishnu. Brhan-naradiya says 'Mahadeva is Hari Roopi and Janardana as Rudra Roopi'.

Even though, Shaiva sects claimed (in their Puranas) Shiva as the supreme god, there have been many secular instances of showing both gods as one – 'Hari-Hara' and 'Shankara-Narayana' and temples were built where both sects worshipped a single god who represented both Shiva and Vishnu. In coastal districts of Karnataka, both Vishnu and Shiva Sahasranamas are recited in some Shiva temples. In South India, Swamy Ayyappa (of Sabarimalai) is a popular god and is considered to have been born out of the union of Shiva and Vishnu (in 'Mohini' form).

There are several groups who believe in the essential oneness of 5/6 deities they consider as personifications of the 'Supreme Being'. These deities are Shiva, Vishnu, Ganesha, Shakti, and Aditya (Sun). Among these, there are sub-groups who consider one of these deities as the prominent deity. This is also reflected in temple architecture, where one deity is prominently placed in the girbha-griha (sanctum sanctorum), and the other gods have smaller temples around the temple of the main deity. *(This concept is called 'Panchayatan' elaborately discussed in Chapter 11).*

Shaaktas worship Shakti – the female divinity (in the form of Devi, Lalita, Durga, Kali, etc.) as the Mother Goddess. (For details see Chapter 9). The concept of a feminine divinity as the 'Supreme Goddess' has evolved over a period of time and 'tantric' forms of worship have also come into existence. The form of offering also changed with animal sacrifice becoming slowly optional and finally extinct. (However it still continues in a few temples of Kali and other village goddesses).

Apart from these major sects, there are also several minor denominations like Saura, Ganapatya, and other sub-sects. These sects differ primarily in the way they perceive the God they worship as the 'Supreme God' along with the traditions and rituals that accompany the worship of that God. Simultaneously, there is another way of dividing major sects among Hindus, based on the Veda they follow in conducting rituals and modes of worship. However, there are several groups of practicing Hindus who do not claim to belong to any denomination at all.

BHAKTI MOVEMENT IN HINDUISM

The Beginnings of Idol Worship

By the seventh century (CE) several changes took place in religious practices. The deity was no longer treated as an abstract form of Brahman by each sect, but was represented by an idol (or an image) housed in a temple (Lingam as in the case of Shiva) – a clear departure from Vedic religion. The form of worship in these sects was different from the Vedic sacrifice, and evolved as a ritual of 'Puja'. The sacrificial ritual of Vedic religion gradually led to devotional form of worship (later termed as Bhakti).

The Concept of 'Bhakti'

'Bhakti' involves total surrender and devotion to god. Bhakti is an important component in Hindu religion and is defined in various ways by different schools of thought. (Chapters 6, 7, 8 and 9). Gita was the first religious text to explicitly use the word 'Bhakti' to denote a religious path and treated it as one of the three yogas to realize god (Chapter 10). 'Bhagavata Purana' elaborated on this concept extensively and mentions nine specific activities to be followed by a Bhakti-yogi. 'Bhakti-marga' is often used to describe religious devotion and complete dedication to god.

Here the intention of the worship through Bhakti was considered as attainment of 'Moksha'. This had a far wider appeal than the Vedic religion which was confined to the Upper castes. The performance of acts through Bhakti required very little investment (when compared to Vedic sacrifices) – Puja, offerings to god in the form of food or fruits, keeping of fasts and vows, visits to temples, pilgrimage to holy places, etc. Many of these were also optional and varied from sect to sect and individual to individual. Both Vaishnavism and Shaivism strengthened the notion of Bhakti as a form of worship focused on the individual.

From the twelfth century onwards, there was active participation of several groups of saints who spread the Bhakti movement (Chapter 7) throughout India, during different periods of time. These saints sung devotional poems and songs in praise of their respective gods and spread the message of Bhakti from place to place. The devotional songs and poetry, focused on the individual's search for liberation from rebirth and attainment of Moksha. The relationship between the deity and devotee was considered as one of love and devotion.

Saints who Spread Bhakti Movements

Prominent saints of Bhakti movement of the period include Jnaneswar (Maharashtra), Jayadeva (Orissa – who wrote 'Gita-Govinda'), Kabir (Sufism), Samartha Ramadas (Maharashtra), Annamacharya (Andhra), Tulsidas (who wrote Ramacharit-manas), Chaitanya (Bengal), Namadev (Maharashtra), Purandaradasa and Kanakadasa (Karnataka), the 12 Alvars (Tamil Nadu), … The list is almost endless.

There were several women devotees in Bhakti movement who became famous through their devotional songs – Andal (Tamil Nadu), Mira Bai (North India), and Akka-Mahadevi (Karnataka).

'Veerashaiva Sect' in Karnataka

The Veerashaiva sect (founded by Basavanna) emerged in the twelfth century with some advocacy of social reforms. The sect's more liberal attitude got support from the lower classes. The sect attacked religious hypocrisy in Brahmanism. It questioned theories like rebirth and norms of caste. It advocated a better status for women. Shiva was worshipped in the form of a Linga – each member of the sect carrying a miniature 'Linga' and worshipping it twice a day. Cremation was replaced with the system of burial of the dead. (Veerashaivism is elaborated in Chapter 8).

Thus Hinduism as a religion, with nearly a billion followers, exhibits a very wide canvas of beliefs, sub-sects, gods and philosophies. This is certainly unique, when we compare Hinduism with other world religions. This book makes an attempt to provide a bird's eye view of Hindu religion, along with its philosophies and practices, with a view to help the general reader to understand Hinduism in all its finer aspects.

2

The Essence of Hindu Scriptures

Hindu religion is perhaps the only religion in the world, which boasts of an enormous amount of religious literature. It is well neigh impossible for any one person to become proficient in understanding and mastering this vast religious literature during one's life time.

The basis for the Hindu religion and philosophy consists prominently of the Vedas and Upanishads (called as Srutis), the epics, Smritis, the Puranas and a host of other religious texts. This chapter briefly summarizes the essence of these scriptures.

THE VEDAS

The Vedas are considered as 'Eternal Truths' and 'the only original source of knowledge' and hence form the basis of all our scriptures. They are among the most ancient religious texts still in existence in the world. They have enriched the Hindu religion, philosophy and culture, with rich ideas associated with the concepts about life and spirituality.

Vedas were perceived by our ancient 'Rishis' during meditation. This amounted to a vast body of knowledge. These were handed down from teacher to student by word of mouth for centuries. The 'Rig Veda Samhita' is considered to be the earliest available Vedic text. There are strong linguistic similarities between the Rig Veda and the Persian holy book *Avasti*.

It is said that 'Sage Veda-Vyasa' (also called Krishna Dwaipayana) collected all the Vedic hymns (mantras), edited and divided the vast

Vedic knowledge in to four volumes – the Rig Veda, the Yajur Veda, the Sama Veda and the Atharva Veda (probably around 1500 BCE – which is literally 3500 years ago). In each volume, Veda-Vyasa brought about a harmonic rhythm, both in arrangement and classification of contents. He divided each volume roughly into 4 sections:

1. *Samhitas*: The part containing the sacred Veda-mantras–chants/hymns,
2. *Brahmanas:* Description of Vedic Rituals and Rules of Conduct,
3. *Aranyakas:* Theology – relating to 'Subjective Worship' and
4. *Upanishads:* Philosophic Revelations.

Each section represents a phase in the development of the religious consciousness of the Aryans. The first two sections are called 'Karma-Kanda' (Ritualistic portion) and the last two are called 'Jnana-Kanda' (Knowledge portion). (For important details pertaining to Vedas see Annexure 9).

Content of the Vedas

Among the Samhitas, the Samhita belonging to the Rig Veda is the largest and considered to be the oldest extinct text of Vedic literature. It is spread over 10 mandalas and consists of 1028 suktas (hymns) dedicated to 33 different gods. Each mandala corresponds with the name of a Rishi, who was bestowed with its revelation. The first and tenth mandalas are considered to be later day compositions, according to modern scholars.

The Rig Vedic hymns offer prayers to Gods belonging to earth, heaven and space, most notably Indra, Agni, Soma, Varuna, Vishnu and other gods. Varuna was also addressed as Mitra-Varuna. The gods Vishnu and Rudra were given minor importance in these hymns.

Yajur Veda lays down various sacred invocations (known as yajus) which are chanted during sacrificial rites. Sama Veda consists of a collection of chants (samas) which are sung at the rituals related to soma ceremonies and are lyrical in nature. The first three Vedas are called 'Thrayi'. The Atharva Veda contains mostly chants which are magical in nature, formed a part of Rig Veda for a long time. It was sung during ceremonies like coronation of kings, marriage and obsequies. They also contain medicinal formulae to deal with sickness and diseases.

Rishis Connected with the Vedas

Veda-Vyasa after division of the Vedas, entrusted the propagation of each Veda to a 'Maharishi' especially trained for the purpose–

1. Rig Veda to Paila,
2. Yajur Veda to Vaishampayana,
3. Sama Veda to Jaimini and
4. Atharva Veda to Samantu.

The Yajur Veda later split in two parts: Shukla Yajur Veda and Krishna Yajur Veda. Shukla Yajur Veda is said to have been given to sage Yagnavalka by Surya, the Sun God. The Rishi for Krishna Yajurveda is Vaishampayana. Each Veda has several shakhas (branches) depending on the number of Rishis who propagated them.

Vedas and Gayatri Mantra

'Aitareya Aranyaka' describes the association of the three Vedas in the Gayatri Mantra ('Bhu Bhuvah svah') where Bhu stands for Rig Veda, Bhuvah for Yajur Veda and Svah for Sama Veda. Upanishads reduced the 'essence of Vedas' further into the word Om ('a-u-m'). The Kathopanishad says: That the goal, which all the Vedas declare, which all austerities aim at, ... is Om'.

Sutras: The Sutra section, (which is often included under Vedic corpus) has three categories of texts: the Grihya-sutras, concerned with domestic rituals; Shrauta-sutras, concerned with public rituals performed for establishing status in society; and the Dharma-Sutras, which state the rules of what was regarded as sacred duty and social obligations.

Upa Vedas: Ayur-Veda (subject of medicine), Dhanur-Veda (subject of Archery), Gandharva-Veda (subjects relating to music and dance) and Shastra-Shaastra (Military science) are given the status of 'Upa-Vedas'.

Vedangas: In order to understand the hidden meaning of the Vedas, and help people apply the Vedic thought properly in their life, 6 shaastras called 'Vedangas' came into being. They are – Shiksha (Phonetics), Vyakarana (Grammar), Chandas (Prosody), Nirukta (Vedic Etymology and Dictionary), Jyotisha (Astrology), Kalpa (Rituals). Grammar written by Panini is considered as one of the most important works in Sanskrit.

PRASTHANA TRAYA

The three authoritative works on Hinduism (collectively called Prasthana Traya) are considered to be:

1. Upanishads,
2. The Bhagavad-Gita and
3. Brahma Sutras.

No study of Vedanta (the philosophical aspect of Hinduism) is considered complete, without a study and deeper understanding of these three works.

Every prominent Acharya (who propagated his own brand of Vedantic philosophy), has written authoritative commentaries on each of these three works to propound his own respective school of thought. Among them, Adi Shankara's commentaries on 'Prasthana Traya' are considered to be the most authoritative works on Indian philosophic thought.

The Upanishads

The Upanishads form the essence of the Vedas and are found in the last section of each Veda and therefore the philosophy of the Upanishads has come to be called Vedanta (end part of Veda). While the Vedas focus on rituals, Upanishads focus on spiritual insight and philosophical teachings. Upanishads are the oldest and most authoritative sources of Indian philosophic thought. They are believed to have been perceived by a galaxy of famous Rishis like Aruni, Yagnavalka, Shandilya, Balaki,

Shvetaketu and others. They give prominence to discussion relating to 'Adhyatma Tatva' (relating to Brahman and Atman).

Major Upanishads

Out of over 108 Upanishads (according to some scholars the number now exceeds 200), that are extant today, 12 are considered to be the most important: *Isha, Kena, Katha, Munduka, Prashna, Mandookya, Aitareya, Taithiriya, Chandogya, Brhadaranyaka, Kausitaki and Swhetaashwatara* Upanishads. Of these, *Chandogya, Brhadaranyaka, Aitareya, Kausitaki and Taithiriya,* – these five are considered to be the most ancient among them.

The various concepts discussed in the Upanishads are presented in a cryptic poetic style, which lend themselves into a wide variety of interpretations. Some of these Upanishads discuss the nature and qualities of Brahman as the Supreme Being. However not all Upanishads present the same point of view. We can only conclude that these Upanishads explore different aspects of the same Truth.

The Concept of Brahman

This concept of Brahman is not the same as the God Brahma (belonging to the Trinity aspect of Brahman) who deals with creation alone. Brahman is that which creates the world (Srishthi), that which regulates life in this world (sthithi), and that in which everything gets absorbed after death (Laya).

Nirguna (without characteristics) and Saguna (with characteristics) are the two different aspects of the same Brahman. Brahman is also described as 'Sat-Chit-Aananda'. (the characteristic of Saguna Brahman). Sage Yagnavalka called this as 'Akshara Brahman'. Saguna Brahman is also termed as 'Iswara' (taken to mean as the Supreme God). Brahman is to be understood through Jnana and Iswara to be worshipped through 'Karma' Upasana.

Ishopanishad beautifully describes this aspect through the 'Shanti Mantra':

'Om Poorna-madam. Poorna-midam...' – That (Brahma) is Poorna (the whole), This (Iswara) is Poorna, Poorna is born out of Poorna. If

Poorna is removed from Poorna, the remaining is still Poorna. Both Brahman and Iswara are complete in all respects. Even when Iswara comes out of Brahman, Brahman is still whole or complete in all respects. Most of the Vedantic philosophies consider Iswara as Vishnu.

Philosophies Enunciated by the Upanishads

Many of the philosophies discussed in the Upanishads, aim at liberating the soul (spirit/Atman) from the body so that it can attain communion with God. The core teaching of Upanishads is summarized in 3 words: 'Tat Tvam Asi' [You (Atman) are That (Brahman)]. The philosophy of Upanishads is based basically on some of the following principles:

1. Brahman is the one unifying principle behind this world.
2. Knowledge of the Brahman reveals the way to self-realization,
3. Doctrine of Karma is the basis of all Indian Philosophy,
4. Man's worldly and otherworldly goals need not be opposed to each other.
5. Understanding the metaphysical significance of the sacred word 'Om', leads one to the path of enlightenment.
6. The concepts of one god, unity of souls and the world – in one all compassing Reality.

Some of the other concepts discussed by these Upanishads are:

1. The relationship between Paramatma and Jeevatma,
2. The concepts of Jnana and Karma,
3. Karma and Punarjanma (Reincarnation),
4. Varnashrama Dharma,
5. Moksha,
6. Methods (Sadhana) used in obtaining Moksha.

The essence of the teachings of some of the Upanishads is briefly given below:

1. ***'Brhadaranyaka Upanishad'*** (belonging to Kanva shakha of Shukla Yajur Veda) is widely accepted as the most important of all Upanishads. It largely contemplates on the relationship between the Atman and the Brahman. It further goes on to

give philosophic backing to this concept and also describes the various rituals of worship and meditation. It contains a detailed discussion between sage Yagnavalka and 'Brahmavadini' Maitreyi regarding 'Adhyatma Tatva'.

2. ***'Mandookya Upanishad'*** regards the word 'Om' as the basis of all existence. Gaudapada expands the concept of 'Om' in his work *Mandookya Karika* thus:

   Pranavo hi aparam Brahma, pranavascha parah smrtah ।
   Apurvohyantaro bahyoo na parah pranavo vyayah ॥

   [Pranava is Omkara, It is considered as apara-Brahma as well as para-Brahma. Omkara is that which has no birth, no characteristics and no dissolution.]

3. ***'Swhetaashwatara Upanishad'*** identifies Saguna Brahman (as Iswara the Supreme Being) with Shiva/Rudra and describes the qualities of Shiva as the Supreme God. It also contains the three basic principles of Shaivagamas – Pashu (Man), Pati (God) and Pasha (bonds) and the relations between them.

Consequently, the concept of Vedanta separated into 6 separate sub-schools of philosophy, each interpreting the meanings of Upanishads in their own way and producing their own commentaries. They are described in Chapters 5 and 6.

The Bhagavad Gita

Importance of the Gita

Gita forms an important part of the epic *Mahabharata* (Bhisma Parva) and is considered the most sacred work in Hindu religion and philosophy and brings out the essence of the Vedas and Upanishads. 'Swhetaashwatara Upanishad' treats Shiva as the Supreme God. In comparison, Gita which is also considered as an Upanishad gives primacy to Vishnu. It consists of 700 slokas spread over 18 chapters.

Gita is considered the essence of the Hindu philosophy and Dharma. It describes the virtues, glories and the secrets of the Eternal

Truth (God) and indicates the paths through which one can attain self-realization. Gita also has reconciled the various facets and schools of Hindu philosophy.

The philosophies and insights provided in the Gita (is believed by scholars) to reach beyond the scope of religion and are intended to cover the entire humanity as a whole. The teacher of the Gita is Sri Krishna, (who is also referred to as 'Gita-charya' /'Yogacharya') and is considered as the manifestation of 'Para-Brahman' himself. Krishna describes the best yogi as the one who constantly meditates upon Him.

The book of Gita may be broadly divided into three parts of six chapters each. The first part deals with Karma or Action, the second with Bhakti or devotion and the last part deals with Jnana or spiritual knowledge, each path is considered essential for a person to attain communion with God.

The Goal of the Gita

Shoka Mohadi Samskara karma Nivrutyartham Gita Shastram

The goal of Gita is not just to propagate Dharma, but also to show the way for one to come out of the misery of 'Samskara karma' and follow the path of self-realization. All doubts that may arise in a person are put as questions through 'Arjuna' and they are cleared through answers given by 'Krishna'.

Like Upanishads, the ultimate goal of the Gita is to devise paths to realize Moksha/Mukti. Different Upanishads enunciate different paths to realize this Moksha – Jnana, Nishkama Karma, Bhakti, etc. Gita tries to reconcile all these paths. For this purpose, the various concepts of Akshara/Saguna Brahman, Jnana, Karma and Bhakti explained in various Upanishads in different ways, get crystallized in the Gita. The Tatva of 'Bhagavata sect' is also highlighted here.

Gita further emphasizes 'Nishkama Karma' – duty done without expecting any benefits:

Karmany evadhikaaras-te ma phaleshu kadachana |
Ma karma-phala-hetur bhur ma te sango'tsv akarmani ||

[You have a right to perform your prescribed duty, but you are not entitled to the fruits of action. Never consider yourself the cause of the results of your activities and never be attached to not doing your duty (Gita 2.47)]

Essence of the Gita

According to Gita, the goal of life is to free the mind and intellect from complexities and focus on the glory of the 'Self' by dedicating one's action to the divine. This goal can be achieved through meditation, action, devotion and knowledge. Gita emphasizes three Yogas – Karma Yoga, Bhakti Yoga and Jnana Yoga (they are discussed in Chapter 3 and explained more elaborately in Chapter 10). While each path differs in the process, the fundamental goal is the same – to realize the supreme Brahman as being the ultimate Truth. The essence of Gita may be summarized as follows:

> *Sri Krishna says: I am the source of all spiritual and material worlds. Everything emanates from Me. The wise who realize this engage in devotional service to Me, and worship Me with all their heart. Consequently, they experience fulfillment, bliss and realize Me. (Gita, 10 – 8 and 9)*

Gita is thus a unique work, (which has no comparison in any other religion), as it describes the purpose of human existence, the immortality of the soul and its relationship with God. Further, it prescribes the three paths which helps one to attain communion with God.

Commentaries on the Gita

Gita is one religious work which has attracted the largest number of commentaries by scholars down the ages. Some of the earliest commentaries on the Gita are not available to us at this point of time. All the prominent Acharyas, have written commentaries on the Gita, essentially to propound their respective schools of thought: Adi Shankara (Advaita), Yamuna and Ramanuja (Visisthadvaita), Madhva (Dvaita), Abhinava-Gupta (Shaiva tradition), Nimbarka (Dvaita-Advaita), and Vallabha (Shudha-Dvaita).

In modern times, notable commentaries were written by Bal Gangadhar Tilak, Aravinda Ghosh, Mahatma Gandhi, Swami Prabhupada (ISKCON) and Mahrishi Mahesh Yogi (Transcendental Meditation). The commentaries by Tilak and Gandhi helped inspire the freedom movement.

(The essence of the Gita has been discussed in Chapter 10)

The Brahma Sutras

Sage Badarayana (sometimes he is also identified with another Vyasa), organized the teachings of the Upanishads, in a logically coherent sequence, in what are known as 'Brahma-sutras'. These sutras are also known by other names – Vedanta Sutras, Shaaririka Sutras, and Bhikshu Sutras. Ramanuja and Madhva believed that sage Badarayana was also Veda-Vyasa. This seems unlikely as Veda-Vyasa lived during the Mahabharata period (1500 BCE) and Brahma Sutras critique both the Jaina and Buddha Darshanas and hence could have been written only after 500 BCE, (but certainly not later than 200 BCE). In addition to Jaina and Buddha Darshanas, the Brahma Sutras criticize most notably Sankhya, Vaiseshika, and Lokayata Darshanas.

Upanishads deal with diverse topics and concepts such as Nirguna Brahman, Saguna Brahman, unity of Brahman with Atman, Jnana, Karma, Bhakti, etc. All the Upanishads also do not present a common point of view or philosophy with respect to some of these concepts. Since none of the Upanishads singly deal with all aspects of the Brahman, the Brahma Sutras gained importance as they contained the essence of all the Upanishads and dealt with the concept of Brahman in all its finer aspects (which constitute Atma-Tatva or Brahma Jnana). Apart from the nature of the Brahman, they deal with abstract philosophical concepts like the nature of the Universe, its creation, the soul and its forms.

Content of Brahma Sutras

The Brahma Sutras are 555 in number spread over four chapters. Each Sutra is very short and pregnant with meaning relating to 'Adhyatma

Tatva'. We cannot identify even one syllable or letter which is out of place or context. The smallest sutra is just one word: 'Anushcha' (2.14.13).

In ancient times, each sutra was individually analysed and explained by the Guru, by keeping in mind the meaning reflected in the Vedas as well as the meanings ascribed by the various acharyas with respect to their individual philosophies. The different steps of logical analysis of any such concept, is given in 'Nyaya Darshana' in chapter 5 relating to 'Shad Darshanas'.

Samanvaya – The Concept of Brahman

The first chapter is called 'Samanvaya', as it deals with propagation of the unitary concept of God known as the Para-Brahman and the relationship between God, Universe and Atman – 'That which has created the universe is Brahman. He is responsible for cause and effect in this Universe. He is Aditya and pervades the Universe. He is also bliss, but he is different from Jeevatma'.

Sruti and Smriti are the only means of understanding the concept of this Brahman. Badarayana uses the term 'Sruti' in relation to Upanishads and Smriti here means *Gita*, *Mahabharata*, and *Dharma Shastras*. He further states that 'Brahma Jnana' cannot be understood either by logic or by any other type of subjective analysis.

Avirodha – Criticism of Other Philosophies

The second chapter (known as 'Avirodha'), deals with detailed analysis and rejection of all statements which are in opposition to Vedic thought. It extensively discusses 'Sankhya' and rejects premises made in Sankhya, which are contrary to Vedic thought. It summarizes its criticism of other similar philosophies advocated by Vaiseshika, Buddha, Jaina, Pasupata and Bhagavata schools.

This chapter also gives importance to creation of the Universe. It also discusses the cause (Brahman) and effect (Universe) theory. It further states that the Universe is not different from Brahman. It states that Atman is eternal. Happiness and sufferings of the soul are the result of their individual Karma.

Sadhana – The Path to Brahma Vidya

The third chapter (known as 'Sadhana'), deals with the methods (Brahma – Vidya) of realization of the Brahman. Badarayana compares the relationship between Brahman and Atman to Sun and the sunlight (rashmi). When clouds cut out sunlight, it does not affect the Sun in any way. Similarly Brahman does not get affected by the actions of Jivas. Through knowledge (Brahma Jnana) and upasana alone, the Jivas can achieve realization. The chapter also deals with Karma to be performed by people of various varnas.

Phala – Results

The fourth chapter (known as 'Phala'), deals with the details of eternal bliss obtained as a result of realization of the Brahman. Characteristics of the Jiva which has attained bliss are discussed in detail. In the state of such supreme bliss, Atman becomes one with Brahman (Pure water remains pure when it joins pure water). However, it does not have the power of creation like Brahman.

'Brahman is the beginning and the end of everything. Different souls get created, live their life as per their Karma and finally become one with Brahman' – is the essence of the theory propounded by Brahma sutras. The Brahma sutras are often seen in the light of the theology devoted to the worship of God Vishnu.

Commentaries on Brahma Sutras

The Sutras simulated many interpretive commentaries over the next two millennia. The different schools of Vedanta have built their philosophies on the foundation of these Sutras. Teachers of all major Vedantic schools have written commentaries on the Brahma sutras, as a means of understanding the Upanishads and propagating their own individual schools of thought.

Probably, the earliest interpretation of Brahma sutras is the work of Bhaskara, who advocates the 'Bheda-abheda-vada' – where in the individual soul is seen as different and also not different from God (Brahman). Adi Shankara advocates the theory of a Nirguna Brahman (and identified it with the Atman), as well as the theory of Maya.

Nimbarka combines both dualism and non-dualism (Dvaita-Advaita-vada). Ramanuja commenting on the Brahma sutras claims that everything is Brahman, but also acknowledges the reality of individual souls and the material world. Madhva claims absolute difference from Brahman and the individual souls (Dvaita-vada).

Other major commentaries on the sutras are by Yadva Prakasha (1140 CE), Srikantha (1270 CE) , Sripati (1400 CE), Vallabha (1479 CE), Shuka (1550 CE), Vignana Bhikshu (1600 CE), and Baladeva (1725 CE), (For details see Chapters 6 and 7).

SMRITIS

Smritis, literally mean 'that which is remembered'. Smritis contain 'the Rules of Dharma' (and hence termed as 'Dharma Shastras') and supplement and explain the sociological and ritualistic injunctions of the Vedas. Even though there are innumerable texts which are considered as Smritis, the most important of them according to many scholars are those of Manu, Narada, Parashara and Yagnavalka.

They lay down the laws which regulate the national, communal, family and individual obligations in general and also special situations. They lay down the dharma as well as duties for kings, other officials and also for people belonging to different Varnas. They also deal with the 'Dharma' to be followed by people in four Ashramas (Brahmacharya, Grihasta, Vanaprastha, and Sanyasa).

The three important parts in Smritis are the rules relating to –

1. Achara (ceremonial duties),
2. Vyavahara (social transaction/civil and criminal related litigation) and
3. Prayashchitta (penance or expiatory rites/punishments).

Manu says

One is born alone and dies alone. One enjoys the fruits of his deeds alone. It is Dharma alone which comes to one's help in the end. Neither one should cling to life nor court death, but live a life of non-attachment, and do one's duty properly. One who sees the self in all beings attains equality with everything and realizes the state of Brahman.

THE EPICS

In ancient India the kings who ruled over India either belonged to Surya-vamsha (the Solar Race) or Chandra-vamsha (the Lunar Race). *Ramayana* depicts the story of Sri Rama who belonged to Surya-vamsha and lived in Treta-yuga. *Mahabharata* depicts the stories of kings who belonged to Chandra-vamsha and lived in Dwapara-yuga. These two works, essentially reflect to some extent, the histories of dynasties of the kings who ruled India at that time. Apart from Vedic gods, we see the worship of Shiva, Vishnu and Shakti during the epic period. The age of the epics is generally placed between 1500 to 1000 BCE.

Universally regarded as among the worlds' greatest epics; *Ramayana* and *Mahabharata* are the two great Sanskrit works, which reflect the essence, culture and ethos of the early part of Hindu civilization. Valmiki's *Ramayana* has 24,000 slokas (stanzas), spread over 7 chapters (kandas). Linguistically, the period of *Ramayana* is placed just after the Vedic period. *Mahabharata* (dictated by Veda-Vyasa and said to have been written down by Lord Ganesha) is a much bigger epic having 100,000 slokas spread over 18 chapters (Parvas). Innumerable short stories, myths and fables are inter-woven into the main frame work of the story of the *Mahabharata*, thus making it into the largest epic in the world.

Through their stories, these two epics propagate various human values and the ultimate triumph of good over evil forces. These two epics in turn, have become a never ending source of stories which are told and retold in many languages both within India and outside.

Ramayana

The epic *Ramayana* tells the story of Sri Rama, who went into exile for 14 years along with his brother Lakshmana and wife Sita. Ravana, the demon king of Lanka, abducts Sita. Rama fights Ravana and brings back Sita. The story is full of morals and thought provoking lines. The moral of the story highlights the importance of being truthful always and never to deter from the path of good in one's life.

Rama as the hero of the epic represents qualities such as honour, courage, valour and single mindedness in facing great difficulties so that he could fulfil his fathers' words of promise. The other prominent characters of *Ramayana* – Lakshmana, Sita, Hanuman and even Ravana are portrayed in all their glory.

The story also highlights several ideals – truthfulness, obedience to elders, total affection between brothers, the 'swami-bhakti' of Hanuman, etc. – which have inspired people for the past several thousand years.

Mahabharata

The epic *Mahabharata (dated about 1500 BCE)* is considered sacred by the Hindus and is known as *Panchama Veda* as it is said to contain the essence of the four Vedas. It is described by various scholars as 'Sruti, Smriti, Purana, Itihasa, Adhyatma Shastra, and Maha-Kavya (epic)' all embodied in one single work. It contains about one lakh slokas, which makes it the greatest epic in the world.

It is also considered a very sacred work, because of the presence of *Bhagavad Gita* and 'Vishnu Sahasranama' which are considered 'holiest of the holies' and vehicles of 'Moksha Sadhana' for an individual to attain salvation.

Mahabharata describes the story of the epic struggle between two dynasties – Pandavas and Kauravas and the ultimate triumph of 'Good over Evil'. *Mahabharata* dwells on life's important goals and declares that one should never deviate from the path of one's Dharma.

Mahabharata is also considered to be an embodiment of 18 virtues (values): *Dharma (represented by Dharmaraja); Bhakti, Jnana, Vairagya, Pragna, Medha, Dhruthi, Sthithi, Yoga, Prana, Bala, (represented by Bhima); Shravana, Manana, Nididhyasana, (represented by Arjuna); Sheela, Vinaya, (Nakula-Sahadeva); Adhyatma (Druapadi); and Paratatva (Sri Krishna).*

For the past several thousand years, *Ramayana* and *Mahabharata* have been important sources of inspiration for the common people as well as several poets and authors, who have written innumerable literary works in Sanskrit and several other languages.

THE PURANAS

Puranas are said to contain the essence of the Vedas. Historians generally date the beginning of the composition of the Puranas to the early centuries of the Christian era. The Puranas were essentially written keeping the masses in view (as they could not understand the higher levels of philosophical thought) and also to impress upon them the necessity of following one's Dharma to obtain divine grace. They emphasize the worship of various gods (in their respective Puranas) – Brahma, Vishnu, Shiva, Surya, Ganesha, Skanda, etc. These Puranas recount the mythological legends of Gods and Goddesses, their interactions with humans, their battles with the demons and the rituals of worship of the respective gods.

The Puranas were also used as a means to propagate the religion of the respective sects. These Puranas were meant to be recited orally in public (in public places like Mutts and temples) to attract larger audiences. These Puranas were also critical of those who followed other 'Shramana' sects like Buddhism and Jainism. The Puranic religion lent itself to assimilation of new deities, mythologies and rituals. This was the time when 'Purusharthas' (Dharma, Artha, Kama and Moksha) and 'Trivarga Sidhanta' gained prominence.

'Amara Kosha' tells us that a Purana should contain the following five core elements – Srishthi (creation), Upa-srishthi (counter-creation), the lineage of Gods, Manvantar (time period of Manus), and histories of dynasties of kings:

> *Sargascha prati-sargascha vamsho manvantaraani cha* ।
> *Vamshaanucharitam cheti lakshananaam tu panchakam* ॥

These puranas are further classified as Maha-puranas, Upa-puranas and Oupa-puranas, each being 18 in number. The Upa-puranas and

Oupa-puranas are based on the Maha-puranas. The Maha-puranas are further classified as Satvic, Rajasic and Tamasic according to the gunas (characteristics) highlighted in them.

1. *Satvic group of Puranas*: Vishnu, Naaradiiya, Bhagavata, Garuda, Padma, and Varaaha.
2. *Rajasic group of Puranas*: Brahmanda, Brahma-Vaivartha, Markandeya, Bhavishya, Vamana and Brahma.
3. *Tamasic group of Puranas:* Matsya, Koorma, Linga, Skanda, Agni and Shaiva.

The **Upa-puranas** are: Adi, Narasimha, Kumarakruta-skanda, Vayu, Doorvasa, Narada, Kapila, Vishnu-dharma, Oushanasa, Brahmanda, Kaalika, Varuna, Maheswara, Saamba, Soura, Parashara, Maricha, and Bhaskara.

The **Oupa-puranas** are: Sanatkumara, Bruhannaradiya, Aditya, Surya, Nandikeshwara, Koorma, Bhagavata, Vasistha, Bhargava, Mudgala, Kalki, Devi, Maha-Bhagavata, Bruhadharma, Paranandа, Vahni, Pashupati, and Harivamsha.

AGAMAS

Agamas are non-Vedic collection of Shastras, which deal with all the Dharmic activities to be carried out in life. Some of the Agamas are also known as 'Tantras' as they deal with rituals and practices to be followed for worshipping each deity. Besides Hindu agama texts, agamas are found in both early Jain and Buddhist scriptures also.

The subject matter in 'Agamas' is largely divided into four parts:

1. Jnana (relating to Adhyatma Tatva);
2. Yoga (practices leading to Moksha);
3. Kriya (matter relating to specific Puja-vidhis of deities, temple rituals, festivals, etc.); and
4. Charya (details of steps to be followed in real life).

Even though there are numerous agamas, majority of them are classified as those belonging to either Shiva, Vishnu or Shaakta sects.

The followers of these sects are expected to follow the guidelines laid down in their respective 'agamas' while worshipping their deities.

Shaiva Agamas

Shaiva agamas are 28 in number. They are also known as 'Pasupata' agamas. They are also considered as important sources used in the development of 'Shaiva Sidhanta' philosophy in South India (See Chapter 8).

Vaishnava Agamas

The 'Purusha Sukta' perceived by 'Narayana Rishi' of Rig Veda is considered to be the original source for Vaishnava and Bhagavata sects that consider Vishnu as the supreme God.

The two most important Vaishnava agamas are 'Vaikhanasa' and 'Pancharatra'. There is a vast amount of literature (Samhitas) pertaining to these agamas. They prescribe in detail the methods of idol worship, description of various types of deities, meditation, details of Mantras, and 'prayaschitta'.

3

The Essence of Hindu Dharma

THE CONCEPT OF DHARMA

The concept of 'Dharma' is quite unique to Hindu Religion. It was perceived by the ancient 'Rishis' as a solution to several eternal problems confronting the human race. It is presumed that the various interpretations of the concept of 'Dharma' evolved over a period of several centuries and cover a wide spectrum of meanings. 'Dharma' cannot be defined in a single word or sentence, as it is a Sanskrit expression of widest import. It can only be explained or interpreted.

Dharma has been interpreted both in religious as well as ethical contexts. In ancient texts, the concept of 'Dharma' was given a variety of meanings. 'Dharma' meant –

1. Duty as enjoined by the Vedas,
2. Virtue attained by doing it,
3. Good attainable by performing Vedic injunctions – especially rituals, religious practices, etc.

Besides, religious texts interpreted 'Dharma' differently in different contexts:

1. *Performing one's duty sincerely is the real Dharma* – replies Dharmaraja in answer to Yaksha's question in Mahabharata.
2. Gita says *that by doing his own duty in life, a man reaches perfection.*

3. Bhishma in *Mahabharata* says – *that which ensures the welfare of living beings is Dharma.*

The above interpretations lead us to believe, that the ancient 'Rishis' did not equate 'Dharma' with religion at all. They in fact, conceptualized 'Dharma' more as an ethical code, which can be interpreted even beyond the ambit of religion itself. Only much later, it was codified in canons in the form of 'Dharma Shastras'.

Buddhist texts also use the term 'Dharma' (rendered as Dhamma) in the sense of regularity of activities, virtue or justice though these conceptions are different from Vedic texts. Jains considered Dharma as 'activity' and 'adharma' as inactivity.

'Dharma' is a collective term which encompasses righteous conduct in every sphere of human activity. The supremacy of Dharma has been an article of faith with the ardent followers of Hindu religion. Actions taken by individuals or society at large, which are not in conformity with Dharma, will ultimately lead to conflicts, fights, loss of happiness and peace, to individuals as well as society itself.

Interpretation of Dharma in the Present Day Context

Dharma has been described by various wise-people in different ways as it is used in different contexts with a variety of meanings:

1. To the common man, Dharma is 'duty in life without complaint'.
2. To a knowledgeable person, it is the accepted way of life by the society when followed properly as it brings peace and prosperity to all.
3. To a devout Hindu, Dharma is the divine law which governs all material affairs.
4. Dharma can also be described as the established and accepted code of conduct of – righteousness and good behaviour.

Justice Rama Jois in his book on 'Dharma' has given a wide variety of interpretations of the word 'Dharma' – Justice (Nyaya) in the context of what is right in a given circumstance, moral values of life, pious obligations of individuals, etc.

Interpretation of Dharma in Different Contexts

The concept of Dharma lends itself to a whole spectrum of interpretation in different contexts. Even though it is normally considered as the righteous way of life, the concept changes with a person's age, class, occupation, gender, etc.

For example, the 'Brahmacharya dharma' is different from 'Grihasta dharma' and 'Stree-dharma' is different from 'Purusha dharma'. Similarly 'Samaja Dharma', 'Rashtra Dharma', 'Raja Dharma', 'Kula Dharma', 'Jaati Dharma' are used in different contexts.

Sapta Dharma (Seven Categories of Dharmic Duties)

Dharmic duties of a person are usually classified into seven categories:

1. *Nitya Dharma:* Duties enjoined on a person in his daily life – honesty, sincerity, integrity, etc. – also separately mentioned below under the heading 'Essence of Dharma'.
2. *Sva-Dharma:* Enables a person to develop a code of conduct of his own, but such a Dharma should not come into conflict with the Dharma followed by others. Sva-Dharma, also enables a person to develop his talent and capacities professionally to the fullest extent – talent in music, arts, sports, etc.
3. *Varna Dharma:* Conditions that come with duty in a person's professional life – Raja Dharma for a king, Adhyapaka Dharma for a teacher, Kshatriya Dharma for a warrior, Vysya Dharma for a trader, etc.
4. *Ashrama Dharma:* Duties relating to the four 'Ashramas' described herein separately.
5. *Nimitta Dharma:* Dharma practiced on specific occasions – while performing rituals, Diksha, Vrata, Puja, fasting, pilgrimage, etc.

6. *Apad-Dharma:* When a person cannot perform his regular Dharma under testing circumstances – Saving a life by telling falsehood to a murderer, a doctor assuring a dying person that he will recover and will live long, killing a person or animal in self defense, etc.
7. *Yuga Dharma:* Following social norms of the period as they keep changing from 'yuga to yuga' (period to period). For example several orthodox rituals followed earlier are no longer followed now. Travelling overseas – was prohibited a century ago. It is no longer considered an anti-dharmic activity.

THE ESSENCE OF DHARMA

The essence of Dharma has been discussed in many scriptures. Truthfulness, forgiveness, purity, absence of enmity, straightforwardness, maintaining persons dependent on oneself, sharing wealth with others, to be free from anger and procreation of children from one's wife alone – are considered as the nine cardinal principles of Dharma. Observance of these principles leads to real happiness and harmony in life.

Manu Smriti is more precise when it advocates the five paths of Dharma: (These have to be followed by every person as 'Nitya Dharma')

1. ***Ahimsa*** means non-violence. The concept of 'ahimsa' is as old as the Vedas. The Chandogya Upanishad uses the word to mean a code of conduct and bars violence against all creatures *(sarva-bhuta)*. It also names ahimsa as one of the five principal virtues.

   However, later on, ahimsa also came to mean kindness towards all living beings including animals. It is an important tenet of Karmic theory as well as Dharma, as one may be born even in the form of animals and hence one should respect all living beings.
2. ***Satya*** loosely translates into English as Truthfulness. The concept of 'Truth' is not merely correctness but is more metaphysical

in nature. 'Patanjali's Yoga Sutra' says: 'When one is firmly established in speaking the truth, the fruits of action become subservient to him'. Brhadaranyaka Upanishad says *Asato-ma sad-gamaya* (lead me from delusion to truth).

The philosophic meaning of the word also refers to 'Brahman' which is also termed as 'Truth' – defined as – 'That which has no distortion, that which pervades the universe and that which is beyond distinctions of time, space and person'. Pursuing the path of truthfulness and in search of the 'Ultimate Truth' is also a path of Dharma.

3. ***Asteya*** means non-stealing, non-coveting others wealth, and non-hoarding. It also implies not-acquiring illegitimate wealth. All human beings are exhorted to adhere to 'Asteya' as a path of dharma. It is also one of the 'Yamas' or disciplines.
4. ***Shoucha*** means purity. Purity is required at three levels for a person, if he has to follow the path of Dharma – physical, mental as well as spiritual levels, which in turn has to result in purity in thought, speech and action. Spiritual purity leads to salvation and realization of god.
5. ***Indriya-nigraha*** means control of the senses. One's sensual desires sow seeds of conflicting emotions in one's mind and thus the person becomes a slave of his senses. The instability of the mind has to be controlled through 'Indriya-nigraha', self-discipline, development of detachment to sensory objects and practice of renunciation.

Important Quotations Relating to Dharma

These are some of the important quotations from the Hindu scriptures, which highlight the various aspects of Dharma –

1. *Satyam Jnanam Anantam Brahma* – Brahman is the Truth, Knowledge and Infinity.
2. *Ahimso Paramo-dharmah* – Non-violence is the greatest kind of Dharma.

3. *Satyam Vada* – Tell the Truth.
4. *Anrutham na vadet* – Never tell untruth.
5. *Matru Devo Bhava, Pitru Devo Bhava, Acharya Devo Bhava* – Treat your mother, father and teacher as God.
6. *Karmanyevadhikaraste...* – Your right is to perform your duty

According to 'Vidura Neeti' – Yagna, Adhyayana, Daana, Tapas, Satya, Kshama, Ghruna (Daya), Alobha are considered the eight paths of Dharma. As already discussed, Smritis prescribe the code of conduct to be followed by persons in practicing Dharma. In ancient times, power was conferred on the Kings to rule in accordance with Dharma.

PAAPA AND PUNYA

The concepts of 'Paapa' and 'Punya' are unique to Hindu Dharma. These can be compared to 'Bank Accounts' in the life of an individual. It is said that only these two follow the individual through Samsara and Karma, from one life to another. They are also responsible in the choice of their subsequent births.

'Paapa' can be described as the accumulation of the effect of bad deeds in the life of an individual. Similarly 'Punya' can be described as the accumulation of the effect of good deeds by an individual. By following the precepts prescribed by Dharma, an individual can accumulate Punya and work towards salvation.

One popular sloka says that 'in all the 18 Puranas, Vyasa propounds the same two Tatvas: 'Helping others is Punya and harassing others in Paapa'.

Astadasha Puraneshu Vysa-sya Vachana-dvayam ।
Paropakaarah Punyaya, Paapaya Parapeedanam ।।

Hence whatever action leads to Paapa, is considered to be against Dharma. Whatever action yields Punya is definitely Dharmic in nature. If we follow the paths of Dharma, then it leads one on the path of self-realization. It also helps in making the society to retain its Dharmic identity.

TRIVARGA SIDHANTA

The Concepts of Dharma, Artha and Kama

'Trivarga Sidhanta', comprises of *Dharma, Artha* and *Kama* and is termed as the sum and substance of the 'Hindu Philosophy of Life'. The concept of close relationships between the three 'Purusharthas' developed over a period of several centuries. At a later stage, Moksha (liberation) was added as the fourth 'Purushartha'. The concepts as per 'Trivarga Sidhanta' are:

1. ***Dharma*** is termed as *that which sustains.* Dharma lays down duties and obligations to be followed by everyone.
2. ***Artha*** is termed as *that which one seeks.* In a broad sense Artha covers one's professional activities and material wealth which sustains one's life in this world. 'Artha' came to be understood as 'wealth' and the second 'Purushartha'.
3. ***Kama*** means *Desire.* Kama is also taken to mean as pleasure. It drives man in the pursuit of happiness. (which is termed as the basic and natural instinct of man).

The ancient philosophers, who propounded this doctrine, understood that the fulfilment of desires was essential for any person, and unless these desires are regulated by Shastras, they would bring out undesirable results. Hence Dharma Shastras prescribed that fulfilment of either Kama or Artha should always conform to Dharma and should never be inconsistent with it. Manu specifically says that Kama and Artha must be rejected if they are contrary to Dharma. In case of conflict, Artha and Kama should always give way to Dharma.

The scriptures state that morning is the precious time to carry out activities leading to 'Dharma', the afternoon should be spent in activities relating to acquisition of 'Artha' and evening should be spent in activities for satisfaction of 'Kama'. In the early part of life importance is to be given to satisfaction of wants, the middle part in acquisition of wealth, and the later years to be spent in Dharmic activities.

YOGA

Yoga essentially means path or method. A person in order to attain his 'Adhyatmic' goal in life (self-realization/Mukti/Moksha), can follow any one method (Yoga) prescribed by the scriptures – Bhakti Yoga, Karma Yoga, Raja Yoga or Jnana Yoga. These methods have been elaborately dealt in Gita, Yoga Sutras and 'Hata-Yoga Pradeepika'. Practice of one yoga, does not exclude a person from practicing other paths too. (See also Chapter 10 on Gita)

Many schools believe that different types of Yogas blend themselves and aid the 'Sadhaka' in pursuit of his goal. For example, practice of Jnana-Yoga may help a person to practice Bhakti-Yoga better.

1. ***Bhakti Yoga:*** *(The path of love and devotion to a particular god):* Many devotional schools teach that 'Bhakti' is the only practical path for the ordinary devout, to achieve Mukti or Moksha in today's world. *Bhagavata Purana* teaches nine primary forms of Bhakti. Ramanuja, Madhva, Chaitanya and several other saints propounded 'Bhakti' as a superior path to salvation.
2. ***Karma Yoga:*** *(The path of disinterested action):* In Gita, Sri Krishna, teaches that we should perform our different activities without being attached to the fruits of these activities. He further explains that karma done without expectations, motives, or in anticipation of its outcome, purifies the mind and leads one towards the spiritual path.
3. ***Raja Yoga:*** *(The path of Meditation):* is a part of the 'Sankhya' tradition and is described in Patanjali's 'yoga Sutras'. Raja Yoga deals with the disciplining of the mind through meditation, which further leads one to spiritual liberation. Raja yoga is sometimes referred to as 'Astanga-yoga' as its practice disciplines the body also.
4. ***Jnana Yoga:*** *(The path of spiritual knowledge and wisdom):* Adi Shankara gave primary importance to Jnana yoga as leading to knowledge of the 'Brahman', where as Ramanuja regarded knowledge, only as a condition of devotion. In Gita, Sri Krishna

says that 'Jnana' consists of properly understanding 'Kshetra' (the body) and 'Kshetra-jna' (the knower of the body-the soul). Jnana Yoga teaches four means to salvation –

(*i*) *Viveka* (ability to discriminate),
(*ii*) *Vairagya* (detachment from worldly pleasures),
(*iii*) *Shat-samapt* (6 virtues) and
(*iv*) *mumukshutva* (intense longing for liberation).

HINDU DHARMIC RITUALS

A vast majority of Hindus practice religious rituals on a daily basis. These may vary from person to person depending on his level of initiation into these rituals. They also vary between individuals, families, locations, castes and societies across the country.

1. Lighting a lamp at home before a family deity or in a temple,
2. Worshipping/Conduct of Puja on a daily basis,
3. Meditation/Dhyana,
4. Visit to a temple either daily or on a particular day of the week,
5. Breaking a coconut in front of a deity,
6. Conduct of 'Sandhya-Vandana',
7. Conduct of homa or sacrifice,
8. Worshipping of the *Tulsi plant*,
9. Conduct of daily Arati before the family deity,
10. Giving alms to the poor/Feeding the poor,
11. Taking *Ashirvad* of elders

These are some of the rituals which are followed by a majority of followers of Hindu Dharma.

Elaborate rituals are also performed to mark major transition points in the lives of individuals. Orthodox families invite priests to perform some of these rituals –

1. Ceremonies are performed during pregnancy to ensure the health of the mother and the child growing in the mother's womb.

2. After the birth of the child, a number of rituals are performed – like the naming ceremony, first feeding with solid food, ear piercing, the first hair cut (shaving of the head before the family deity), etc.
3. Upanayana – the sacred thread ceremony which initiates a person in to 'Brahmacharya'.
4. Marriage ceremony – the actual practices vary among various castes and linguistic groups.
5. Death and funeral ceremonies – here also actual practices vary: cremation and burial – both practices are in vogue as per their respective castes and traditions.
6. Ceremonies performed every year (Shraadh Karma) to appease the souls of the departed elders, and help them on their path to Moksha, as well as to seek their blessings.
7. 'Pitru Paksha Shraadha' also known as 'Mahalaya Shraadha' relates to ceremonies performed during the 'Krishna Paksha' of Bhadrapad month in South India or during 'Aswin' month in North India. During this period, rituals are performed to offer food to all the departed elders (relatives, ancestors, parents, etc.) through the priests. The aim is to get liberation for the departed souls.

GOTRA

The concept of Gotra appeared in later Vedic times. It literally means cow-pen (go–tra), where cattle belonging to the whole clan was kept. It was used as a means of identifying a particular clan. The term 'gotra' broadly refers to people who are descendents in an unbroken male line from a common male ancestor (probably a Rishi). Hence people belonging to the same 'gotra' are prohibited from marrying among themselves.

According to Panini and several Sutras, Viswamitra, Jamadagni, Bharadwaja, Gautama, Atri, Vasistha, Kashyapa and Agastya are the 8 Rishis who established their clans originally. But these grew over a period of time and there are now 49 established gotras among Hindus.

A Gotra is different from a Kula (jati) who belong to a group of people who follow the same set of dharmic traditions. Marriage within a Kula is always preferred.

FOUR ASHRAMAS

This concept which came into practice in the later Vedic period refers to the four stages in the life of an individual. The four Ashramas are –

1. ***Brahmacharyashrama*** – The first period of a religious student's life (between 8 and 20 years) before he gets married. Brahmacharya may also be followed by any person, who practices chastity.
2. ***Grihasthashrama*** – The period when a person lives with his family and earns honestly for a living.
3. ***Vanaprasthashrama*** – The period when a person renounces worldly pleasures and retires to the forest and leads an ascetic life. Nowadays, it is possible that a person can lead a life akin to the Vanaprastha Ashrama, by attaching to some monastic order/temple and serving the society.
4. ***Sanyasashrama*** – The period when a person renounces the world and family completely and lives the life of an ascetic and spends time in meditation and prayer.

RENUNCIATION

Realization of god can be achieved through the path of 'Renunciation'. Renunciation in the present day context does not imply renunciation of home and family ties, but renunciation of one's desires, affection and attachment. Renunciation should result in surpassing the mental obstacles, lead to greater devotion to god and a smoother sailing in the path of self-realization.

The scriptures say that a person need not become a 'Sanyasi' and renounce the world in order to realize God. One who is having a family also, can realize God through utter devotion (Bhakti), prayer, meditation, japa, worship, singing of bhajans and hymns that glorify

God (but without the desire for obtaining any object). One has also to adopt the well established practice of 'Renunciation' of the following Acts (through mind, speech and body):

1. All forms of evil Acts (Nishiddha Karma) which are prohibited by scriptures – theft, adultery, deception, fraud, utterance of false-hood, oppression, violence, taking of prohibited drinks and food, wrong-doing, cursing in the name of God, etc.
2. All acts (including auspicious acts like worship, sacrifice, etc.) done with a selfish motive and for getting objects of enjoyment – like women, progeny, wealth, etc. The desire for honour, fame, and social prestige, are considered products of 'prarabdha-karma'.
3. Expecting money or service from others, acceptance of gifts or service from others with a selfish interest is to be totally renounced.
4. All acts enjoined in the scriptures (worship of Gods, service of parents and elders, performance of sacrifices and charities, sustenance of the body, etc.) should be performed by duly renouncing every form of desire.
5. One should have a sense of detachment for all work done through mind, speech and body as well as over all worldly objects and family ties, regarding them as impermanent.

Sri Ramana Maharishi says 'All activities of a wise man exist only in the eyes of the others and not in his own, although he may be accomplishing immense tasks, he really does nothing. Therefore his activities do not stand in the way of inaction and peace of mind. For, he knows the truth that all activities take place in his mere presence and that he does nothing. Hence he will remain as the silent witness of all the activities taking place.'

SIGNIFICANCE OF 'OM'

Om is one of the most widely chanted Hindu religious symbols and is considered a very sacred Mantra. Its form is worshipped, contemplated upon, or used as an auspicious sign throughout the length and breadth of the country. Uttering its sound is considered auspicious, while beginning any task that we wish to undertake.

This sound is considered to be divine in nature and has the most profound effect on one's body and mind, as well as one's surroundings. It is also repeated as a Mantra and meditated upon. It fills the mind with peace and makes it focused. People meditate on its meaning and attain realization.

It is also considered as the universal name of 'God or Brahman – the supreme being'. The formless and attribute-less Brahman is represented by the silence between two 'Om' chants. 'Om' is also called 'pranava' that means 'that' (symbol or sound) by which the Lord is praised.

The three syllables of Om: a-u-m, also symbolise:

1. The three states of consciousness (waking, dream and deep sleep),
2. The three deities (Brahma, Vishnu and Maheswara),
3. The entire essence of the three Vedas,
4. The three sacred words (Bhuh, bhuvah, Suvah), which are part of the Gayatri Mantra, etc.

Om represents all these and beyond. Most Mantras and Vedic prayers start with Om as the first sound. It is also used as a greeting among many communities – Om Hari Om, etc. Prayers also end with the phrase: 'Om Tat Sat'.

VARNASHRAMA DHARMA

This word has been narrowly interpreted as a caste based system which in turn was said to be based on the birth of a person. But it implies the division of the society into four categories according to natural tendencies and work done by the persons concerned. They may be broadly classified as – Thinker Class, Ruler Class, Trader Class and Worker Class. This type of division was present in all societies and cultures even though they were not categorized by names as done in India.

There are several instances of prominent personalities taking up vocations unrelated to their Varna – King Vishwamitra who became a Brahma-rishi, Valmiki who wrote *Ramayana*, Veda-Vyasa who divided the Vedas and wrote *Mahabharata*, Prince Sidhartha who later became Gautama Buddha, the famous Sanskrit poet Kalidasa, etc.

But over centuries, it has degenerated into caste system which has generated much heat and hatred among various castes. Swami Vivekananda States:

> *In religion there is no caste. A man from the highest caste and a man from the lowest may become a monk in India and the castes become equal. ... The caste system is opposed to the religion of Vedanta... The plan is to make everybody a Brahmana, the Brahmana being the ideal of humanity...Let everyone be taught that the Divine is within and every one will work out his salvation... The solution is not bringing down the higher, but by raising the lower up to the level of the higher....*

(Swami Vivekananda – on India and Her Problems, Chapter VI)

Mahatma Gandhi wrote:

> *There are varnas, but none of the varnas are superior to the others. Varna does not connote superiority, it connotes different functions and different duties. Caste distinctions in so far as they imply superiority, of one over another have to be abolished altogether. That is merely a phase or a grade of untouchability. But in so far as caste in the sense of Varna fulfills a nature of law of conservation of human energy and true economies, it is good to recognize and obey the law. (Harijan. Feb 2, 1934)*

A host of social reformers have worked incessantly over the past century, to eradicate the evil effects of the caste system in India. With urbanization, modernization and globalization of the Indian economy, caste based Indian society, is slowly evolving into a class based society.

The society today, recognizes only three classes – the rich class, the middle class and the poor class. Caste is now used to get social benefits (in employment and education). For marriages, the tradition has been to search within a caste, though inter-caste marriages have not been uncommon. But caste based politics has come to stay on the Indian political scene.

However, the principles enunciated by Hindu Dharma are as relevant today, as they were thousands of years ago. They help everyone to lead a pious life in the pursuit of peace, happiness and self-realization.

4

Origins of Vedic Religion
(*and Re-dating of Various Periods*)

SOURCES OF ANCIENT INDIAN HISTORY

Chronology of the early part of 'Ancient Indian History' is almost impossible to construct due to lack of historical evidences. The early Vedic people are presumed to have led a pastoral existence and hence did not leave behind them any solid material remains. In such cases historians generally look for other evidences – mainly linguistic and literary sources. The problem with literary sources from Ancient India is that they belong to a span of time (probably several centuries) rather than a specific time period. This is true of early Vedic literature.

There is another dimension for the lack of sources on early Vedic religion. This has been remarkably brought out by 'Alberuni' in the opening chapter of his book:

> *The Hindus believe that there is no country but theirs, no nation like theirs, no king like theirs, no religion like theirs, ... They are by nature niggardly in communicating what they know, and take the greatest possible care to withhold it from men of another caste from among their own people, still more of course from a foreigner. (E C Sacahu – ed. and tr. – Alberuni's India, pp 22–3)*

One may or may not agree with Alberuni's statement, but the fact remains that we would (at this distance in time) have been more enlightened, if the learned people of that period had kept proper and accurate records of their history, achievements, etc.

Ancient Indians are usually charged with a lack of historical sense. They did not maintain records like the Greeks. Early Vedic people observed the lunar calendar (with adhika masa) which was not reliable. Besides, the concept of time in ancient India was cyclic. All human activities were continuously repeated in each cycle. (Even today we follow a 60 year cycle in our lunar Hindu almanacs). They adapted the solar calendar only from the sixth/fifth Century (BCE).

The language spoken by early Vedic people was archaic Sanskrit, which had several words common to languages, spoken by various groups of people of Central Asia at that time. This has led to several distortions in writing the 'History of Ancient India'.

THE PURANAS AS HISTORICAL SOURCES

We have a semblance of history in the Puranas, but they do not contain exact dates of events and sometimes the time periods are exaggerated (like the periods of the four yugas). Statement about events, are made in a future tense, although they were written much after the events had happened. Besides, there is no sense of demarcation between history and mythology, by the Puranic writers.

This ambiguity in chronology is offset to some extent, in the later part of ancient Indian History, as Buddhist literary works are considered usually reliable. These works reckon from the date of the death of the Buddha – where there are three alternative dates – 544/486/483 BCE, – one of the last two dates seems more probable.

From the sixth century BCE onwards, with the establishment of kingdoms like Anga, Magadha, etc. in the Gangetic Plain, historical records help in tracing the history of Hindu religion with greater accuracy. Sources such as biographies of kings, records of foreign travellers, etc. help in dating Indian history only from 300 BCE onwards. From the first century BCE, precisely dated inscriptions put up by various dynasties are available and historically these dates are accepted universally.

DISTORTIONS IN WRITING ANCIENT INDIAN HISTORY

The writing of Indian History began with the colonial perceptions of the Indian past, which were invariably influenced by the then prevalent (European) ideas about history. European historians who came to study Indian History (in the eighteenth and nineteenth centuries) started searching for history, but could not find any, that conformed to their view of what a history should be. Hence there was bound to be distortions in the history written by them. The reasons for these distortions were many:

1. They were baffled by an ancient religion that was so completely different from their own – It was not monotheistic, there was no historical founder, no single sacred text or dogma and finally, no church like organization to control the religious beliefs. Patronage of kings extended to more than one religion, whereas, this was not the case in their countries.
2. These scholars were mainly Christians and firm believers of the Bible and brought up in strict Christian beliefs, traditions and practices. Hence they could not understand an ancient civilization much older than their biblical concepts of Creation (dated 4000 BCE) and the 'Great Flood' (dated 1500 BCE) mentioned in the Bible. This also led to dating of various periods like the Vedic period and the Epic period far later than the actual periods.
3. However these periods were dated just before the Buddhist times, as Buddha had rejected several of the Vedic concepts.
4. Many of these historians could not understand the Hindu concepts of Karma and Rebirth, as they were grounded in a tradition which believes that the life of a person ends at death and one has to await the final judgement.
5. Some of the European Sanskrit Scholars were also non-believers and rationalists. They compared Vedas etc with Old Testament for chronology/parallel stories/concepts, etc. For example, Griffith – the most authentic translator of the four Vedas – in his preface of Rig Veda says that the hymns lack 'poetical aspects'/it is not poetry like Old Testament.

6. These historians had also been brought up on the European classical concept of 'the hegemony of Europe' and according to them, the greatest civilizations were the Greek and the Roman Civilizations. Consequently every new cultural discovery in other countries was viewed against the norms and standards of Greek and Roman Civilizations:

One example of connecting even unconnected events with Greece is given below: .... *The most important paintings at Ajanta... suggest the possibility that the Ajanta school of pictorial art may have been derived from Persia and ultimately from Greece* – 'Early History of India' (Oxford 1924 pp 442)

Another Indian historian has made out the following additional points, which she has considered responsible for distorting ancient Indian History by European scholars:

1. 'To the imperialist Europe, India was an enigma that did not fit into the neat categories of 'fair skinned civilized Europeans and dark skinned savage aboriginals.... The indologists presented the highly developed culture and civilization of India as a product of fair skinned invading European Aryans who had civilized the dark skinned aborigines...' during the Rig Vedic Period.
2. Some of the prejudices that European scholars had against ancient Indian scholars is reflected by Max Mueller who considered the Aryans of the Rig Veda as the nearest intellectual relatives and fellow workers of Europeans and observed that 'Sayana' the fourteenth century commentator of the Rig Veda had no original sense of the Vedic hymns.
3. The British after facing the fury of upper caste soldiers in the revolt of 1857 attempted to represent themselves as a part of the same Aryan family. E.B. Havel called India under the British as new 'Aryavarta'. Even some eminent Indians unfortunately supported this view. 'Keshab Chunder Sen' stated that 'in the advent of the English nation in India; we see a reunion of parted cousins, the descendents of two different families of the ancient Aryan race'.

4. The Christian missionaries of the nineteenth century, used the 'hostility between the Aryas and the Dasas in the *Rig Veda* to argue that the lower castes were the descendents of the Dasas who were oppressed by the Aryan Brahmins. They directly linked the disabilities suffered by the lower castes in the nineteenth and twentieth centuries to the Aryan invasion. However, Dr. Ambedkar who was fighting for the rights of depressed classes described this theory as 'pre-concocted and perversion of scientific investigation by western scholars'.

However it was unfortunate to note that these European perceptions gradually influenced the way in which Indians themselves viewed their own history, religion and culture. Most Indian historians of early twentieth century were either participants in the national freedom movement or were influenced by it. These historians tended to endorse a majority of the views of the European historians, but only included certain concepts like 'nationalism' which was alien even to kings of ancient India.

Previously, there was an emphasis to divide Indian History into three major periods: Hindu, Muslim and British, which the later day historians changed to Ancient, Medieval and Modern; however the time periods have remained the same. It is therefore surprising that these dates are commonly accepted by a majority of Indian historians also. This indicates a mindset of even the present day historians resisting to see history in a totally different light.

In spite of new evidences and epoch making archeological discoveries, our history textbooks have changed little, giving our children a totally distorted view of our glorious past and we still find every boy and girl in India repeating *Aryans came to India in 1500 BC ....*

The dating done by many historians even today is as shown below:

1. Harappan Culture: 2600 – 1700 BCE
2. Composition of Vedic literature: 1500 – 500 BCE
3. Epic Period: 800 BCE
4. Urbanization in Gangetic Plain, Rise of Magadha, Mahavira, Gautama Buddha: 600 BCE

According to even our own historians, the Vedic period started around 1500 BCE and continued to around 500 BCE. Even this seems improbable as the Epic period (which was usually dated around 800 BCE) had ended even before the period of the Buddha in the sixth century BCE. The foregoing analysis helps us to critically analyze the origins of Vedic religion.

ORIGINS OF VEDIC RELIGION

The Myth that Aryans came from Central Asia

On the basis of certain evidences, historians have placed the origins of Vedic religion to around mid-second millennium BCE. We need to look into the controversies of whether Aryans came from Central Asia or whether they were wholly indigenous people of north-west India. The presumption that Aryans came from Central Asia, first advocated by European Historians has no basis if we consider the following evidences:

1. If Aryans had come from Central Asia, they would have brought with them the 'cuniform' script, which was already prevalent in that area at that time. The fact that Aryans did not use any script for the next millennium shows that Aryans were not familiar with that script. The earliest script that the Aryans used was the Brahmi script.
2. The fact that Rig Veda does not contain any reference to any region, society or religion of central Asia also points out that the people of early Vedic period were not familiar with that region in any way and hence could not have come from any region of Central Asia.
3. The Aryans were not nomadic tribes as is believed by many historians. They were highly cultured people who had already a cohesive society, religion and a religious text in the form of 'Rig Veda.'
4. The Rig Veda shows greater familiarity with the North-West India – Eastern Afghanistan, the swat valley, and Punjab – what later came to be called as 'Sapta-Sindhu' region.

5. This shows that Aryans were natives of north-west India and had to migrate east (onwards to Gangetic plains) because of several reasons – climate becoming hostile due to climatic changes, drying up of river Saraswati, increase of population, migration of other people from western parts, etc.

The 'Bactria-Margiana Archeological Complex' (BMAC) Discoveries

This archeological complex discovered by Soviet Archeologist 'Viktor Sarianidi' as late as 1976 shows the remains of a 'Bronze Age Culture' of Central Asia, which covers an area comprising of South East Iran, Baluchistan and Afghanistan. The complex exhibits many of the hall marks of an independent and literate civilization which existed in the second millennium BCE (1900 – 1500 BCE). The evidence suggests that they had also developed writing. However there is no archeological evidence of an invasion or destruction of this culture.

These people used fortifications which were then unknown to Aryans. If Aryans had come from Central Asia through the traditional route, they were bound to have come into contact with the people of this culture. If this was the case, then wars between the two groups would have been chronicled in Rig Veda. But such evidence simply does not exist. As stated earlier, the BMAC civilization was also not destroyed by wars. The BMAC complex is also very poor in horse remains or representations, which are often seen as a sign of Aryan presence. From this also we can conclude that Aryans did not come from outside India and they were the natives of this country.

Hence we may draw conclusion that the Vedic Aryans were basically cultured people of north-west India, who were pastoral in the beginning but later started practicing agriculture. Their religion and culture was probably common (in some form), with many groups of people of Central Asia through historical, religious and cultural links and also probably through trade (like horses). This view is substantiated by certain evidences given below.

1. We find a historical record in the form of a treaty drawn on clay tablets between two chieftains of northern Syria (approximately belonging to the fourteenth century BCE) which calls upon certain gods as witnesses and among them are found the names of some Vedic gods identified as Indra, Mitra, and Varuna.
2. The inscriptions of 1600 BCE belonging to Kassite rulers of Babylon also mention some gods who are identified as Surya and Maruths. These gods are also worshipped in Rig Vedic hymns which are considered the earliest available Vedic religious literature.
3. Calling gods as witnesses is also an Indian tradition which was probably practiced in many areas which had links with early Vedic culture.
4. Some of the people of Central Asia were Assyrians/Anatolians who had 1500 gods, few from Egypt, few from Babylon, few from India and the rest from a pool of local gods, so we cannot actually say they were Aryans.
5. Rig Veda has also many things (including closeness of language) in common with 'Avesta' the oldest religious text of Iran. In fact, both these texts have the same names for several gods and even for social classes.
6. The above points have led historians to believe that Aryans came from Central Asia. In fact this can be counter argued, saying a branch of Aryans might have migrated from north-west India to parts of Central Asia.

From north-west India, Aryans started migrating to Gangetic plains, as mentioned in the 'Brahmanas'. By the time of the *Mahabharata*, the centre of authority had shifted from 'Sapta-Sindhu' region to western gangetic plain. The migration can also be deduced from the change in 'Saraswati based Rig Vedic literature' to 'Ganges based Puranic literature' by the first millennium BCE.

As already discussed, probably this migration was due to drying up of the river Saraswati and climatic changes spread over a millennium. There was also a gradual shift from wheat cultivation to rice, and rice came to be increasingly used in rituals.

Development of Indian Philosophic Thought

The development of the Indian philosophic thought is also closely connected with the developments that took place in the Vedic religion over a period of several millennia. Hence, in order to understand the processes under which various systems of philosophies developed in India, it is also important to understand the periods in which these philosophies developed. The history of development of 'Indian Philosophic Thought' may be divided into 5 periods starting from the Vedic Period. The periods indicated in the brackets are as ascribed by historians and which are subject to revision.

1. Vedic Period (1500 BCE – 500 BCE)
2. Epic Period (800 BCE)
3. Sutra Period (500 BCE – 200 CE)
4. Scholastic Period (200 CE – 1700 CE)
5. Modern or Contemporary Period (1700 CE – 2000 CE)

Due to several recent discoveries and evidences, we will have to take a relook at these periods and rectify the above dating given for these periods.

RE-DATING OF THE VEDIC PERIOD

(Earlier Dating: 1500 BCE to 1000 BCE, Re-Dating: 2300 BCE to 1400 BCE)

The Vedic period covers the rise and development of the Aryan culture and civilization. This is the period when the vast corpus of the Vedas and a few important Upanishads developed. The period of development of the Vedas might easily have taken several centuries, – probably a greater part of the second millennium BCE. Let us discuss some available and new evidences:

1. **Drying up of the River Saraswati:** Rig Veda mentions river Saraswati several times as 'the mighty river Saraswati'. This means that the river Saraswati was a perennial river at the time of the Rig Veda. It is said to have completely dried up by 1900

BCE due to severe drought brought out by climatic changes. This evidence helps us to conclude that the date of Rig Veda should be earlier than 1900 BCE.

2. **Archeological Excavations at Dwaraka:** Recent archeological excavations of the legendry coastal city of Dwaraka, (belonging to the *Mahabharata* period and said to have been founded by Sri Krishna), show that the city of Dwaraka was submerged in the sea around 1443 BCE (roughly 3,400 years ago). This fact also finds a mention in the *Mahabharata*.
3. **Division of Vedas by sage Veda-Vyasa:** A most important internal evidence, is that sage Veda-Vyasa collected all the Vedic hymns and divided them into 4 volumes. Since sage Veda-Vyasa lived during the *Mahabharata* period, it can be generally concluded that the Vedic period had come to an end by that time (1500 BCE).
4. **Re-dating of the Vedic Period:** Therefore, the Dwaraka discovery pushes back the Vedic period by at least another 800 years. Consequently we have to conclude that the Vedic period started around 2300 BCE and had concluded before the starting of the Epic period around 1500 BCE. The Epic period might have easily lasted around 500 years and concluded by 1000 BCE.

RE-DATING THE EPIC PERIOD

(Earlier Dating 800 BCE, Dwaraka excavation Dating: 1500 BCE and hence Epic period is placed between 1500 BCE to 1000 BCE):

The Epic period is re-dated from 1500 BCE (as per Dwaraka excavation) and probably ends around 1000 BCE. The Epic *Mahabharata* came to be written during this period. The original Version of *Mahabharata* written by sage 'Veda-Vyasa' was said to contain 8,800 slokas in its 'Jaya Samhita' version. It later expanded to 24,000 slokas and called as 'Bharata' – named after one of the early-Vedic groups of people. Some scholars credit this Bharata version to Vyshampayana. This work again expanded and became *Mahabharata* with one lakh slokas. Some scholars credit this version to 'Ugrashrava Sauti'.

The process of expansion of the epic may have been mainly due to the contribution of several scholars over generations (through addition of Upa-Kathas – sub-stories) and might have lasted easily for more than five hundred years. This epic contains narrative, descriptive and didactic material. Scholars credit the narrative portion relating to Kaurava-Pandava conflict to later Vedic period (1500 BCE), descriptive portion to post Vedic times (1000 BCE) and the didactic portion to still later periods.

Even though, the story of *Ramayana* took place earlier, the standard Sanskrit text of *Ramayana*, seems to have been composed after *Mahabharata* according to some scholars. Hence historians have not been able to date it to any particular period. These two epics idealized the social, religious and political aspects of the life of the people of the (epic) period and contain within them the broad principles of Hindu religion.

The sacred work *Bhagavad Gita*, as a part of the *Mahabharata*, ranks as one of the most authoritative texts (and considered as one among the 'Prasthana Traya' works) in Indian philosophical literature.

POST EPIC PERIOD

(Present Dating: 1000 BCE – 200 CE)

Several scholars have called the next period as the 'Sutra Period'. But since the Epic and Vedic periods get pushed back by 800 years due to the archeological discoveries and dating of the submerging of 'Dwaraka', let us call this period from 1000 BCE to 200 CE as the 'Post Epic Period'. During this period several important Upanishads, Sutras, Darshanas, Dharma Shastras, some of the Puranas and other religious scriptures came into existence. Kautilya's 'Artha-shastra' is another important work of this period.

During this period, scholars wrote various 'Sutras' which helped to systematize, preserve and transmit the rich philosophical thought that came to be accumulated in the vast religious literature. 'Grihya Sutras', 'Srauta Sutras' and 'Sulva sutras' came to be written during this period. The most notable work among them is the 'Brahma sutras' also called 'Vedanta Sutras' by sage Badarayana. These Sutras later laid the foundation for the various systems of philosophies in India.

The concept of 'Varnashrama Dharma' developed and Smritis prescribed duties for people belonging to each Varna. Outside influences started creeping in during this period. It also saw the rise of Jainism and Buddhism as independent religions.

The corpus of 'Sangam' literature in Tamil, also came into existence in the early centuries of the Christian era. It is a major source of information relating to the social, economic and political life of the people of the region.

SCHOLASTIC PERIOD

(200 CE to 1700 CE)

This is the period of commentaries on the Sutras. The six classical systems of Indian philosophy known as the 'Shad-Darshanas' fully developed during this period. This period also witnessed the emergence of different schools of Vedanta. Majority of Puranas were also written during this period.

The period also witnessed eminent scholars and great philosophers like Adi Shankara, Bhaskara, Ramanuja, Neelakanta, Nimbarka, Madhva, Vallabha, Vignana Bhikshu, Baladeva, Srikara and others write authoritative commentaries on the 'Brahma sutras', to enunciate their respective philosophies.

The three important branches of Vedanta – Advaita, Visisthadvaita and Dvaita developed during this period. The Acharyas, who developed these branches of philosophy, also founded their own Mutts (on the lines of Buddhist monastic orders) to develop and spread their respective philosophies and practices. In contrast to the earlier periods, this period saw the phenomenal development of criticism of opposing philosophies. The later part of the period also saw the rise and spread of Bhakti movements in various parts of India.

MODERN (CONTEMPORARY PERIOD)

(1700 CE – 2000 CE)

This period saw the decline of classical systems of Indian philosophy, with the rise of the influence of Muslim and British cultures in India. There was also philosophical and religious renaissance in the form of establishment of institutions like 'Arya Samaj' 'Brahmo Samaj', and 'Prarthana Samaj' by English educated Indians. There was also a concerted effort to eradicate some of the evil practices that existed in the name of Hinduism.

The period also saw the teachings of several eminent Indian philosophers, scholars and religious personalities like Sri Ramakrishna Paramahamsa and Swami Vivekananda; Aurobindo, Radhakrishnan, and several others, who synthesized and crystallized the Indian philosophical thought as a single and unique brand of philosophy. Some of these philosophers are profiled in Annexure 2.

Several monastic orders to uphold the broader principles of Hinduism came to be established in different parts of India. Notable examples of such orders are –

1. Ramakrishna Mission,
2. Chinmaya Mission,
3. Prajapita Brahmakumaris,
4. International Society for Krishna Consciousness (ISKCON), etc.

In this chapter, an attempt has been made to give a historical background relating to the periods of development of various religious and philosophical works. This would further help the reader to understand these concepts discussed in subsequent chapters.

5

Evolution of Indian Philosophic Thought (Part I)

THE SHAD DARSHANAS

An Introduction to the Indian Philosophic Thought

'Indian Philosophic Thought' refers to various traditions of philosophic thought (which includes a very broad spectrum of Hindu, Jain and Buddhist philosophies) that originated in India and evolved over a period of several millennia. Indian philosophy is considered to be the oldest in the world and has the longest history of continuity and development right from pre-historic times to the present day.

The unique nature of Indian philosophy is that it is not just based upon reason, but also religion. It places greater emphasis not only on 'Truth' but also on the 'Ultimate Reality'. It has also enriched the life of man, not only in India, but across the world.

Vedas constitute the very basis of Indian philosophy. Vedic hymns are philosophical to the extent that they attempt to explain the mysteries of the world, through reason, from which arose the concept of religion. Part of the Rig Veda (Rig Veda Samhita – collection of Vedic hymns to the gods), philosophically is the most ancient and important Vedic text. These hymns give us an idea of what Aryans thought about the origin of the world and the underlying order of nature. The subsequent thought process has also been considerably influenced by some of the Upanishads and other philosophies which arose from them.

The major theme of 'Indian Philosophical Thought' down the ages has a common underlying theme of righteousness (Dharma) and explaining the process of spiritual emancipation. All philosophers and scholars explained in the beginning of their treatises, how their philosophical thought helped to serve the human ends (termed as Purusharthas).

Classification of Indian Philosophic Thought

The various philosophies coming under the umbrella of Indian philosophical thought, is classified in this book (for the sake of convenience) into four categories and discussed in this, as well as subsequent chapters under the following headings:

1. Part I: Shad Darshanas (Six classical schools of Philosophy and also a brief discussion of some of the Nastika schools) – in this Chapter 5.
2. Part II: Vedanta – Advaita, Visisthadvaita, and Dvaita – in Chapter 6.
3. Part III: Bheda-abheda Sidhanta and Bhakti – in Chapter 7.
4. Part IV: Shaiva and Veerashaiva Sidhanta – in Chapter 8.
5. Jain and Buddhist philosophies are discussed in Annexure 1, as they were originally considered as part of 'Indian Philosophic Thought' and have considerably influenced the development of several Hindu philosophic concepts also.

However, due to the limited scope of the book, the philosophies advocated by various saints and other minor schools of philosophy are not included in this book.

Public Debating of Philosophies

Public debating (which also meant freedom of speech as well as religion) was a custom in Ancient India, and is found reflected both in the Upanishads and the earliest Buddhist texts. Public debating coupled with religious tolerance, was the main reason, for so many philosophies to emerge in India, over the course of time. During the course of these debates, rigorous methods of logical arguments were developed by scholars.

A notable feature of first millennium (BCE) appears to have been lively intellectual and philosophical debates between various thinkers across the spectrum – from Buddhism, Jainism and various shades of beliefs within the Vedic Religion. These debates helped in the gradual evolution of well defined philosophical systems in ancient India.

The method used in such discussions was variations of the 'dialectical method'. A proposition ('Prameya') was made by a leading scholar. There were arguments either supporting it or rebutting it. Alternatively, a negative statement as formulation was first enunciated, discussed and then rebutted. Finally an assessment of arguments on both sides was made. Development of consensus was usually attempted. This procedure showed openness to ideas and debate, even when the two sides did not concur. In cases when two opposing sides met for discussions, the two sides would normally agree on a neutral umpire – usually a renowned scholar, to give his verdict.

Evolution of Indian Philosophic Thought

The ancient Indian sages viewed philosophy as a practical necessity to explain the purpose of man's life on Earth as well as to understand the different facets of life itself. As already discussed, all major phenomena observed by them regarding nature, as well as cyclical nature of human life (birth, youth, old age, death, etc.), made them conclude that Nature and also life itself is governed by an unitary and underlying order (termed as Universal Truth) which is all pervasive and omniscient. Rig Veda speaks of such a mysterious force as the all powerful Brahman (the Supreme Being/God) – transcendent, timeless and beyond all kinds of human knowledge.

Even though the early Vedic people worshipped gods as personifications of nature, (especially for prosperity, material wealth, health, etc.) the concept of god underwent a gradual change, as the transition of Vedic people from a pastoral life to a settled life began. The hymns of the 'Rig Veda Samhita' contain the following themes pertaining to the Vedic gods.

1. Different gods having independent powers and functions,
2. These gods as different forms of a single entity,
3. A single entity which is totally different from these gods but controlling these gods,
4. An indeterminate thing termed as 'That' (later termed as Truth or Brahman), which is beyond all gods and not even perceivable by them.

This description gives us an idea of the process of evolution of the philosophical thought in the Vedas.

Development of Philosophy through Inquiry

The primary objective of Indian philosophy came to explore the nature and different aspects of this Truth. Several rational methods of inquiry were adopted. The process of exploration of truth started for a person at the student stage itself. One example from Chandogya Upanishad (6.13) is reproduced below:

Guru: 'Fetch me a fruit of the Banyan tree.'
Sishya: 'Here is one, sir.'
Guru: 'Break it'
Sishya: 'I have broken it, sir'
Guru: 'What do you see?'
Sishya: 'Very tiny seeds, sir.'
Guru: 'Break one'
Sishya: 'I have broken it, sir'
Guru: 'Now what do you see?'
Sishya: 'Nothing sir'

Guru: 'What you do not perceive is the essence and in that essence, the mighty Banyan tree exists. In that essence is the self of all that is. That is the Truth. That is the Self. And you are that Self, Shvetaketu.'
(Extracted from *The Wonder that was India* – A.L. Basham)

Evolution of Central Themes in Indian Philosophy

The next stage in the thought process was the evolution of the concept of 'Purusha', (identified with the ultimate 'Brahman' of which the Universe is made). The 'Shathapatha-Brahmana' (of Shukla Yajur Veda) speculates on the beginning of the Brahman – creation of the three worlds and the gods, and even going beyond the worlds. Subsequently, the concepts of Brahman (God), Dharma, Karma and Moksha became the central themes around which various systems of philosophy developed.

All these philosophies emphasized that the ultimate goal of human life is to merge with God (by whatever name it is called - Salvation, Eternal Bliss, Mukti, or Moksha) and the only way to attain this goal is to lead a moral life and practice Dharma. Thus the goal of every school of philosophy came to design a righteous path which will guarantee the attainment of salvation.

Hence, in the Indian context, philosophy became the theoretical aspect, and Dharma the pragmatic aspect of Hindu religion. The essence of the Vedic thought is found reflected in the Upanishads.

This chapter discusses the various systems of philosophy (termed as 'Classical Systems') within the main framework of Hindu philosophy.

NASTIKA SCHOOLS

Origins of Nastika (Heterodox) Schools

From the beginning, there were certain groups who did not believe in God, but who believed in concepts related to Karma, and Rebirth. There were groups who did not even believe in Karma and exhibited a totally materialistic point of view. We get indications of existence of such groups in Rig Veda. One Rig Veda Sukta refers to people who do not believe in the existence of Indra (God). Chandogya Upanishad refers to an 'asura' who believed that the body itself was the atman. Brhadaranyaka Upanishad in one of its arguments first opposes the premise that 'everything is born out of, and finally gets absorbed by the (Pancha) bhutas'.

'Jabala' in *Ramyaana* argues that there is neither heaven nor hell and conduct of 'Shraadha' for the departed soul is a waste. *Mahabharata* describes such groups as Charvakas, Lokayatas and Hytukas. It also says that even some Brahmans (like Ajagara) who had studied the Vedas, used to argue that the Atman was not different from the body. But even such people preached other good qualities of Dharma like 'Ahimsa', and were against violence – leading us to believe that such groups were not taking up such positions for selfish reasons.

Mention of these Nastika groups is found in Padma Purana, Skanda Purana, Kautilya's Artha-Shastra, and in some Buddhist texts (Ex. Deergha Nikaya) also.

Rise of Opposition to Vedic Sacrifices and Other Practices

Even though a majority of the groups which were expounding their own philosophies, accepted the authority of the Vedas, some groups from the beginning had started questioning various ideas, religious practices and inconsistencies they perceived in the Vedic religion (termed as elite and orthodox Brahmanism) – elaborate Brahmanical rituals, worship of deities, animal sacrifices, questioning of postulates related to existence of Atman or the soul, etc. In short, the very authority of the Vedas was questioned by some of these groups.

Prominent among them are the Ajivakas, Lokayatas, Charvakas, and the Shramana schools (which later developed independently into Jain and Buddhist schools) all of which are now classified as belonging to Nastika schools of philosophy.

Then there were followers of 'Agnana-vada' (Agnosticism). This school maintained a total skepticism, holding no doctrine at all as to the nature of 'Reality' or the possibility of knowledge about any kind of philosophy. They merely preached friendliness and avoided argument as a way to happiness. Other schools considered them as 'simple wandering ascetics, who dismissed knowledge as useless'. They also described them as 'ignorant teaching the ignorant of incoherence and confusion'. All these schools primarily reject the authority of the Vedas. Jainism and Buddhism also rose as a consequence of opposing certain views in Vedic religion.

Sources Relating to Nastika Schools

However, original works containing the philosophies of some of the major Nastika schools (like Lokayata and Charvaka) are not available at this point in time and we can only understand them by their descriptions in later works opposing these philosophies like 'Sarva Darshana Sangraha' by Madhava and a drama entitled 'Prabhoda Chandrodaya'. Obviously these works see the Nastika philosophies in a negative light. However, S.S. Das Gupta and Devi Prasad Chattopadhyaya have independently tried to construct the Lokayata and Charvaka philosophies through research of works relating to other ancient schools of philosophy.

Impact of Nastika Schools on Indian Philosophical Thought

It may be noted that the existence of Nastika schools gives important evidence of a materialistic movement within Hinduism. Further, it is also important to note, that Charvaka system was responsible for putting the then Hindu beliefs to a detailed analysis of logic, reasoning and independent thinking. All these Nastika schools have made significant contribution to the 'Indian Philosophic Thought' by either propounding new theories, or questioning old ones, or critiquing other schools through development of methods like analysis and inference.

Consequently, every system of philosophy started its philosophical treatise by first fiercely contradicting the views contained in the Charvaka and other Nastika systems. From this aspect, we can conclude that the Nastika schools were as powerful as the other philosophical schools in ancient times.

The Ajivaka School

The Ajivakas were followers of a philosophy of predetermination – that destiny controlled every action of man and nothing could change this. They specialized in predicting the future, believing that a future of a person is unalterably fixed. Ajivakas pioneered the theory of atoms and other combinations and it is presumed that the other schools (especially Jain, Vaiseshika, and Buddhists) borrowed and adapted the concepts from them.

The Ajivaka Philosophy

The Tamil text 'Manimekalai' gives an idea of the atomic theory as developed by them. 'The atoms are of four kinds (probably of four physical elements), and souls, happiness and unhappiness. These atoms are invisible but when the physical kinds of atoms combine they can be perceived by the soul. The ratios of combination are fixed according to the name. The substances are characterized according to properties: earth is hard and has downward tendency (probably refers to gravity). Water is cold and has also downward tendency. Heat burns and has rising tendency. Air has horizontal movement. Earth has all the sense qualities except sound which is the quality of air, etc.

The Lokayatas

The word is derived from the phrase: 'Lokeshu Ayata' which means – 'that which is prevalent in this world'. This also means that 'Lokayata' was a popular group at that time. 'Lokayatas' (naturalists) though materialistic, did not believe in reincarnation, and recommended pursuing happiness in this life. They believed that sensation was the only means of acquiring knowledge.

Kama (pleasure) is the only aim in life. They also advocated kindness to all living beings. But they condemned Vedic rituals and giving of gifts (dana). They also criticized those people who had taken 'Sanyasa'. The Lokayatas were later known as Charvakas, whose philosophy derived from materialism and challenged the views of Vedic Brahmanism, Buddhist and other philosophical schools.

The Charvaka Philosophy

The Charvaka is a materialistic and atheistic system. According to this system, there is no world other than this world. Perception is the only form of knowledge and matter is the only reality. Whatever is arrived by means of direct perception of the senses is the ultimate Truth. Whatever is not perceivable or cannot be experienced is non-existent.

The objective of life is pursuit of wealth, happiness and pleasure only. Pleasure and pain are the central themes of life. There is no pleasure without this body. Hence we have to look after our body to live happily. Life is made of four elements - Earth, air, water and fire, which are eternal. No one can survive death. Thus the life of a human being ends at death. When he dies, each element of his body returns to its original state, where as his senses (Chetana) vanish in to space. Since no one can see atman, there cannot be an atman separate from the body. No one survives after death and hence the concepts of Reincarnation, Atman and God have no meaning.

One Charvaka school (Jayanta's Nyayamanjari page 467) however, believed that there is a real entity (Tatva - Reality), which persists as long as the body lives and is destroyed by death, with no future life. One of the main reasons for the decline in the believers of this system could be that this system opposed the existence of God.

CLASSICAL SYSTEMS OF INDIAN PHILOSOPHY

The Astika Schools (Shad Darshanas)

Apart from the above Nastika schools, several Astika schools (orthodox) came into existence at the same time as the Nastika schools and the philosophies propounded by them are called 'Classical systems of Hindu philosophy'. The objective of all these schools generally was to devise paths for liberation of the soul from the cycle of births and deaths.

They claim the Vedas as their authority and give importance to the Upanishads. These systems are termed the Shad-Darshanas (six schools) - Nyaya, Vaiseshika, Sankhya, Yoga, Purva-Mimamsa, and Uttara-Mimamsa (which also popularly came to be known as Vedanta).

The Astika systems are again grouped in to three groups for historical and conceptual reasons: Nyaya-Vaiseshika; Sankhya-Yoga; and Mimamsa-Vedanta; Competition and integration between these different schools of philosophy was intense in the formative years. Many of these schools influenced the other Astika schools and some of the Nastika schools (especially Buddhist philosophies) and in turn were also influenced by them. By second century C E, only a few schools (Jain, Buddhist, Shaiva and Advaita) survived in India. Sankhya and other schools were assimilated by other schools.

Common Features of Shad Darshanas

All the Astika systems of philosophy display some common features:

1. They place emphasis on making a positive impact on the life of man.
2. They further emphasize that philosophy should aid man to realize the main ends of human life: 'Purusharthas' (Dharma, Artha, Kama and Moksha).
3. They reflect the view that philosophy should lead a person from darkness and ignorance to light and wisdom.
4. The concepts of 'Truth' and 'Reality' should be verifiable. They should be substantiated through reasoning and experience. An experience may be sensory, conceptual, logical or intuitional.
5. Man's sufferings are a result of Karma and ignorance, which can be conquered through knowledge and devotion.
6. There is essential spirituality in all persons.

These schools were also influenced to a great extent by Jain and Buddhist philosophies. They accepted the view that life on earth is full of sufferings. They argued that the freedom from births and deaths is to be gained only by – control of passions, acts of devotion, self-sacrifice and renunciation – as these are the only means of attaining true knowledge. Let us discuss the individual philosophies of these six schools briefly:

I. NYAYA DARSHANA

(The School of Logic)

Nyaya system (as a method) was propounded by the ancient sage Gautama. It deals with 'analysis based on logic' as the process of reasoning and inference. This system had fully developed by 250 BCE and was often used in debates with Buddhist and other teachers, who were also well versed in the use of logic. The school introduced the concept of 'Vada' for debate or argument, which is described as 'a constructive discussion guided by the laws of logic'. Two other concepts 'jalpa' (for dispute) and 'vithanda' (for argument used to destruct the position of the opponent) came to be used.

The System of Logical Analysis in Nyaya

The description of detailed procedure –(consisting of five essential steps – statement, middle term, example, application and conclusion), for argument is attributed to 'Charaka'. His form of proof, though with some modifications remained the basis for debate and argument in India till modern times.

One such example is given below:

1. Man is impermanent *(statement)*
2. Because of being a sense object *(middle term)*
3. A pot is a sense object and it is impermanent *(Example)*
4. And as a pot so also man is a sense object *(Application)*
5. Therefore impermanent *(Conclusion).*

Charaka enumerates 5 faults which must be avoided in a proof:

1. 'Nyuna' (deficiency),
2. 'Adhika' (redundancy/irrelevance),
3. 'Anarthaka' (meaninglessness),
4. 'Aparthaka' (disorder), and
5. 'Viruddha' (contradiction).

The 'Nyaya Sutra' which is a later day (200 CE) composition, lists 16 categories (padarthas): pramana, prameya, samshaya, prayojana, dristanta, Sidhanta, avayavas (steps), tarka, nirnaya, vada, jalpa, vithanda, hetva-abhasa (false middle term), chala, jaati and nigrah-sthana (defeat situation) for advancement of 'Nyaya' methodology.

The Nyaya Philosophy

Vade Vade Jayate Tatva Bodhah (One will understand the Tatva – philosophy, through arguments). The Nyaya philosophy believes in plurality of souls. Ignorance results from identification of self with the body. Nyaya subjects all concepts propounded in religious philosophies – life, world, Atman, God, etc. – to a logical analysis and attempts to supply logical description of each concept. Nyaya deals mainly with the following four subjects:

1. Theory of knowledge (Jnana Tatva),
2. Theory of the Physical World (Bhouta Tatva)
3. Theory of Individual self and liberation (Atma Tatva and Moksha),
4. Theory relating to God (Paramatma Tatva).

The Nyaya School believes that the soul is eternal and is different from the body. God creates, preserves and destroys people – according to their karmas accumulated in previous lives. Transcendental knowledge (Knowledge of the 16 categories – padarthas – mentioned above) leads to 'Liberation' from the cycle of births and deaths, for the individual soul. Nyaya and Vaiseshika schools both believe that God creates the world anew at every cycle and invests each individual soul with a body so that it might work out its destiny and attain liberation through spiritual knowledge.

Until fourteenth century (CE), the subject of Nyaya Shastra was treated as a part of religious philosophy. Gangesha (in the fourteenth Century), bifurcated the metaphysical aspect, and gave Nyaya an independent status of a 'Shastra' (discipline) and called it 'Naveena Nyaya' in his famous work 'Tatva Chintamani'. It is believed that this work has attracted the most number of commentaries in Sanskrit language and has considerably influenced the evolution of the subject of 'Logic' in other philosophies as well. Many scholars have compared this Logic with the subject of Logic developed in the West and opine that the Indian Logic covers far wider areas than the Western system of Logic.

Other important works on Nyaya Darshana: 'Nyaya Sutra' (Gautama), 'Nyaya-manjari' (Jayanat), 'Nyaya-sara' (Bhasa-ranjan), 'Tatva Didhiti Teeka' (Gadadhara) and 'Vartika' (Udyotaka).

2. VAISESHIKA DARSHANA

(The Atomist School)

The school is named after the word 'Visesha' meaning 'special' (identified through the quality of discrimination). The school believes that knowledge of reality, results from discrimination (visesha) of qualities (dharmas) which make the attainment of 'supreme good' possible. This Darshana came into existence (probably around 350 BCE) as an opposing philosophy to 'Vignana Vada' of Buddhist schools.

This system of induction and inference, developed by Kanada and Prashasta-pada, places emphasis on the evolution of nature as also physical sciences (atomicity of elements) and called the atom as eternal and distinct from the soul. Creation, preservation and destruction – all are considered as a result of change of form of the atoms. The school further explores the importance of Pancha-bhutas as well as mind and soul in the cognitive development of man.

A virtuous life guided by the principles of Dharma, enables an individual to lead a fulfilling life which will finally result in liberation. Dharma here is defined as that which brings 'abhyudaya' (exaltation which also means Heaven).

Originally the 'Vaiseshika Sutra' of Kanada did not contain any reference to God. But later followers of this school included God as 'Iswara' and as an additional Tatva. God is also described as the reason behind the cause and effect theory. Even though God does not interfere in the worldly affairs, the world moves as per rules laid down by the God. The souls take rebirth according to Karmic principles. Some of the principles enunciated by this school were later adapted by both Ramanuja and Madhva when they propounded their respective philosophies.

The 'Vaiseshika' principles were also widely used by 'Charaka' (100 CE), in his medical work 'Charaka Samhita'. Vaiseshika differed from 'Nyaya' in one crucial respect – While Nyaya accepted four sources of valid knowledge, Vaiseshika accepted only 'pratyakshika' (perception) and 'laingika' (inference). Although Vaiseshika school had originally developed independently from 'Nyaya', the two eventually merged because of their closely related metaphysical theories (especially the doctrine of inference). The combined Vaiseshika – Nyaya school, suffered a natural decline by the fifteenth century CE.

Some of the important works on Vaiseshika Darshana are: 'Vaiseshika Sutra' (Kanada), 'Padartha dharma Sangraha' (Prashastapada), and 'Sapta Padarthi' (Shivaditya – tenth century CE).

3. SANKHYA DARSHANA

(The Enumeration School)

Sankhya is considered as the oldest school of Indian philosophy and the essential points of this Darshana (like Prakriti-Purusha) can be traced to 'Swhetaashwatara' Upanishad. Mahabharata for the first time describes three different types of Sankhya Tatva (principles).

This system is said to have been first advocated by sage Kapila muni. Sankhya comes from the words 'Samyag-akhyate' which literally means 'that which explains the whole'. The word 'Sankhya' is interpreted in three ways – Enumeration, Inquiry, and Discussion. The school converts various philosophical concepts into numbers and on the basis of this, tries to explain the concepts of life and liberation. Hence it is also called the 'Sankhya' school.

The Sankhya school does not believe in God as the creator of the world, but advocates a strongly dualistic line stating that the union of the Nature and the Soul (Prakriti and Purusha) as responsible for evolution and creation of the Universe. Purusha (defined as self/Atman/Soul) is regarded as the centre of consciousness where as the 'Unconscious Prakriti' is the source of all material existence. 'Avidya' (ignorance) causes the attachment of the soul to the body and spiritual knowledge leads to enlightenment and freedom.

The school categorizes 'Tapatrayas' (obstacles and problems) which every one faces in life into three forms:

1. Adi-daivika: The unseen divine forces over which we have no control – natural calamities like floods, earthquakes, tsunami, supernatural powers, etc.

2. Adi-bhoutika: The physical factors around us which happen daily – accidents, crime, pollution, problems created by others, etc.
3. Aadhyatmika: Problems which arise from our bodies and minds – diseases, jealousy, anger, frustration, etc.

Sankhya classifies 'liberation' into two categories –

1. '*Jivan-mukti*': is liberation obtained (through Viveka Jnana) when the soul is present in the body,
2. '*Videha-mukti*': is liberation obtained after the soul leaves the body. That means the 'Purusha' here becomes free from all body bondages.

Sankhya offers a framework (it enumerates 25 principles) for all levels of manifestation – Prakriti (nature), Purusha (as soul), buddhi (intellect), three gunas (Satvic, Rajasic and Tamasic), manas (mind), Indriyas (organs of the body), Pancha-bhutas (Five elements), etc.

Sankhya forms the philosophical basis for the Yoga school and has strongly influenced other Vedantic schools also. The Sankhya school and the Jain schools of philosophy have similar ideas regarding pluralism. Even though Sankhya does not touch upon the existence of God, the Yoga school as a continuation of the Sankhya philosophy discusses several aspects relating to God.

The notable works on Sankhya philosophy are: 'Sankhya Sutra' (Kapila), 'Sankhya Karika' (Iswara Krishna), 'Sankhya Karika Bhashya' (Gaudapada), and 'Sankhya Pravachana Bhashya' (Vignana Bhikshu).

4. YOGA DARSHANA

(Path/Application School)

The word 'Yoga' has been used in Upanishads as a way of controlling the senses (Indriya Nigraha), very much like the method used in the control of the horses. By the time of Panini, the word 'Yoga' came to be used for 'Ekagrata' (Concentration of the mind). Gita uses the word yoga to refer to concentration of the mind and as also a way of controlling the senses.

Some Hindu sects have interpreted the concept of yoga to suit their respective philosophies. Shaiva and Shaakta sects have developed 'Mantra Yoga' as a method of worship. The Upanishad 'Yoga-Tatva' describes four kinds of Yoga –

1. Mantra Yoga,
2. Laya Yoga,
3. Hata Yoga and
4. Raja Yoga

The sage Yagnavalka in his Sutra states that sage 'Hiranya Garbha' was the first 'Yogacharya' who systematized 'Yoga Darshana' based upon the Sankhya philosophy, by amalgamating the various concepts used by different sub-sects. Patanjali wrote the 'Yoga Sutras' based on the system developed by 'Hiranya Garbha'.

'Yoga Darshana' refers to a path of spiritual realization and often referred to as 'Sankhya-Yoga' as it also contains practical methods to realize the truths of Sankhya philosophy. Yoga Darshana is also known as 'Raja Yoga' as it presents the eight fold path towards self-realization.

Nyaya, Vaiseshika and Sankhya schools provide the philosophical basis for explaining various metaphysical concepts like Jiva, life, happiness, misery, creation, preservation, destruction, Universe, Moksha, etc. All these schools believe that Moksha (liberation) is the final end of the cycle of births and rebirths. In this context it is 'Yoga Darshana' which provides an accepted path to attain this liberation.

Even though Sankhya Darshana does not believe in the existence of God, Yoga Darshana as a continuation of Sankhya philosophy, gives importance to the existence of God and calls Him the twenty sixth Tatva ('Iswara Tatva'). Yoga Darshana believes that in order to obtain 'Viveka Jnana' described in Sankhya, one has to practice the correct path of Yoga. 'Patanjali' advocates that a perfect control over body and the senses is required for gaining knowledge of the 'Ultimate Reality'. Hence he gives importance to the physical and mental rejuvenation of the individual. He says: *Yogah chitta vritti nirodah.*

Followers of Yoga believe in the Sankhya doctrine. But according to them, God does not take responsibility in creation, preservation and destruction of the Universe, but acts as a teacher of truth (Yogacharya) to earnest aspirants at the beginning of every cycle. Yoga gives importance to purity of the mind, thought and action. It involves systematic witnessing of one's inner states through meditation, so as to experientially go beyond all of them, to the centre of consciousness. Yoga advocates a path of eight steps 'Astanga-marga' in 'Yoga Sadhana' – yama, niyama, asana, pranayama, pratyahara, dharana, dhyana, and Samadhi. A Sadhaka has to attain perfection in these steps in order to attain self-realization/liberation.

Yoga as a Darshana as well as a path of control over the body and mind is a very powerful tool. Yoga has become so popular across the world, people of all religions practice yoga as a way of improving their mental state as well as their physical health. For this reason, Yoga has entered the dictionaries of all the major languages of the world.

The notable works on Yoga Darshana include: 'Yoga Sutra' (Patanjali), 'Yoga Sutra Bhasya' (Vyasa), 'Tatva Vaisharadi' (Vachaspati), 'Rajamarthanda' (Bhoja Raja), and Maitrayani Upanishad.

5. MIMAMSA DARSHANA

(School of Inquiry)

Mimamsa is a Sanskrit word for investigation (through 'pramanas' like Pratyaksha, Anumana, Shabda, Upamana, etc.) and focuses on the nature of Dharma. The school is considered as the most orthodox of all the philosophical schools, as its professed aim was to systematize the doctrine of the Vedas, since it believed that the source of knowledge (Vedas) is being neglected. It advocated that the nature of Dharma, is not accessible to either reason or observation and hence must be deduced from the revelations contained in the Vedas. After a lot of deliberations, It developed two systems of study – each of which later split into a separate school of philosophy – Purva-Mimamsa and Uttara-Mimamsa:

1. **'Purva-Mimamsa'** school considers the 'Vedic Rituals' as a system of actions to bring about the desired results. It developed a detailed philosophy relating to rituals, worship, ethical conduct, and propounded the basic philosophy of 'Karma'.
2. The second school considered that the knowledge of the Brahman (as the Ultimate Reality), is itself enough to lead to supreme bliss and salvation. This school is called **'Uttara Mimamsa'** or **Vedanta**.

Purva-Mimamsa: This system was propounded by sage Jaimini, a prominent disciple of Veda-Vyasa. Dharma was considered as virtue, morality or duty pertaining to the correct performance of Vedic rituals (performance of Karma). The followers of this system did not believe in a Creator God, but believed that the world was eternal. Individual souls went to heaven and enjoyed happiness as a result of virtues accrued to them through performance of good deeds and various rituals and ceremonies, while living on the Earth.

The Purva-Mimamsa school regards the Upanishads as subordinate to Karma-Kanda – the ritualistic portion of the Vedas. It propagates 'Karma' as prescribed by the Vedas to be performed by every individual. It further classifies such Karma into four categories:

1. *Nitya Karma*: Sandhya Vandana, Agnihotra, etc.
2. *Naimittika Karma*: Karma performed at a given time – like performing tarpana during eclipses, special baths taken during 'sankramana' and other 'punya-kalas', etc.,
3. *Kamya Karma*: Karma performed for fulfilling desires – Special Pujas done for specific objectives, Undertaking fasts, Conduct of Vratas, etc., and
4. *Nishidda Karma*: Non-performance of actions prohibited by Vedas – a list of such prohibited actions is given in the Chapter 3, (Essence of Dharma – under Renunciation).

The school believes that the soul gets purified through the above Karmas. It further believes in 'Trivarga Sidhanta' (Dharma, Artha and Kama) and does not believe 'Moksha' as a 'Purushartha'. The followers of this school believe that 'Moksha' is that aspect of the Atman which has no connection with the body. In that aspect, the Atman experiences neither happiness nor misery. (This is not the same as bliss experienced by the Atman as understood by the Vedanta schools).

The Purva-Mimamsa school again got divided into two branches one advocated by 'Kumarila Bhatta' and another advocated by 'Prabhakara'. However both advocated that liberation or Moksha can be attained by faithful following of Karma as prescribed by the Vedas.

The Purva-Mimamsa school exercised near dominance on Indian philosophical thought for centuries and is credited as a significant force responsible for the decline of Buddhism in India. It was successful in refuting the theories of all Nastika and Non-Brahmanical schools.

Evolution of the Vedanta School

However, the Purva-Mimamsa school did not go into the discussion on various theories advocated by other schools on metaphysical concepts like God, Atman, creation, preservation, destruction, birth, death, rebirth, etc. These concepts were developed in depth by the 'Uttara Mimamsa' school, also popularly known as the 'Vedanta school'. The Purva Mimamsa school gave importance to 'Karma Kanda' of the Vedas, while the Uttara Mimamsa school gave importance to the 'Jnana Kanda' of the Vedas.

Vedantic schools derived their philosophies from the 'Brahma Sutras' of sage Badarayana. However, these schools also derived much of their philosophies from two other sources – Upanishads and *Bhagavad Gita*.

Even though debates between the various schools continued for centuries, Uttara Mimamsa or Vedanta has got maximum attention for the past 1500 years, (probably due to the tremendous strength of philosophies enunciated by various acharyas) to the point of being projected as the dominant philosophical school of ancient India.

We will discuss the three major philosophies advocated by the Vedantic schools in our next chapter.

6

Evolution of Indian Philosophic Thought (Part II)

VEDANTA

Evolution of Vedantic Thought

With the decline of Buddhism in India and as a part of an amalgamation process, a wholly diverse set of religious beliefs, traditions and philosophies started emerging in India. Vedas and Upanishads came to be interpreted in a variety of ways and philosophies emanating from them were collectively called Vedanta.

Earlier, the word Vedanta referred to only Upanishads. Subsequently, Vedanta came to be referred to schools of philosophy that interpreted the Upanishads. In this way, there are many schools of Vedanta. These Vedantic schools mostly dealt with the nature of the 'Ultimate Reality' (Brahman) and interpreted the paths to self-realization – described in various ways as Liberation/Moksha/Mukti/Eternal Bliss, etc.

These schools did not develop in isolation. The process included discussions and refutation of each others' points of view and also views of other schools and sects. Acharyas, who propounded their respective philosophies, had continuous debates with scholars of opposing schools. When they were successful in defeating them, they forced the defeated scholars, to convert to their school and made them their disciples.

The Central Theme of Vedanta

The central theme of all these systems of Vedanta is based on the concepts of Brahman, Dharma, Karma and Moksha and the relationships between them. Vedanta deals with some of these metaphysical concepts in all its finer aspects. It holds 'Brahman' as the ultimate reality, underlying the whole universe. The means of liberation (Moksha) is to experience the identity of the individual self (Atman) with the larger Cosmic Identity (Brahman/Divine) or as in the case of Dvaita, enjoying eternal bliss.

All the Acharyas (who propounded their respective schools of philosophy), based their philosophies on the 'Brahma Sutras' (of Sage Badarayana). Though they differed in the interpretation of various concepts, they essentially agreed on the means of liberation – that obtaining 'Divine Grace' is the result of leading a holy life which is free from attachment. Besides 'Brahma Sutras', the Gita has played a major role in the evolution of the Vedantic philosophies, as all these Acharyas have also written extensive commentaries on the Gita, and explained the meaning of the Gita through their philosophies.

By the time Vedantic philosophy evolved, there was a growing belief in the worship of individual gods as personal gods and hence these philosophies also dealt with the relationship of the individual soul and God (in the form of Vishnu).

Historical Background for Evolution of Major Vedantic Schools in South India

By the fifth century (CE) the South Indian religious scene presented a diverse picture. Popular Hindu local sub-sects existed along with Vedic religion, as also Buddhism and Jainism. Buddhism was dominant in Tamil Nadu and Andhra. Jainism was dominant in Southern Karnataka.

The, sixth century Tamil Buddhist text *Manimekalai* advises a leading character, to study the various Hindu schools of philosophy (Sankhya and Vaiseshika) along with Ajaivaka, Charvaka, Buddhist and Jain philosophies. The intension was that such a study would help in rebutting the Hindu philosophies by Buddhist scholars. In the context of such fears of Buddhist and Jain takeover, a large Hindu revival started to gain momentum and reached its peak in the seventh century and continued for several centuries. There were also some Bhakti movements, which preached that caste and sex was no bar in expressing devotion to God.

On the philosophical side, this period saw the rise of different Vedantic schools of philosophy. Vedanta also brought about a reformation in the Vedic religion with a focus on the teachings of the Upanishads. Devotion and Worship gained prominence among common people, as against Vedic sacrifices which were dominant earlier.

Schools of Vedanta

The main schools of Vedanta fall under the three broad categories – Advaita (as advocated by Adi Shankara), Dvaita (as advocated by Madhva), and Visisthadvaita (as advocated by Ramanuja). It is important to note that all the three acharyas hailed from South India.

The philosophies propounded by the three Acharyas may be considered as three ways of understanding the same Truth. While all the three Vedantic philosophies might seem different or contradictory to each other, we may consider them as three stages of development of the same consciousness.

Among the many minor schools of Vedanta (ex. Bheda-abheda), mention may be made of Srikara, Nimbarka (Dvaita-Dvaita), Vallabha (Shudha-Dvaita), Chaitanya (Bhakti) and Neelakantha. Apart from these schools there were schools followed by a number of other religious sub-groups – Shaiva, Veerashaiva, Shaakta, Kalamukha, Pasupata, etc. Some of them followed non-Vedic and Tantric forms of worship also.

Comparison of the Three Main Vedantic Philosophies

It is extremely important to note that the three main Vedantic philosophies were propounded by the three Acharyas under different circumstances and during different time periods. These Acharyas molded their philosophies differently in order to suit them to meet the demands of the particular situations which they faced. However, these philosophies have stood the test of time for nearly a millennia and this alone is sufficient proof as to the strength of these philosophies.

The three Vedantic schools differ on important metaphysical questions like the nature of the Brahman, its relationship with the soul and the material world. All the three Acharyas declare that Vedas have an independent validity and are the ultimate source of knowledge of the Brahman.

Advaita Sidhanta

Adi Shankara in his 'Advaita Sidhanta' believes that the only true reality is the Brahman – 'Nirguna Brahman', even though he appears as 'Saguna Brahman' in this world. This Truth is concealed by 'Avidya' (ignorance) and 'Maya' (illusion) and the highest reality or existence of Truth cannot be two but must be one and 'Atman' is that Reality. The aim of human birth is to experience this Truth. Atman experiences a false sense of plurality, under the delusive power of Maya. A soul becomes liberated from Samsara (the cycle of rebirths), when it realizes that the world is an illusion and identifies itself with Brahman.

Visisthadvaita Sidhanta

Both Dvaita and Visisthadvaita schools believe in Saguna Brahman (who is endowed with all the unique qualities), and that the Universe is a part of God. Ramanuja modifies Shankara's position saying that there is a plurality in individual souls whose identity remains intact with Brahman after realization. According to him, the world is real and not Maya, but constitutes the body of God. Ramanuja identifies the Saguna Brahman as Vishnu and emphasizes devotion to god, as a way to salvation. Moksha is release of the souls from the cycle of births and deaths and then enjoying eternal bliss with Brahman.

Dvaita Sidhanta

Madhva differs from both these views, saying that there is a fundamental difference between Atman, (the human soul) and Brahman (the Ultimate reality). The world is real as also is God, the Ultimate Reality. Brahman is identified as Vishnu, the Supreme Being, who controls the world and all the souls. The divine grace can be obtained through Bhakti – 'Devotion to God'. All souls are not eligible for Moksha/Mukti, (which is release from the cycle of births and deaths). Karma, Jnana and Bhakti are all different levels of Moksha Sadhana. Even after Mukti, the souls remain different from God and enjoy bliss based on their nature and levels of devotion.

Comparison of the Three Philosophies

Swami Agamananda in his introduction to the book *The Quintessence of Vedanta of Sri Shankara* compares the three Vedantic schools as follows: 'Of the three Acharyas, Ramanuja and Madhva are realists. To Madhva as well as Ramanuja, God and the individual soul are transcendent entities to be known and understood only by Sruti. Their interpretation of Sruti is in harmony with the realities of everyday life. Both propounded Bhakti yoga as the path to reach the eternal Truth. Madhva supports pluralism. Ramanuja agrees with him substantially, but he invests his system with a monistic garb, by explaining that the souls and the material world are the body of God, so that there is only one Reality, God of whom the rest are parts...

Although Madhva agrees with Ramanuja in regard to God, soul and matter as being equally real and distinct from one another, Madhva differs from Ramanuja in the following respects: God does not wear the other two categories – soul and matter – as his body. God pervades them. Souls are distinct from one another and this distinction is eternal. In the state of liberation, though each soul is filled with bliss, the degree of this bliss may not be identical'.

Reconciling the Three Philosophies

It is rather difficult to reconcile the three divergent views on God. According to some scholars, Shankara is in the right from the point of view of a 'Jnani', Ramanuja from the point of view of a 'Bhakta' and Madhva as far as 'worldly affairs are concerned'.

These three major schools of Vedanta in turn, directly as well as indirectly influenced the philosophies of various Acharyas who propagated the different types of Vaishnava Bhakti movements of North India. This aspect is discussed in Chapter 7 pertaining to 'Bheda-abheda' Sidhanta.

I. ADVAITA SIDHANTA

(Manoism or Non-Dualism)

Brahma Satyam jagan mithya jivo Brahmaiva na parah

[Brahman is the only Truth (reality), the world is unreal, Jiva (atman) is Brahman itself and not different (from it). This in essence is the philosophy of Advaita Sidhanta]

Origins of Advaita

The origins of 'Advaita Sidhanta' (strict non-dualism with the universe as illusion) lie in Upanishads and sages Yagnavalka, Uddalaka and Badarayana are considered to have advocated some thoughts of early Advaita (as it appears in their works). Some sort of Advaitic tradition might have been developed in the early part of first millennium (CE) as Adi Shankara himself refers to such a tradition.

Historically Gaudapada (sixth century CE) first propounded it as an idealist philosophy (in his work 'Mandukya Karika') and called it Ajativada – which would negate the principles of almost all the schools of thought which were prevalent in that period. Gaudapada's disciple was Govinda Bhagavatpada, who in turn was the Guru of Adi Shankara. The philosophy of Advaita was later elaborated, systematized and propounded as the most important school of Vedantic thought by Adi Shankara.

Adi Shankara had to basically face several different and opposing philosophies and sects – the 'Shoonya vada' of Madhyamica school of Buddhism; the ritualistic philosophy of 'Purva Mimamsa' school, which believed in Karma Kanda and held that the Vedic sacrifices were paramount; the continuing enmity between Shaiva and Vaishnava sects; the 'Bheda-abheda' vada of several scholars before him, and finally the totally unorganized Tantric philosophies which held sway over all the existing sects. Adi Shankara took all these into consideration while propounding his philosophy.

Adi Shankara is considered as the only Indian philosopher who has been much admired and equally much criticized for his views on various aspects (especially Maya Vada) of his philosophy. The reason for this is that every subsequent scholar has taken Shankara's views as the basis for either propounding his philosophy or denouncing Shankara's views. This in itself is a considerable achievement (of Shankara) which perhaps no other scholar in India has been able to achieve.

Accomplishments of Adi Shankara

Though he lived only for 32 years, Adi Shankara's accomplishments are considered as super human in nature. His notable contributions to Indian philosophical thought are his authoritative commentaries on ten major Upanishads, as well as the Gita and the Brahma Sutras. He has also authored many other important works like Viveka Chudamani, Upadesha Sahsri, etc. He is also credited with many other works like 'Soundarya Lahari', 'Bhaja Govindam' and a host of other 'Stotras' used in the worship of various gods.

Adi Shankara is credited with the revival of 'Sanatana Hindu Dharma' when it was being threatened from diverse forces from both within and without. His teachings form the main philosophical basis for the followers of 'Smarta' tradition within Hinduism. The propagation of 'Panchayatana' form of worship is attributed to him. (It is explained in Chapter 11).

He was the first among the Hindu saints to establish a monastic order – Dasanami sampradaya, (on the lines of Buddhist monastic orders). He travelled the length and breadth of India and established four mathas in the four corners of the sub-continent to propagate his teachings and philosophy. They are located at Badrinath in the North (Himalayas), Puri in the East (Orissa), Dwaraka in the West (Gujarat) and the most important matha at Sringeri in the South (Karnataka).

Essence of Advaita Vedanta

The classical Advaita philosophy recognizes a kind of unity in multiplicity. It is based on the following eight concepts: Brahman, Universe, Maya, Iswara, Jiva (Atman), Srishthi, Samsara-bandana and Moksha. It advocates that Brahman is the only reality underlying all objects and experiences.

The essence of Advaita Vedanta can be summarized as follows:

'This world as it appears is an illusion because of Maya. Ignorance (Avidya) of this reality is the cause of all suffering. Due to the influence of Maya, Brahman (Nirguna Brahman) appears as Iswara (Supreme God with attributes/Saguna Brahman), separate from the individual and the world.

In reality, there is no difference between the individual soul (Jiva/Atman) and Brahman. The veil of Maya is removed only when one attains Brahma Jnana (true knowledge of the Brahman), which lies in understanding of this reality.

Brahman is without a second, changeless, immutable, all pervading and perfect. (Satyam Jnanam Anantam Brahma). It is not a physical entity as it pervades the entire world and is without name, form or qualities (Anaam, niraakar, nirguna). According to Sruti, there is no difference between Brahman and Atman. Brahma Jnana results in attainment of liberation of the individual'.

Let us now understand the Advaita Philosophy in a little more detail:

Jnana Kanda and Karma Kanda

Shankara divides all Sruti into two parts: Karma-kanda – the ritualistic portion and Jnana-kanda – the portion which deals with the knowledge of the Brahman, the Supreme Being. The followers of Karma-kanda, follow the injunctions of Sruti strictly as a question of faith. Shankara believes that the Karma-kanda part of the Vedas, is meant for those who are yet in the adolescent stage in the pursuit of Truth.

Shankara is a strong proponent of Jnana-Yoga. The goal of Jnana-kanda is realization of the Brahman – the ultimate Truth, which is beyond word and speech. Although Brahman is beyond description, Rishis, based on their personal experience described it as 'Sat-Chit –Aananda' (Sachidananda):

1. 'Sat' means Existence – pure and absolute,
2. 'Chit' means Knowledge – pure and absolute and
3. 'Aananda' means Bliss – pure and absolute.

Pramanas (Proofs)

Shankara bases all his teachings on 'experience'. Of the 'pramanas' (proofs), he gives the first place to experience, then to Sruti and finally to mere reasoning. He points out that the term 'experience' should include all levels of consciousness – waking, dream (swapna) and deep sleep (nidra/sushupti). We would then realize that what seems to be real in one stage, is unreal in the other two. Whatever is perceived, is not necessarily real. Only Brahman, which undergoes no change and which does not cease to exist is real.

Brahman

Brahman is also one without a second, all pervading and the immediate awareness. Consciousness is the very nature of Brahman. This absolute Brahman is also known as 'Nirguna Brahman' or Brahman without qualities, but he is simply called Brahman. However, Brahman can be experienced indirectly in the natural world of experience as a personal God, known as 'Saguna Brahman' or Brahman with qualities. It is usually called Iswara (and it can be any god according to one's preference).

Three Levels of Truth

Truth is defined at three levels:

(*i*) Paramarthika level – Brahman is the only reality and nothing else.

(*ii*) Vyavaharika level – apparent existence where Jiva, Iswara and material world all appear to be true.

(*iii*) Pratibhasika level –existence of the material world is actually false. (It appears to exist when in reality it does not exist like the illusion of the snake over a rope or dream).

The 'External World' at the 'Vyavaharika' Level

Shankara is opposed to pluralism (dualism) and does not accept the ultimate reality of the external world. This appearance of plurality is due to ignorance. Brahman appears as the manifold objects of experience because of its creative power Maya. The world is neither totally real nor totally unreal. It is just like self and reflection of the self in the mirror. While the self is real the reflection is unreal.

Similarly, any distinction between subject and object is unreal and the notion of an external world is purely conventional (Vyavaharika). He gives an example of two pots existing in space. When the pots are broken, the space continues to exist without any alteration. In reality, space permeates everywhere.

'Avidya' and 'Maya'

To explain this apparent plurality, Shankara introduces the concepts of 'Avidya' (ignorance) and Maya (illusion) which prevent the individual from seeing the Truth. The Truth cannot be perceived through existing human senses. The physical body appears to be real, when the Jiva (soul) identifies itself with the body. When this identification is destroyed by spiritual knowledge, the Jivah feels its presence everywhere.

Maya has both individual (vyasti) and cosmic (samasti) aspects. The cosmic aspect belongs to Iswara and the individual aspect known as 'Avidya' belongs to Jivas. But Iswara is not controlled by Maya, where as Jiva is overpowered by 'Avidya'. Maya is responsible for the creation of the world. Avidya conceals the Brahman from the Jiva. As a result Jiva functions as a 'Karta' (doer) and 'bhokta' (enjoyer) of a limited world.

Satva Shuddhi and Realization

All knowledge is within us and we may not be aware of it. It is only when a person is established in 'Satva-shuddhi', when attachment drops away he begins to perceive that this world is not eternal. Through a Guru, he meditates upon the truth of the Vedanta and finally realizes one's own identity with the Brahman. Then, Avidya and all its products (samsara-bandana) leave him once for all.

Shankara further says that we cannot know the nature of time, space and cause as long as we are in it. It ceases to exist when we transcend it. A person himself is responsible for his sorrow, failure and misery in life.

Iswara

According to classical Advaita Sidhanta, the existence of the empirical world cannot be conceived without a Creator (Saguna Brahman) who is all-knowing and powerful. The creation, sustenance and dissolution of the world are overseen by Iswara, who is actually the manifestation of the Brahman. Brahman with the creative power of Maya is Iswara.

Iswara as Vishnu

There is debate and controversy on Shankara's choice in the worship of a personal God (Iswara). Shankara's devotional composition 'Bhaja Govindam' answers this point. This song invokes the almighty in the aspect of Vishnu and instructs all people to remember and worship 'Govinda' all the time. The song is not only a summary of 'Advaita Vedanta' but also underscores the view that devotion to God 'Govinda' is an important part of the general spirituality.

Another important point which stresses that he preferred Vishnu as the personal God, is that he has written an authoritative commentary on 'Vishnu Sahasranama', explaining the intricate meanings of each of the thousand names of Vishnu.

Sub-Schools of Advaita

After Shankara, two sub-schools of Vedanta arose – Bhamati and Vivarana. The major issue that distinguishes these two schools is their position on the nature of 'Avidya'. Bhamati school considers Jiva as the locus and object of Avidya. Vivarana school considers Brahman as the locus of Avidya.

Advaita Vedanta is summarized in the following popular phrases:

1. *Ekam Evadvitiyam Brahma* – there is one absolute reality without a second.
2. *Brahma Satyam, Jagan Mithya* – Brahman alone is real and the world is unreal.
3. *Aham Brahmasmi* – who I really am, is that absolute reality. (Brhadaranyaka Upanishad)
4. *Tat Twam Asi* – Thou are that (Brahman). (Chandogya Upanishad)
5. *Pragnanam Brahma* – Brahma is Prajna (Jnana Rupa – Aitareya Upanishad)
6. *Ayamatma Brahma* – This Atman is Brahman (Mandookya Upanishad)

These are also known as 'Mahavakyas' which a guru initiates the disciple in to Advaita Vedanta.

2. VISISTHADVAITA SIDHANTA

(Qualified Non-Dualism)

Sarva dharmaan parityajya mamekam saranam vraja |
Aham tvaam sarva-papebhyo mokshayisyami ma suchah ||

['Relinquishing all ideas of righteousness, surrender unto Me exclusively; I will deliver you from all sinful reactions, do not despair'. (Gita 18.66)]

This is considered as the most sacred Sloka known as 'Charama Sloka' and also considered one among the 'Rahasya Traya' by Sri Vaishnava community. Sri Ramanuja has interpreted this Sloka thus:

The Sadhaka has to renounce all methods of religion (prescribed by Dharma –Karma yoga, Bhakti yoga or Jnana Yoga) along with 'Phala Tyaga' (renouncing expectation of rewards), Karma Tyaga and Kartru-tva (both action and its ownership) and take exclusive shelter in the Supreme Lord Krishna, who promises his devotees that he will personally redeem and deliver them from all sins. There is no need to despair.

This Sloka exemplifies the essence of Visisthadvaita – Ananya Bhakti (Unswerved/Undistracted Devotion), Tyaga (Renunciation), and Sampoorna Sharanagati (Total surrender to God). Visisthadvaita prescribes that every follower of the faith has to properly understand the meaning of this Sloka and lead his life accordingly.

Ubhaya Vedanta

'Visistha' means qualified or distinguished. It is distinct from Advaita as the distinction being 'although Brahman is one, the Universe is real'. (Advaita calls the Universe as 'Maya' – illusion). Visisthadvaita tries to provide a Vedantic base to the then popular conception of a personal god (Vishnu) and a genuine identity to the devotional sects (Vaishnava Panthas) which were then very active in Tamil Nadu.

It is this synthesis between 'Classical Vedantic Philosophy' and the Tamil Vaishnava devotional faith, ('Ancient Sanskrit Vedantic Thought' and Tamil devotional verses called 'Nalayara Divya Prabhandam') that Visisthadvaita philosophy is categorized as *Ubhaya Vedanta.*

Historical, Social and Religious Background

When compared to Adi Shankara, Ramanuja faced a different set of issues and circumstances. Ramanuja's philosophy is best understood, if we take into consideration, the historical, social and religious circumstances that prevailed in South India at that time.

1. For centuries, a kind of social and religious transformation was taking place in Tamil Nadu with the gradual decline of both Buddhism and Jainism. Religious Bhakti movements gained the support of the masses.

2. There was also quite an opposition to the Vedic religion (which was confined to the upper castes and purely Brahmanical in nature and was dominated by sacrifices) from the lower strata of the society.
3. Islam had taken its roots in India and had become a ruling religion in large parts of the country. There were forced conversions as well. Besides, Islam was teaching the necessity of praying to a single God compared to numerous Gods worshipped by different Hindu sects.
4. There was also no unity among the various sub sects in Hindu religion. Some of the Tantric and Shaakta groups (like Kapalikas, Kalamukhas and Pasupata) followed Tantrism and had become extremely powerful.
5. The Tamil Kings tended to give a greater support to the dominant religious group, which in many areas was Shaivism. This led to confrontations with the Vaishnava groups, who were attempting to reorient their rituals to bring in a wider range of worshippers from all classes. The 'Bhagavata Purana' projected a Vaishnava world view.
6. In the later part of the first millennium (CE), the Vaishnava Bhakti movements were spearheaded by 'the twelve Alvars' who came from different social strata. They advocated that caste and sex was no barrier to devotion and worship of God. Their poetry and devotional compositions were very much popular with the masses.
7. One of the leading proponents of Vaishnava panthas was 'Nathamuni' (tenth century) who compiled the devotional compositions of all the Bhakti saints and poets, as a canon, known as the 'Nalayira (4000) Divya Prabandha' in Tamil. This work came to be considered as a source of revelation equal in authority to the Vedas among the Sri Vaishnava community.
8. Ramanuja states in his works, that there were several acharyas prior to him, who propagated Sri Vaishnava Sidhanta. He mentions some of their names in his works – Tanka, Dravida, Guhadeva, Bharuchi, etc.

9. Bhaskara, who had written a commentary on the 'Brahma Sutras', opposed the non-dualism and 'Maya-vada' of Adi Shankara and advocated the Bheda-abheda Vada. Ramanuja's Guru Yadava Prakasha also subscribed to this view.
10. Yamunacharya (belonging to eleventh century CE, in his work 'Siddhi Trayam'), also opposed the Advaita philosophy. He argued that Shankara's doctrine was contrary to all experience and also contrary to the Upanishads. Even though they state that Brahman exists, they do not imply that 'everything except Brahman is illusory'. He also tried to synthesize the teachings of the Upanishads with the 'Vaishnava Tatva' of Alvars.
11. Hence there was necessity in uniting the various sub-sects in Hindu religion (especially the lower castes) through the promotion of the worship of a single God, synthesizing Vedantic philosophy with the teachings of Alvars.

Ramanuja took all these points into consideration while suitably modifying his philosophy to suit the needs of the then society.

LIFE OF RAMANUJA

Formative Years

Ramanuja in his formative years was largely influenced by the teachings of the Vaishnava panthas. His Guru was 'Yadavapraksha' (of Kanchi) a well known (Advaita and Bheda-abheda) scholar. But there were many disagreements between them regarding interpretation of Vedanta and Upanishads. He left this guru and went in search of the then famous sage 'Yamunacharya' who had opposed the 'Advaita doctrine'. But he had died by the time Ramanuja reached Srirangam. Ramanuja accepted him as his 'Manasika Guru' and learnt his philosophy from a disciple 'Mahapurna' and started preaching the philosophy of Visisthadvaita.

Exile to Melukote

History records the persecution of 'Vaishnavites' in Tamil Nadu by the religiously intolerant Chola rulers, especially 'Kulothunga Chola'. Some of Ramanuja's followers were blinded or put to death and Vishnu idols were thrown into the sea. This resulted in Ramanuja's subsequent exile to Melukote in Karnataka. Under the influence of Ramanuja, the Hoysala (Jain) king 'Bittideva' embraced Sri Vaishnavism and called himself as 'Vishnu Vardhana'. Ramanuja is believed to have lived for a total period of 14 years during his two trips to Melukote.

Works on Sri Vaishnava Sidhanta

Ramanuja provided a good framework to the Bhakti cult. He authored nine works in Sanskrit. The most important of these are *Vedartha Sangraha*, *Sri Bhashya* (a commentary on Brahma Sutras), and the *Bhagavad Gita Bhashya*. Among the followers of Ramanuja, *Vedanta Deshikar* (thirteenth century CE), stands out for his several authoritative (120) works on Sri Vaishnava Sidhanta.

Ramanuja as a Social Reformer

Ramanuja besides being a saint, was also a social reformer. His famous statement was 'If I can bring deliverance to so many, I do not mind being condemned to hell'. He spread his message to all social classes without discrimination. He established the 'Yatiraj matha' at Melukote and popularized the 'Sri Vaishnava' sect.

Basis of Ramanuja's Philosophy

Ramanuja's philosophy is seen as a contrast to three leading competing views of his time: Advaita (Non-dualism), Bheda-abheda (Difference and non-difference) and Dvaita (dualism). (During his time Dvaita – dualism, had not yet attained the status of a separate philosophy). Ramanuja argued that the views of these philosophies lead to intolerable contradictions and further conclusions that go against common sense.

His argument is that you cannot quote only some passages out of Vedic texts, which support Advaita (However, he says that even these affirm plurality). His view is that you have to take the Vedic texts as a whole to understand their meaning. His interpretation is that they not only affirm the reality of plurality, but also the ritual and moral obligations (of Dharma).

Ramanuja does not accept the view that only Brahman is true and that everything else is Maya. He argues that if consciousness exists, then it follows that difference and plurality as well exists. He further argues that qualities attributed to the Brahman (ex. Satyam Jnanam Anatam Brahma) means in reality Brahman has these qualities. If anything is subject to 'Avidya' (ignorance) it means that you recognize the existence of an individual other than Brahman who is ignorant.

He disagreed with Shankara's philosophy that spiritual knowledge was the primary means of liberation from rebirth. It was only one of the means and pure devotion (Bhakti) was a better way of pleasing the Divine being, projected as loving and forgiving. He also stressed the need of the individual soul – Atman to unite with the Universal soul – the Brahman, for attainment of liberation from rebirth.

He based his philosophy on the Upanishads, the Brahma Sutras, the *Bhagavad Gita*, the Pancharatra Agama, and the divine experiences of the Alvars.

Essence of Visistha-Advaita Vedanta

Visisthadvaita accepts plurality both of matter and souls. Ramanuja interprets the world as the manifestation of the Brahman, and differs from the 'Maya' theory of Shankara. Again, he does not accept the impersonal and 'Nirguna' Brahman of Shankara, but rather an eternal personal Brahman (having definite form, name and attributes – rather the Saguna Brahman). He identifies this Brahman as Vishnu, who can be easily approached through Bhakti and devotion.

He taught that 'Reality' has three aspects – God (Vishnu), Jiva (Soul), and Matter (Prakriti). One part of Brhadaranyaka Upanishad (III.v) supports this view point. [Hiriyanna (in The Essentials of Indian Philosophy) argues that 'since the ultimate aim of Brhadaranyaka Upanishad is teaching of Advaita, we cannot substantially say that this Upanishad ultimately accepts Visisthadvaita']. Ramanuja further argues that Vishnu is the only independent entity where as Jiva and Prakriti are dependent on Vishnu for existence.

According to Ramanuja, the individual Soul and the Universal Soul (God) are not the same, although they are not separate from each other. There is one God and he is the only Reality. He is all powerful, all-knowing and all merciful. He has infinite auspicious qualities like grace, compassion, bestowing blessings, etc. Vedas are the only source through which his existence and his nature as the Creator, Moral Controller, Saviour and Destroyer can be known. He is in fact the Universe, even though he remains separate from his creation.

Each Soul, according to its individual Karma passes through many births and deaths, until it realizes its relationship with God. The highest ideal and the final goal is – to love and worship God, and completely surrender one-self to God. The evil and suffering of the Soul are the results of one's own Karma. It may be overcome by devotion to God through prayer, meditation and performing pious deeds in the service of God. Then, by the grace of God, the Soul attains release/liberation (Mukti). Thus Ramanuja added the concept of devotion, worship and faith as new dimensions of Vedanta.

Interpretation of *'Tat-twam-asi'*

Ramanuja interprets this famous quotation from Chandogya Upanishad, which the Advaitins use to propagate their philosophy (Thou are That – which expresses an absolute identity of the individual self with the Brahman). Ramanuja's interpretation of the phrase is as follows: 'Thou' and 'That' signify an underlaying unity, while containing distinctive qualitative content. Hence 'That' in this context brings to the fore the quality of the underlying substantial unity of all individuals in Brahman, while 'Thou' emphasizes that we as individuals, are qualities or distinctions in this underlying unity' (Sri Bhashya 1.i.1, *Great Sidhanta* pp 129)

Brahman and Atman

All individuals are Brahman by virtue of constituting its body, but all individuals retain an identity in contradistinction to other parts of Brahman, particularly the soul of Brahman. Ramanuja gives examples of 'sharira' and 'shariri' (body and soul), and 'sesha' and 'seshin' (dependent and dependent upon) to elucidate his statement.

Ramanuja maintains that there is a way in which the individual-self (Jeevatma) is identical with the ultimate-self (Paramatma). Each Jiva shares with Brahman an essential nature of being a knower. However due to Karma, this true nature is obscured from us. In other words our likeness in one respect with Brahman does not imply that we ourselves are omnipotent, omniscient or all good.

Even though there exists one all pervading 'Brahman (termed as Vishnu)', this Brahman has all imaginable qualities, especially consciousness. Similarly the plurality of the universe is also real – matter and souls are all parts of the all pervading Brahman.

There are two states of the universe –

1. Vyakta (manifest) and
2. Avyakta (un-manifest).

In the un-manifest state, all the qualities of Brahman exist in the subtle state. From this initial state, creation takes place through the wish of the Brahman, and the world comes to the manifest state. Through spiritual knowledge, the souls can come out of the cycle of births and deaths, attain liberation and go to the world of Brahman and become one with Brahman in all aspects, except the three aspects of creation, preservation and destruction of the Universe.

Vishnu as a Personal God

Ramanuja considers Brahman as the union of two deities – Vishnu (or Narayana) as the Father and his consort Sri (Lakshmi) as the Mother. This is an important concept (by which Ramanuja considers Brahman as 'Ubhaya-lingam' – the unity of both the sexes – the father and the mother), which accounts for Brahman's creative potency. He further feels that Brahman is antagonistic to all evil, lacks all faults (papa, heya, mala or dosha) and is comprised of innumerable auspicious qualities. (Vedanta Sangraha and Sri Bhashya).

Moksha

Ramanuja says that attaining 'Moksha' is the purpose of every soul. Any soul, (in whatever body it has taken man, woman, and animal) can attain Moksha and there is no discrimination. We should be aware of our true nature as also the nature of the Brahman. When all impediments to this awareness are removed, the individual attains Moksha. Ramanuja subscribes to the view held by Sruti: 'Awareness of Brahman is bliss' (Taittiriya Upanishad 2.6). He further holds the view that mere theoretical knowledge is not sufficient to procure liberation.

Bhakti

Ramanuja advocates two methods of attaining Moksha –

1. *Bhakti (devotion):* Bhakti or pure devotion and worship, help an individual to counteract one's Karmas, and please Brahman. He emphasizes Bhakti Yoga as propounded by Sri Krishna in the Gita. Bhakti is still dependent on the efforts of the Bhakta.
2. *Prapatti (sharanagati/surrender):* He further says that surrender to God is the only way to spiritual emancipation, but does not rule out other paths.

Visisthadvaita recognizes the following principles:

1. *Tatva Traya* (Three Principles): Chit (Atma) and Achit (inanimate objects) form the body of the Brahman known as Iswara (Vishnu).
2. *Rahsya Traya* (Three Secrets):
   - (*i*) *Tiru mantra (*Om Namo Narayanaya) to be initiated through a Guru by means of Vaishnava Diksha;
   - (*ii*) *Dvaya –*
     - *Sriman Narayana Charanam Sharanam Prapadye Srimate Narayanaya Namaha*
     - The two aspects of the God – Sri (Lakshmi) and Narayana. The Sadhaka has to approach Narayana through his consort Lakshmi.

(*iii*) *Charama Sloka* – As already quoted at the beginning of the section on Visisthadvaita, the following Sloka of Gita (18.66) is known as Charama Sloka:
Sarva dharmaan parityajya ....

Vadakalai and Tenkalai Schools

After Ramanuja, the Sri Vaishnava tradition split into two schools – the northern school (Vadakalai – founded by Vedanta Deshikar) and the southern school (Tenkalai – founded by Manavalama muni). The northern school holds that Vedic observances are essential to proper Sri Vaishnava practices. The southern school emphasizes the importance of emulating the examples of the twelve Alvars.

The two schools also differ in the form of divine grace and individual effort. Both schools agree that divine grace is necessary for liberation, but they disagree as to the conditions under which divine grace is dispensed. The northern school believes that the divine grace is tied to the efforts of the individual. The southern school believes that the divine grace is dispensed freely as liberation is the sole responsibility of God.

In conclusion we can say that, Visisthadvaita declares Brahman, Jeevatma, the world as all real and propounds that Bhakti, Tyaga and Sharanagati as the three paths for attaining Moksha.

3. DVAITA SIDHANTA

(Dualism – Bheda Vada)

Hari-Sarvothama – Vayu-Jeevothama

[Lord Vishnu is the Supreme God, while Vayu (the God of Life) is supreme among the Souls]

Madhvacharya (thirteenth century CE) opposed both the Advaita and Visisthadvaita philosophies, and put forward a straightforward dualistic (Dvaita) theory. It is also known as 'Tatva Vada' (Philosophy of Reality), 'Vaishnava Sidhanta' and 'Bimba-Prati Bimba Vada'. There were sects which propounded Dvaita Sidhanta even earlier to Madhva.

But it was Madhva who provided a complete philosophical basis to Dvaita Sidhanta. Madhva and his subsequent followers of the Dvaita school like Jaya-tirtha (fourteenth century) and Vyasa-tirtha (fifteenth century) have made substantial contributions to 'Dvaita philosophy' as also the system of logic and epistemology.

Dvaita offers an alternative system of Vedantic interpretation in direct contrast to the dominant Advaita view which was prevalent at that time. Dvaita stresses a strict distinction between God (Brahman) and Jivas (Individual souls). Like Ramanuja, Madhva advocated a Vaishnava pantha, which believes that God as the Supreme Being (Brahman) is endowed with attributes, and that Saguna Brahman is Vishnu.

Subsequently, Dvaita Sidhanta school has seen a galaxy of great scholars and leaders of Vaishnava Bhakti movements in subsequent centuries – the saint poets like Purandaradasa and Kanakadasa; as also popular saints like Sri-Pada-Raja and Guru Raghavendra Swamy. Madhva's Dvaita philosophy also greatly influenced the philosophies of several acharyas – Nimbarka, Vallabha and Chaitanya to name a few.

Confusion of Identities

There is a tendency among some Western philosophers to confuse Madhva who propounded Dvaita Sidhanta, with another Madhava (Vidyaranya) who was an Advaitin and Guru of Hakka & Bukka, the founders of Vijayanagar Empire. Hence some of the Advaita works of Vidyaranya have been attributed to Madhva by these scholars. In fact, Madhva spent his entire life time opposing Advaita philosophy and hence it is ridiculous to suggest that he was the author of several Advaita works, which were in fact authored by Vidyaranya whose name was also Madhava.

Historical Background

It is important to keep in mind, the historical scenario during Madhva's time.

1. Northern India was being subjected to invasions by Muslim invaders. Forced conversions to Islam were also on the rise.

Some of the Muslim invaders had also started regular attacks on South India and there was constant fear of desecrating of Hindu temples and destroying of Hindu idols by Muslim armies.

2. Northern Karnataka had already seen the rise of the 'Veerashaiva' sect and 'Kalyana Kranti' (religious revolution in Kalyana of Chalukyas), with its attendant consequences which affected the religious and social fabric of the region.
3. To a large extent South India was safer than North India, to the followers of Hindu religion. Hence there was time and space for people to practice their respective religions and for scholars to discuss philosophical issues in peace and tranquility.
4. In Vedic religion, there were two powerful groups –
   (*i*) One group believed in Karma Kanda and rituals. However, the influence of this group had declined to a considerable extent because of the teachings of Adi Shankara and Ramanuja, who were both against animal sacrifices. But in subsequent centuries these rituals were still practiced by quite a few people.
   (*ii*) The other group believed in the Advaita system of Philosophy advocated by Adi Shankara. This was the more powerful group.
5. Shaivism had seen a purge of the negative effects of Kapalikas, Pasupata, Tantric sex and human sacrifices, etc.
6. The Bhagavata Panthas in neighbouring Maharashtra, were not anti-Shaivite in nature.
7. There were efforts to bring tolerance and unity between Vaishnava and Shaiva sects and one could hear secular terms like Hari-hara, Shankara-Narayana, Dattatreya, etc.

Socio-Cultural Scenario of Coastal Karnataka

The coastal districts of Karnataka (known as Parasurama Kshetra) in which Udupi is situated, present a lot of socio-cultural contrasts. The region is known for considerable religious tolerance when compared to other regions of South India.

The temples situated in this region are mainly Shiva temples. Prior to establishment of 'Krishna Matha' (by Madhva), there were no Vishnu temples in this region. The Anantheswara and Chandramouleswara temples at Udupi are Shiva temples. In all these Shiva temples, worshipping of the deity is done as per 'Shaivagamas'.

The only difference is that in some temples like Ananteswara, (the deity is considered as Vishnu in the form of Shiva lingam by Madhvas) both Vishnu sahasranama and Shiva-sahasranama are recited. The priests of these temples belong to Shivalli Brahmin community, who are followers of Bhagavata Sampradaya, but worship both Shiva and Vishnu with equal reverence.

Before the time of Madhva, the only Vedantic school prevalent in these coastal districts was Advaita. Visisthadvaita had not reached this region, even 200 years after Ramanuja propounded his philosophy. However there was considerable influence of Jainism in the area. This is evident by the number of 'Jaina Statues' and 'Bastis' in the area. The Dharmadhikari family of the famous Dharmasthala Manjunatheswara temple is a Jaina by tradition.

Madhva's father (Madhya Geha Bhatta) is said to have worshipped Ananteswara for 12 years for 'Putra-santana-prapti' – to get a son.

Life of Madhva

Madhva is a thirteenth century saint from Udupi, Karnataka, born in a 'Bhagavata Sampradaya' Brahmin family. His Guru was 'Achuta-prekshaka' who had been brought up in the then current Advaita School of philosophy. Madhva did not agree with his philosophy and started preaching his own philosophy according to which the world is real, the individual souls are different from Brahman and Vishnu is that Brahman, the highest entity in the Universe. This was the essence of Dvaita Sidhanta. Followers of Madhva sect believe that Madhva is the third incarnation of Vayu (considered as Mukhya Prana) after Hanuman (*Ramayana*) and Bhima (*Mahabharata*).

Madhva's Works

Madhva's singular contribution was to offer a new insight to Vedantic thought, the Upanishads, Brahma Sutras and the Puranas. Madhva in all wrote 37 works. His most important works are his commentaries on the Gita, Brahma Sutras, ten principal Upanishads, *Mahabharata* and *Bhagavata*. Another Madhva scholar 'Jayatirtha' has composed the commentary on Madhva's works – titled 'Nyaya sudha' – which helps us to understand Madhva's works easily.

Founding of Krishna Matha

Madhva founded the 'Krishna Matha' at Udupi and established eight mathas and appointed his disciples as the 'Peethadipatis' of these mathas. The Swami of every one of the eight Mathas worships Krishna (by turn) for a period of two years (known as Paryaya).

ESSENCE OF DVAITA SIDHANTA

Dvaita Sidhanta also accepts the description of 'Brahman' as 'Sat-Chit-Aananda' but does not subscribe to the definitions given by Advaita at three levels – Paramarthika, Vyavaharika, and Pratibhasika levels.

Madhva argues that 'Although Brahman (Vishnu) is real, souls and matter are different from Brahman'. He opposed the theory of Ramanuja that it is self contradictory, to hold that souls are both different and not different from God. Through devotion, one can attain liberation by the grace of God. The existence of God is as per statements made in the scriptures and cannot be proved through inference.

Madhva makes considerable use of logic and applies Vaiseshika and Sankhya doctrines to propound his philosophy. He accepts three means of knowledge – sensation, inference and scriptures (Pratyaksha, Anumana and Shabda).

Two Levels of Reality

Dvaita recognizes two orders of Reality:

1. *Swatantra* – The independent Reality which consists of Brahman

alone (and this Brahman is described as Vishnu, the Supreme Being).

2. *Paratantra* – The dependent reality which consists of Jivas (souls) and Jada (lifeless objects); time and space; – all of which exist by the will of God.

Although dependent reality cannot exist without Brahman's will, this very dependence creates a fundamental distinction between Brahman (Vishnu) and all else which is the essence of Dvaita view. Dvaita also gives primary importance to the validity of experience as a means of knowledge.

Basic Tenets of Dvaita Sidhanta

The following in simple terms form the basic tenets of Dvaita philosophy –

1. *Vishnu-Sarvothamatva,*
2. *Vayu-Jivothamatva,*
3. *Jagat-Satya,*
4. *Pancha Bheda,*
5. *Taratamya and*
6. *Bhakti.*

Vayu-Jivothamatva is the supremacy of Vayu (the God of Life) among all Jivas (souls). *'Jagat-Satya'* is that this world is real, which is in direct contrast to the Advaita view, which considers the world as an illusion. The other tenets are explained in detail below:

Vishnu-Sarvothamatva

Dvaita gives supremacy to Vishnu over other deities including Shiva and rejecting the popular Hindu concept of Trimurti (Brahma-Vishnu-Shiva). This is unlike Advaita Vedanta, for which the identity of a personal god does not matter (as he is, anyhow, considered as Nirguna).

Dvaita puts Vishnu in the pre-eminent position above all gods on the basis of his perfect personality, unique qualities and characteristics. This view further makes devotion (Bhakti) an essential component of religious belief and practice. Madhva expounds the theory of 'Vishnu Sarvothamatva' in several of his works.

1. In his work 'Anu Vyakhyana', Vishnu is called as 'Guna poorna' as he is full of infinite good qualities and also is free from limitations. Vishnu is also the Creator, Sustainer, Controller, Destroyer, Enlightener and Liberator of everything else. He is distinct from all other beings as they are dependent on Him.
2. In 'Tatva Sankhyana', while enumerating various metaphysical categories, Madhva declares that God is a separate category by Himself (Swatantra).
3. In 'Dwadasha Stotra' Madhva proclaims thus: 'Past actions, ignorance, afflictions, time, modes of nature, etc. are not primary factors of human bondage... The scriptures declare that it is God alone who controls the entire universe of the living and non-living beings in every context'.
4. In 'Anu Vyakhyana' he further says, 'Any proposition which is inconsistent with 'Vishnu-Sarvothamatva' should be rejected as false... Consistency with divine majesty itself is the criterion of Truth'.

Pancha Bheda/Bheda Panchaka

According to Dvaita Sidhanta, there are five fundamental, eternal and real differences (Pancha Bheda) in the Universe and the unique difference between God and Creation. This is a variant of 'dualism and pluralism'. The Universe is called 'Pra-pancha' for this reason.

These five differences said to make the Universe are:

1. *Vishnu and Jivas* – God (Iswara=Vishnu) is distinct from individual souls.
2. *Vishnu and Jada* – God is distinct from matter (inanimate and insentient).
3. *One Jiva and another Jiva* – Every soul is distinct from another soul and this distinction is eternal and is based upon individual capacity or characteristics.

4. *Jiva and Jada* – Individual souls are also distinct from matter.
5. *One form of Jada and another* – Differences exist between matter and matter.

Individual souls are quite distinct from God as well as their mortal/ material bodies. They are eternal and their spiritual essence is not mortal. They are dependent on God in bondage as well as salvation. All living and non-living beings are images of God, but quite distinct from him.

Reality of the World (Jagat Satya)

The concept of 'Pancha Bheda' implies that this diversity of the world (as perceived by our senses) is not an illusion (Maya). The material world is provided by God, as a field of activity for the individual souls for their spiritual development. God pervades the world and transcends all limitations of mortal life. In 'Dwadasha Stotra' Madhva speaks of this diversity of God's creation, as a concrete evidence of his numerous powers.

Taratamya (Difference in Hierarchy)

Madhva points out a system of hierarchy (called Taratamya) present in the Universe. He describes the elaborate hierarchy of Gods, Rishis, Manes, Angels, Men, Animals, and demons who are instrumental in the process of manifestation of this Universe. This is described purely as a spiritual exercise. When love and devotion is greater, the individual soul attains a higher rank in the hierarchy.

According to Madhva, the following is the hierarchy of gods:

1. Vishnu is the Supreme Lord and the Goddess Lakshmi is his eternal consort.
2. Lakshmi is next in the hierarchy of gods and is considered the 'Kriya-Chaitanya' and 'Maya Shakti' of Vishnu. Sita, Rukmini and others are incarnations of Lakshmi, as she follows Vishnu in his various 'Avatars'.
3. Brahma (the Creator) and Vayu (the God of Life),
4. Garuda, Shesha, Shiva;

5. Indra – Kama;
6. Surya – Chandra;
7. Varuna, Agni, Ganesha, Kubera;

Other gods successively occupy the lower rungs. All these gods depend on Vishnu for their creative power. Hence the worship of these gods, should not compromise one's devotion to the Supreme God Vishnu.

Classification of Souls

Madhva traces the problem of evil in the three-fold categorization of souls in the scheme of spiritual gradation. Thus, Madhva divides souls into three classes:

1. *Mukti-yogyas* – These are 'Satvic' souls, which are essentially good in nature and which qualify for spiritual progress and liberation,
2. *Nitya-Samsarins* – Souls with 'Rajasic guna', stagnate in worldly life forever and hence are in the eternal cycle of death and rebirth,
3. *Tamo-yogyas* – Souls are essentially having 'Tamas guna', which are essentially evil souls, who have repulsion to God and good life. They are condemned to hell eternally.

According to Madhva, most of the evils present in this world are the result of evil actions of these evil souls. This has a parallel in the concept of 'Satan' in Christianity.

However, this goes against the traditional Karma theory believed by all other Hindu schools. All Hindu sects believe in universal salvation for all souls – Moksha even after an eternity of births and deaths.

Mukti (Salvation)

Madhva differs from traditional Hindu beliefs in defining Mukti. He believes that souls possess innate characteristics and capacities and hence they are predetermined to meet certain ends (as per classifications described in 'Taratamya'). Even though souls are eternal, they are dependent on God.

God's grace is required to attain Mukti. To obtain this divine grace, the individual has to undertake 'Sadhana' – through Vairagya (renunciation), Jnana (Spiritual Knowledge) and Bhakti (Devotion).

In the state of liberation (Mukti), though each soul is filled with bliss, the degree of bliss may not be identical. Each liberated soul will have a natural conscious body and senses, which enables it to enjoy every degree of bliss. The bliss also depends upon the individual soul's consciousness and the moral freedom it enjoys, which is a result of God's mercy and grace.

BHAKTI (DEVOTION)

Devotion (love of God to the exclusion of everything else) is the sure way of attaining Mukti. As all creation is dependent on God, Madhva has accorded the highest rank to 'sincere devotion and prayer to the God' as the essence of all ethical and spiritual disciplines. It is only genuine devotion that makes God to shower his blessings on the soul. The 'Dasa Panthas' (Purandara Dasa, Kanaka Dasa, Jagnnatha Dasa, and others) propounded this path through their popular devotional songs, sung with the object of reaching the Dvaita philosophy to the common people.

Nava-Vidha Bhakti

In his commentary on Bhagavata Purana, Madhva has elucidated the different modes of Bhakti known as 'Nava-vidha Bhakti':

1. Hearing about God's majesty from learned discourses on scriptures.
2. Singing His praise collectively,
3. Silent remembrance of God through repetition of His name,
4. Service of holy persons and one's fellow beings,
5. Worship of holy images of God,
6. Salutation of His presence in all beings,
7. Attitude of service of God, through all normal duties of one's life,
8. Entertaining intimacy with him as our inseparable companion,
9. Whole hearted surrender to his will.

Different Stages of Bhakti

Madhva describes the four different stages of Bhakti:

1. *The first stage* is that of getting a general understanding of the teachings about God found in the scriptures,
2. *The next stage* is the critical study and correct understanding of the supremacy of God, as per the scriptures,
3. *The third stage* follows deep meditation on God's supreme majesty leading to direct vision of God.
4. *The final stage* is experiencing God's supremacy, which brings salvation. Devotion in the state of salvation is an end in itself.

Interpretation of 'Tat-twam-asi'

Madhva tries to locate his controversial views in Vedanta texts with difficulty. One famous example is his rendering the meaning of the famous phrase of Chandogya Upanishad 'Tat-twam-asi' – You (meaning the Atman) are That (meaning the Brahman). By carrying over the 'a' from the preceding word Madhva rendered the phrase 'atat-twam-asi' meaning 'You are not That'.

CONCLUSION

Madhva further attempts to synthesize the ideas of Bhakti with Dvaita philosophy. He also gives a greater importance to Bhakti than other Vedantic schools. Some parallels have been drawn between Madhva's ideas and the Catholic Church – Krishna with Jesus and Vishnu bestowing grace on a devotee (through Vayu) which parallels that of the Holy Spirit in Christianity.

However, these interpretations of Madhva's philosophy by western scholars appear to be wholly incorrect, as Madhva has provided a comprehensive and elaborate basis for Dvaita philosophy on the basis of Hindu scriptures.

7

Evolution of Indian Philosophic Thought (Part III)

VAISHNAVA BHAKTI MOVEMENTS AND BHEDA-ABHEDA SIDHANTA

Rise of Vaishnava Bhakti Movements in North India

Even though, the three major schools of Vedanta – Advaita, Visisthadvaita and Dvaita, exercised near dominance of Indian philosophical thought for centuries, the Acharyas who spearheaded the Vaishnava Bhakti movements in North India could not accept any of these Vedantic philosophies, because they could not preach their fundamental concepts of 'Bhakti as well as Moksha' to the masses, using any one of these philosophies.

Fundamentally Advaita advocated a 'Nirguna Brahman' and 'Maya vada' which was not acceptable to any of these Acharyas, as all of them believed that the world was real. Bhakti also required extolling the virtues of a 'Saguna Brahman' like Dvaita and Visisthadvaita. But these two philosophies also did not fulfil their purpose, as pure Bhakti/Devotion had to lead to 'Liberation' for the soul and eventual 'Moksha' (which meant attaining oneness or union with God), which was totally against the philosophy of Dvaita.

This gave rise to a broad spectrum of philosophic thought – known as 'Bheda-abheda' Sidhanta – which tried to bridge the gaps between the unitary philosophy of Advaita and dualistic view of Dvaita. The

Bheda-abheda Vedantic schools exercised tremendous influence on the Vaishnava Bhakti movements of the medieval period in India.

The Concept of 'Bheda-Abheda'

'Bheda-abheda' Sidhanta is considered as the oldest Vedantic school and pre-dates even Adi Shankara's Advaita Vedanta. Several scholars have opined that, sage Badarayana wrote 'Brahma Sutras' originally keeping the 'Bheda-abheda' point of view.

In his commentary on Brhadaranyaka Upanishad, Shankara repeatedly criticizes the 'Bheda-abheda' Sidhanta (made by an earlier philosopher called as Bhatrprapancha). The central difference between the two philosophies is while Shankara maintains that Brahman's creation is Maya (vivarta), Bheda-abheda views the creation as a reality.

'Bheda-abheda' Vedanta essentially means that *Atman (the individual soul) is at the same time, both different but also not different from Brahman, the Ultimate Reality.* Thus it tries to reconcile the opposing positions of both Advaita and Dvaita Sidhantas.

Another important concept in Bheda-abheda Sidhanta is 'Jnana-Karma-samuchaya vada' which advocates the necessity of performing ritual acts (Karma) in combination with spiritual knowledge (Jnana), in order to obtain liberation.

This is in total contrast to Advaita Sidhanta that Jnana (Spiritual Knowledge) alone is sufficient for Atman to attain Brahman. This also shows that the ritualistic leanings of 'Purva Mimamsa' school were still heavily influencing the thinking of philosophers even in the medieval period.

'Bheda-Abheda' Philosophers

Acharyas who propounded the different schools of philosophy under 'Bheda-abheda' Sidhanta are many. The most important of them are:

1. Bhaskara (probably earlier to eighth century CE),
2. Yadava Prakasha (eleventh century),
3. Nimbarka (thirteenth century – Founder of Nimbarka Sampradaya),
4. Vallabha (fifteenth century – Founder of 'Pustimarga' sect),

5. Chaitanya (1486–1533, Founder of Gaudiya Vaishnava sect) and
6. Vignana Bhikshu (sixteenth century CE).

However, all these Acharyas have taken different positions in the interpretation of the 'Bheda-abheda' philosophy.

1. Bhaskara

His only available work is a commentary on Brahma Sutras. Bhaskara is the first in a long line of Acharyas (including Ramanuja and Madhva) to refute the principles of Advaita Vedanta. Though Bhaskara does not take the name of 'Adi Shankara', while criticizing Advaita vada, his powerful refutation of the cardinal points of Advaita Vedanta, leads one to believe that he was either a contemporary of Shankara or was thoroughly familiar with Shankara's philosophy.

Almost all the stock arguments used against Advaita are in effect attributed to Bhaskara. Even after several centuries, Advaita Vedantins considered Bhaskara as a thorn in their side. (Shankara-dig-vijaya by Madhava – fourteenth century). The philosophy advocated by Bhaskara is known as 'Aupadhika Bheda-abheda vada' (It is discussed separately below). Bhaskara maintained that the difference between Brahman and the world is due to limiting conditions.

2. Yadava Prakasha

Yadava Prakasha was the first Guru of Ramanuja. Ramanuja had a series of differences with him and eventually left him. The works of Yadava Prakasha have been lost. But his ideas can be understood by Ramanuja's refutation of his theory. Ramanuja depicts him as an exponent of 'Svabhavika Bheda-abheda vada'.

Yadava Prakasha held the view that Brahman has the substance of pure existence (san-maatra-dravya). He further held that Brahman and the world is both different and not different in its very nature and that difference is not simply due to artificial limiting conditions as propounded by Bhaskara. The relationship between Brahman and the individual is not merely one of class but having a relationship of cause and effect.

3. Nimbarka

He is a Vaishnava saint from Andhra, who advocated the 'Svabhavika Bheda-abheda' Sidhanta, which means (Natural Difference – Non-difference) also termed as 'Dvaita-Advaita'(Duality in Unity). He wrote *Madhva-Mukha-Mardana* refuting the Dvaita philosophy. He also wrote a commentary on Brahma Sutras and propounded his philosophy in his work *Vedanta Parijata Saurabha.* His philosophy is discussed separately below.

4. Vallabha

Both Vallabha and Chaitanya (who were contemporaries) provided momentum to Bhakti movements in North India in the late medieval period. Vallabha wrote commentaries on 'Brahma Sutras' and 'Bhagavata Purana' propounding his philosophy called 'Shudha-Advaita' (Pure non-dualism). According to his view there is no dualism whatsoever between a real Brahman and the world as both are like two sides of the same coin.

5. Krishna Chaitanya

He was a saint and social reformer from eastern India. He was a proponent of the Vaishnava school of Bhakti yoga and is the most famous saint, among those who propounded the 'Bheda-abheda' Sidhanta. His followers consider Chaitanya as an avatar of Krishna. Chaitanya was initiated into Madhva tradition from an ascetic 'Iswara Puri', from whom he received initiation in the 'Gopala Krishna' mantra. Later he took 'Sanyasa-Ashrama' from 'Keshava Bharati' a saint of Shankara tradition. This means he was thoroughly familiar with both the Advaita and Dvaita schools of philosophy.

Chaitanya spent the last 24 years of his life in Puri's Jagannatha Temple in Orissa. He worshipped 'Radha and Krishna' and popularized the chanting of 'Hare Krishna' mantra. His six chosen disciples known as 'Six Goswamis of Vrindavan' (Rupa, Sanatana, Gopala Bhatta, Raghunatha Bhatta, Raghunatha Dasa, and Jiva) were instructed by Chaitanya to systematically present the philosophy of Bhakti as taught by him. They and their disciples were instrumental in spreading the Bhakti movement throughout eastern India.

Swami Prabhpuada, founded ISCKON (International Society for Krishna Consciousness), in the twentieth century, which popularized Chaitanya's Bhakti movement in India and the West.

6. Vignana Bhikshu

He was the last major philosopher of 'Bheda-abheda' Vedanta, belonging to the medieval period. He upheld the view that Vishnu was the supreme God. However, he did not follow the path of Bhakti enunciated by the earlier 'Bheda-abheda' philosophers. He tried to synthesize the philosophies of Sankhya, Yoga and Nyaya with 'Bheda-abheda' Vedanta. He wrote a commentary on 'Brahma Sutras' where he propounds the 'Bheda-abheda' Vedanta in terms of 'separation and non-separation'.

Although he argued that the fundamental relationship between Atman and Brahman is one of non-separation, he agreed with the dualistic view of Sankhya philosophy of 'Prakriti' and 'Purusha' saying that it (separation) is temporary in nature. He also argued that the Sankhya Darshana requires an omnipotent God in order to cause the union of the two fundamental Sankhya principles of 'Prakriti' and 'Purusha'. He was also a fundamental critic of 'Advaita Vada'.

Major differences between 'Bheda-abheda' and other Vedantic schools

1. Shankara's Advaita holds that (Nirguna) Brahman is the only reality and the world is unreal (Maya). Ramanuja agreed with Shankara regarding 'Brahman as the only Reality', but differed from him stating that world is also a reality, but formed part of God. Madhva differed from both Shankara and Ramanuja stating that fundamental duality exists between God and Atman. Both Ramanuja and Madhva considered God as Saguna Brahman (in the form of Vishnu).

   In contrast, 'Bheda-abheda' Sidhanta holds that the world is real and not 'Maya' (illusory/unreal) as claimed by Advaita. In this respect, it is in line with the realist schools of both Ramanuja and Madhva. This helped the philosophers who advocated the 'Bheda-abheda' philosophy, to accept the existence of God in the form of 'Saguna Brahman' (as against the concept of 'Nirguna Brahman' held by Advaita).

2. The concept of Saguna Brahman is central to the Vaishnava Bhakti movements advocated by the 'Bheda-abheda' philosophers as the concept of 'Nirguna Brahman' would not have allowed them any freedom of worship and devotion which a 'Saguna Brahman' can generate among the devotees and followers of Vaishnava Bhakti movements.
3. However, the 'Bheda-abheda' philosophers differ from both Ramanuja and Madhva, in the type of relationship between Brahman and the individual souls. It is termed as 'difference and non-difference' by some and 'separation and non-separation' by others, and 'whole and parts' by still some others. They cite the Brahma Sutras (2.3.43), wherein the individual soul is referred to as an 'amsa' of Brahman.

   They also cite various examples of the physical world to illustrate their (meta-physical) points of view – Sun and sunlight, fire and its sparks, snake and its coils, etc. While in each case, the two entities are fundamentally the same, there is also a difference between the two. For example the sunlight (which is given as an example for the soul) may be of the same essence as the Sun (Brahman), though it (soul) cannot be termed as the Sun (Brahman) itself.
4. On the other hand, Dvaita philosophy also would not have served their purpose as, if complete duality exists between Atman and Brahman, then the ultimate unification of the soul with Brahman (in Moksha) which is the ultimate goal of all Vaishnava Bhakti movements would not have been possible.
5. Hence Bheda-abheda Vedanta (and to a certain extent Visisthadvaita) offer alternatives to the two completely opposing philosophies of Advaita and Dvaita –

(*i*) *Worshipping of a Saguna Brahman (Vishnu) through Devotion/Bhakti (as advocated by both Dvaita and Visisthadvaita).*

(*ii*) *At the same time, providing an opportunity for the soul of becoming one with Brahman (Vishnu) in Moksha (as advocated by Advaita), which is the goal of all Acharyas of Vaishnava Bhakti movements.*

However there are subtle differences between each of the Acharyas propounding 'Bheda-abheda' philosophy. These are separately discussed below.

Types of Bheda-Abheda Sidhanta

The Sidhanta advocated by 'Bheda-abheda' philosophers can be classified into following three types:

1. Aupadhika Bheda-abheda, advocated by Bhaskara,
2. Svabhavika Bheda-abheda, advocated by Nimbarka,
3. Achintya Bheda-abheda, advocated by Chaitanya.

1. 'Aupadhika' Bheda-Abheda Sidhanta
(*Difference and Non-Difference Based on Limiting Conditions*)

This Sidhanta was advocated by Bhaskara. It is a little closer to Advaita and is called '*Difference and Non-Difference, based on limiting conditions*'. According to Bhaskara, the Brahman as the Ultimate reality becomes finite and multiple by means of 'certain limiting conditions' (termed as 'Upadhi'). It is like a pure diamond looking red against a red background. Similarly Brahman appears finite, when transformed by limiting conditions.

This transformation is real as the individual entity (the soul) is finite and limited by conditions of bondage, suffering and ignorance. Although the soul is real in this state, (as different from Brahman), the difference is only temporary in nature. Liberation of the soul is precisely the removal of limiting conditions which enables the soul to find its true identity with Brahman.

2. Svabhavika Bheda-Abheda Sidhanta
(Natural Difference and Non-Difference)

At the other end of the spectrum of Bheda-abheda Sidhanta, is the 'Svabhavika Bheda-abheda' propounded by Nimbarka. According to him, Brahman is different and not different from Atman, not because of any artificial limiting conditions. The difference and non-difference exhibited by Brahman, is because of its essential nature. This view was also advocated by Yadava Prakasha.

According to Nimbarka, there are three categories of existence, real as well as co-eternal:

1. *Brahman* – who is Iswara the controller – Niyantar,
2. *Chit (souls)* – the enjoyer – bhoktr,
3. *Achit (Universe)* – object (enjoyed – bhogya)

Iswara is independent and exists by himself, where as the other two categories, though not different from Iswara, are dependent on him for existence.

1. *Difference (Bheda)* is a kind of existence which is separate but dependent – This dependency is termed as 'Paratantra-satta-bhava'.
2. *Non-Difference (Abheda)* means the impossibility of independent existence. It is termed as 'Swatantra-satta-bhava'.

Similarly, the souls and universe though nothing but Brahman, are different from him because of their own peculiar nature and attributes. Nimbarka accepts 'Parinama-vada', which explains the material cause of the world.

This philosophy is different from Ramanuja's philosophy, as according to Ramanuja, chit and achit have no existence apart from Brahman, as their existence is limited only as body attributes of Brahman.

For Nimbarka, Iswara – the highest object of worship is Krishna along with his consort Radha. He refers to five methods of attaining salvation:

1. Karma (Ritual Action) – consciously performed according to 'Varnashrama dharma', results in knowledge leading to salvation.

2. Vidya (Knowledge) – spiritual study and understanding of its deeper meanings enables one in attaining salvation,
3. Upasana/Dhyana/Meditation – is an independent means to salvation.
4. Prapatti (Surrender) – Bhakti/Devotion and surrender to the Lord is a means of liberation recommended to all castes and classes
5. Gurupasatti – Devotion and surrender to the Guru.

3. Achintya Bheda-Abheda Sidhanta (Gaudiya Vaishnavism)

Hare Krishna Hare Krishna, Krishna Krishna, Hare Hare
Hare Rama Hare Rama, Rama Rama, Hare Hare

Chaitanya based his philosophy on Bhagavata Purana and *Bhagavad Gita*. A work in Sanskrit called *Siksastaka* is attributed to him. Even though his philosophy is within the Vaishnava framework, it has marked differences with the philosophy of Madhva.

'Achintya-Bheda-abheda' is a school of Vedanta which propounds the philosophy of 'Inconceivable Oneness with Difference'. This is a position between Advaita vada of Shankara and Visisthadvaita of Ramanuja. It also differs from Dvaita vada of Madhva. The 'Achintya-tva' is the central concept used by Chaitanya to reconcile apparently contradictory notions of difference and non-difference of God and his creation.

Chaitanya considers God as 'Swayam Bhagavan' with his powers as fully real. Chaitanya took the view that the Brahman (in this case Krishna) and the souls are 'inconceivably, simultaneously one and different'. The living soul is intrinsically linked with the Supreme Lord, but at the same time it is not God, as the exact nature of relationship between God and the soul is inconceivable to the human mind. This tries to reconcile the theory that God is simultaneously one with and different from his creation.

God exercises supreme control over his creation – sometimes directly, and at other times indirectly through his different energies

(Prakriti). The analogy often used in this context, is that of the Sun and sunshine. Though both are part of the same reality, having a beam of sunshine in the room is not the same as being in close proximity with Sun itself. Qualitatively Sun and Sunshine are not different, but as quantities they are different. Similarly, even though the soul and God are similar in quality, the soul does not share the qualities of God to an infinite extent.

According to Chaitanya, 'Scriptures' are the chief proof and form the basis of this philosophy – which is summarized in ten maxims called 'Dasa mula'.

1. Krishna is the Supreme and Absolute Truth. He is without a second.
2. Krishna is endowed with infinite potency.
3. Krishna is the nectarine ocean of all Rasas.
4. The Jivas (individual souls) are His marginal or intermediate discrete parts.
5. Marginally situated the Jivas in their fallen state, are under the influence of Prakriti or Maya, the deluding potency of the Lord.
6. By loving service of the Supreme Lord Krishna, the Jivas get freed from the influence of Maya.
7. The Jivas and the material world, are distinct and non-distinct manifestations of the Lord. It is 'Achintya' (inconceivable), as rational attributes of human beings are quite incapable of understanding or even approaching the Divine sphere of the Lord, except by his mercy.
8. Shudha Bhakti (Pure devotion) is the only means of obtaining the Divine love.
9. Krishna Prema (Pure love) is the final goal of spiritual existence.
10. Krishna is the only lovable blessing to be received.

OTHER PROMINENT BHAKTI SAINTS OF MEDIAVAL INDIA

1. **Jayadeva** (twelfth century)

Jayadeva was a Sanskrit poet and scholar from Orissa. He is most famous for his devotional epic song 'Gita Govinda'. It depicts the divine and eternal love between Krishna the popular Hindu God and his consort Radha. This song became an important symbol of Vaishnava Bhakti movement and became popular throughout India within a short span of time.

Two hymns composed by Jayadeva have been incorporated in the *Guru Granth Sahib* the holy book of the Sikh religion. There are records narrating the deep influence Jayadeva's works had on Guru Nanak when he visited Puri. 'Gita Govinda', the immensely popular epic is considered as one of the finest examples of Sanskrit poetry. It was translated into the English language as early as 1792. Since then it has been translated into almost all the major languages of the world.

2. **Sant Jnaneshwar (Jnanadeva)** (thirteenth century)

He was a 'Nath Panth' saint from Maharashtra. He belonged to Vaishnava Sampradaya (devoted to Vittala of Phandarapur). He is said to have performed many miracles. He was only 21 when he entered into 'Samadhi' at Alandi in Maharashtra. His elder brother (Nivruttinath), younger brother (Sopandev) and sister (Mukta) who were all saints, continued his tradition.

Jnaneshwar gave discourses on the *Bhagavad Gita* when he was barely 15 years old. This was written down by another saint 'Sachidananda baba' and is known as 'Jnaneshwari' – a commentary on the Gita in Marathi. It is considered to be a masterpiece in Marathi literature. *Amrutanubhav*, based on Advaita Sidhanta, is another important work of 'Jnaneshwar. Around 1000 abhangas (devotional lyrics) are attributed to Jnaneshwar.

He strongly advocated 'Jnana-yukta Bhakti' (devotion guided by knowledge). He initiated his contemporaries and followers who were associated with the Dvaita school of Bhakti movement into Advaita. He preached that one cannot attain liberation unless he obtains true and divine knowledge of the Brahman.

3. **Namdev** (fourteenth century)

Namdev was a Marathi saint and a follower of sant Jnaneshwar. He emphasized the importance of living the life of a householder, and through devotional meditation attain salvation and enlightenment. He was a devotee of Vittala of Phandarapur and his abhangs are very popular. Over a period of time he transformed from being a devotee of 'Saguna Brahman' to a devotee of 'Nirguna Brahman'. He was a pioneer of the radical Bhakti school. 61 of his hymns have been included in the *Guru Granth Sahib.*

4. **Kabir** (fifteenth century)

Kabir was a mystic and poet saint of India. The name 'Kabir' is also one of the 99 names of God in Islam. Kabir's writings have influenced the Bhakti movements of India. He greatly influenced 'Sikhism' and his legacy is continued by millions of followers belonging to the 'Kabir Panth'.

Kabir was influenced by many religious traditions – old Brahmanical Hinduism, Buddhism, Tantrism, the teachings of various saints belonging to the Bhakti movements and Islam. Kabir vehemently opposed dogmas prevalent in Hinduism as well as Islam. He is held as the first Indian saint to have harmonized Hinduism and Islam by preaching a universal path which both Hindus and Muslims could practice.

According to Kabir, life is an interplay of two principles: Jeevatma (the individual soul) and Paramatma (God). Salvation is a process of fusing these two principles into one. He advocated the natural way to oneness in God. His teachings were a combination of Bhakti and Sufi ideas. The major part of Kabir's work as a 'bhagat', was collected by the Sikh Guru Arjun Dev and forms a part of *Guru Granth Sahib.*

5. **Tulsidas** (sixteenth century)

Goswami Tulsidas was a poet and saint and is popularly known for his work 'Ramacharita manasa'. He is regarded as an incarnation of Valmiki (who wrote the epic *Ramayana* in Sanskrit). The doctrines and proverbs of Tulsidas have had a tremendous influence on the religious mindset of Hindus in North India.

Like Ramanuja, Tulsidas believed in Saguna Brahman and incarnation of Rama for blessing the mankind. Tulsidas believed in single minded devotion and surrender as a way of realizing god 'Ramacharita manasa' is read and worshipped with great devotion in North India. It contains sweet couplets in beautiful rhyme in praise of Sri Rama.

'Hanuman Chalisa' (40 verses in praise of Hanuman) was written by Tulsidas in prison, when he was imprisoned on the orders Aurangzeb. It is said that when he completed the 'Hanuman Chalisa', an army of monkeys descended on Delhi and started creating disturbance which forced Aurangzeb to release Tulsidas. Hanuman Chalisa is reverently repeated by millions of Hindus throughout the country.

6. **Samarth Ramdas** (seventeenth century)

He was a prominent Marathi saint and religious poet. He has produced a considerable body of devotional literature in Marathi. Chhatrapati Shivaji considered him as his spiritual guru. Ramdas established 12 temples of Hanuman in Maharashtra and preached yoga for a healthy society. In his teachings, he emphasized ethical behaviour, devotion and love of god as fundamental to a Dharmic Hindu life. He had a considerable number of disciples and has a large number of followers in Maharashtra even today.

Apart from the above philosophers and saints, who spread the Bhakti movement, there are also other saints (mostly belonging to eighteenth, nineteenth and twentieth centuries) who equally played a prominent role in the spread of Bhakti movements in various parts of India. But their list is too long to be enumerated here.

8

Evolution of Indian Philosophic Thought (Part IV)

SHAIVA SIDHANTA

[*Om Namah Shivaiah*]

The Shaiva Sidhanta holds Shiva as the Supreme God. Apart from Jaina and Buddhist philosophies, Shaiva Sidhanta appears to be the only other philosophy in India which has developed independently of the Vedas and Upanishads, though some saints and scholars (from the twelfth century onwards) tried to compromise and synthesize the views of both Vedic and Shaiva philosophies. Even today, certain concepts evolved by Shaiva Sidhanta like Karmic theory and Maya, are in total contrast to other Indian schools of philosophy.

Origins of Shaiva Sidhanta

Shaiva sects are believed to have been in existence for more than 2000 years in India, even though the actual worship of Shiva dates back to the pre-Vedic period. Shaiva Sidhanta's original form is uncertain. It appears to have originated as a 'monistic' doctrine and acquired a 'dualistic' nature in later years. It probably started as a ritual of initiation to the path of 'Liberation'. 'Agni Purana' contains some rituals connected with the Shaiva sect.

The systematic enunciation of Shaiva Sidhanta is believed to have originated in Kashmir. Sadyojyoti (seventh century) is credited with the systemization of Shaiva Sidhanta in Sanskrit based on 'Rourava Tantra' and other scriptures. A number of Kashmiri scholars wrote treatises on the Sidhanta over a period of several centuries. King Bhoja (tenth century) of Ujjain, is credited with condensing the massive body of Shaiva Sidhanta spiritual texts into one concise metaphysical work known as 'Tatva-Prakasha'.

The Shaiva Sidhanta which originated in Kashmir differs from the Vedic and Puranic concepts concerning the worship of Shiva. There are also other Shaiva traditions like 'Kaula', 'Kapalika' and 'Pasupata' and other Tantric sects which have established their own Sidhantas, rituals and traditions.

However, due to spread of Vaishnava Bhakti movements in various parts of India, the dominance of the Shaiva sects decreased over a period of time, and is now predominant only in South India (especially in Tamil Nadu and Karnataka); as well as among the Tamil speaking population of Sri Lanka and other countries of South-East Asia.

Some of the Shaiva holy places like Kashi, Kedarnath, Sri Shaila, Ujjain, Gokarna and Rameswaram are revered as very ancient and sacred places dedicated to the worship of Shiva. They draw devotees from all parts of India.

Evolution of Shaiva Sidhanta

The Sanskrit theology of Shaivism of North India later fused with the devotional aspect of the Tamil Shaiva Bhakti movement and has now come to be commonly called as 'Shaiva Sidhanta'.

The first known saint who propagated Shaivism is 'Nandinatha' who lived in Kashmir. He laid down the basic tenets of Shaiva Sidhanta in his work 'Nandikesvara Kasika'. The Tamil saint 'Tirumalar' introduced the Nandinatha tradition of Shaiva Sidhanta in his work 'Tirumandiram' in Tamil. A number of devotional saints (whose works are preserved in Tevaram') made Shaivism a mass movement in Tamil Nadu, (in spite of considerable opposition from the Jain and Buddhist religions which were the dominant religions in South India at that time).

The eleventh century Tamil saint 'Nambi Andar Nambi' codified the basic tenets of Shaiva Sidhanta in his authoritative work 'Tirumarai'. It consists of 18,316 slokas. In the twelfth century, 'Aghora-siva' of Chidambaram amalgamated the Sanskrit and Tamil versions of Shaiva Sidhanta. He made a change from the monistic nature of the Sanskrit Shaiva Sidhanta to a dualistic approach, by reclassifying the first five principles or Tatvas. His work on Shaivagamas (Kriya-krama-dyotika) is considered as the standard puja manual in all Shiva temples.

The Tamil saint – Maykandar (thirteenth century), is credited with propounding the pluralistic realism in Shaiva Sidhanta – in which God, Souls and World, are co-existent, and without a beginning; – in his work 'Siva-Jnana-bodham'. He laid emphasis on Sivam, Jnanam and Bodham, declaring Shiva as One, Jnanam as the knowledge of Sivam, and Bodham as the process of experiencing and realizing such knowledge.

Sources for Shaiva Sidhanta

Even though some of the principles of Shaivism are based on Vedas and Upanishads, the following works are considered as the authorities by the various Shaiva sects:

Sanskrit Works

1. Shaiva –Agamas, which are 28 in number,
2. Various works of Umpati Acharya and
3. Works of other Kashmir Shaiva saints
4. Commentary on Vedanta Sutras by Nilakanta

Tamil Works

1. 'Periya Purana' which consists of life histories of 63 Shaiva saints,
2. 'Tirumarai' consisting of Shaiva prayers,
3. 'Tiruvachakam, and Tewaram' – which consist of mystical writings of Shaiva saints,
4. 'Shiva Jnana Bodham' by Meykandar,
5. 'Shiva Jnana Sidhiyar' by Arulanandi,

Essence of Shaiva Sidhanta

Shaiva Sidhanta recognizes that Shiva, Jiva (Soul) and the world are all eternal realities. Shiva is the Lord of souls. Hence he is also called as 'Pashu Pati'. Shiva is all omniscient, omnipresent, all powerful and Lord of this world – which has been created by Him.

The essential elements of Shaiva Sidhanta are – 'Pati (God), Pashu (Soul), and Pasha (the bonds that bind the Soul) and the 36 Tatvas (Principles)' which constitute this world. Shakti is Shiva's 'Chetana' (consciousness), and there is no difference between Shiva and Shakti. Jivas who are many are also eternal and in eternal bondage due to ignorance. Knowledge leads to removal of this bondage.

The bonds that bind the soul, can be removed through rigorous Tapas, proper discipline, help of a Guru, and above all by the Divine Grace of Lord Shiva. Those who attain salvation by annihilating these bonds are known as Siddhas (perfected beings). Moksha means the soul attaining 'Shivatva'.

Shiva as the Supreme Reality

The central doctrine of this philosophy is that Shiva is the Ultimate and Supreme Reality (the Infinite Consciousness). Shiva means the one who is pure, perfect and auspicious. His inherent nature is wisdom. He is 'Pati' (Iswara – Param-Brahman as the Lord of the Universe) and the Supreme Deity. Lord Shiva pervades the whole world by his Shakti – which is his conscious energy. Some Shaiva sects believe in the five aspects of Lord Shiva thus:

1. *Srishti*: Creation – represented by Brahma,
2. *Stithi*: Preservation represented by Vishnu,
3. *Samhara*: Represented by Rudra,
4. *Tirobhava* (*Tirodhana*): Maya – veiling represented by Maheswara and
5. *Anugraha*: Blessing – represented by Sadashiva.

Manifestations of Shiva

God Shiva in his inherent form is formless. He manifests in various forms to bestow grace. His manifested form is classified into three categories (Also see Chapter 11):

1. Arupa (formless): Shiva is meditated upon in this form through 'Om' and other Shiva mantras.
2. Rupa (with a body): Shiva is worshipped as Nataraja and Dakshinamurty.
3. Rupa-arupa (with and without a body): Shiva Linga is an example of this category, which is an intermediate stage between the first two stages.

Shaivism does not encourage the worship of minor deities. It feels that such worship hinders spiritual progress.

Jivas (Souls)

Every living being has a soul of its own. The individual souls are many and are different from one another constituted according to their Karma. These souls possess Jnana Shakti (power of knowledge), Iccha Shakti (power of desire) and Kriya Shakti (power of action). But these capabilities are impaired by the 'pashas' that bind the soul due to ignorance. Souls have a dependent nature. When they depend on worldly things they behave like them. When they depend on God, they behave like divine beings.

The Concept of 'Bheda-abheda' in Shaiva Sidhanta

This dualistic concept appears to be a later day addition (probably in the twelfth century). According to this concept, the individual souls are of the same essence (Satva) as Shiva (showing Abheda), though not identical (showing Bheda) with Shiva. This is a dualistic view present in Shaiva Sidhanta as it draws a fine distinction between souls and God. The difference is not in their essence but in their constitution. The relationship between souls and God is not of oneness but of sameness (essence). The souls may undergo transformation, due to Karma.

In Shaiva Sidhanta, liberation does not mean that the identity of the soul is lost forever, even though it enjoys unity of experience with the 'Supreme Being' (Shiva). This unity of experience is actually not of oneness but of sameness. Hence the soul enjoys a special relationship with Shiva known as 'Bheda-abheda' (Separation and non-separation). It is a dualistic theory which means – 'One (Shiva) being the whole and the other (the soul) being the part of the whole'.

Pasha (The Bonds)

The soul is subject to three impurities (also known as malas). Pasha is also termed as Karmic bondage (birth, death and rebirth). Ignorance leads to this bondage. There are three kinds of Pasha – *Anava, Karma and Maya.* These three bonds bind the souls to functional limitations. Hence they experience 'asat' – the unreality, and turn them into *pashus* (animals).

1. ***Anava – The First Bond:*** Of the three impurities 'Anava' is the natural impurity (sahaja mala), which is born along with the souls. It is the cause of all negative qualities of the soul. It clouds the consciousness and makes them act like individual entities of finite nature (anu) with limited knowledge and limited abilities. It is the cause of 'ego' of the self, which makes a soul think it is different from Shiva and other beings. The concept of 'Anava' is unique to Shaiva Sidhanta and its actions are summarized under seven categories.
2. ***Karma – The Second Bond:*** It is the binding action which is the second impurity. It binds the soul to the consequence of its actions which are mainly driven by desires. Karma means action. Every action has its own result and everyone has to experience the fruits of his action. Law of Karma explains that we have to experience the results of our actions in this life or another life until they get exhausted. Good actions result in good experiences and evil actions result in painful experiences. Fruit of one's Karma is fed to the soul in order to experience it at a suitable time and place decided by God.

3. ***Maya – The Third Bond:*** Maya is considered real, and not an illusion as considered by Vedanta philosophies. The physical body and the material world are created by God. Maya binds the soul to the sense objects through desires and ignorance. Maya acts as an instrument of Shiva. Although a single entity, Maya manifests itself in to two categories:
   (*i*) *Shudda Maya:* Maya in its pure form is eternal and indestructible. It caters to pure souls known as 'Adhikara Muktas'.
   (*ii*) *Ashuddha Maya:* Maya in its impure form caters to impure souls. Both the pure and impure mayas together give rise to 36 'Shiva Tatvas'.

The Shaiva Sidhanta recognizes three types of souls based on their degree of bondage to the Pashas (Impurities). Souls which are bound by all the three bonds, Souls which are bound by 'anava' alone and Souls which become free from 'Maya' during 'Pralaya' (Dissolution of the entire Creation).

SHIVA TATVAS

Pure Maya (Shudha Maya) gives rise to five pure Shiva Tatvas: Shiva Tatva, Shakti Tatva, Sadashiva Tatva, Iswara Tatva, and Shudda-Vidya Tatva. Using these Tatvas, Shiva creates the bodies, organs, world, and objects of enjoyment for pure souls.

Impure Maya (Ashudha Maya) is the cause of 'Prakriti-Maya' from which 31 Tatvas emerge. Out of these, seven Tatvas are required to awaken the soul's capabilities and to drive it to gain experience. These are called 'Vidya-Tatvas'.

Other 24 Tatvas are required for the formation of the physical body, its functions and experiences. They are called 'Prakriti Maya Tatvas' and they are:

1. *Pancha Bhutas:* Earth, Water, Fire, Air and Akasha (Ether);
2. *Five qualities:* (attributed to the Pancha-bhutas) – Odour, Taste, Colour Touch and Sound;

3. *Five organs of action:* the anus, generative organ, mouth, hands and feet; (Karmendriyas)
4. *Five sensory organs:* ears, skin, eyes, tongue, and nose; (Jnanendriyas)
5. *Four internal organs*: Manas, Buddhi, Chitta and Ahankara.

These 31 Impure Tatvas are used by Shiva for creating the bodies, organs, world, and objects of enjoyment for impure souls.

Purpose of Maya

Contrary to the popular belief, the purpose of Maya is twofold:

1. To subject the souls to the conditions of material existence and help them acquire
   (*i*) *Pasa-Jnana* – Sensory knowledge and
   (*ii*) *Pasu-Jnana* – Material knowledge
2. To prepare the souls for final liberation by subjecting them to Laws of Karma and helping them discriminate between right actions and wrong actions. This is a long process spread over several lives, before the souls need to realize the path to liberation.

Karma and Evolution of the Soul

Before taking birth, the soul is in a state of 'Kevalam' enmeshed in the darkness of the first bond 'Anava'. At this stage it is without its three natural aspects of 'Jnana, Iccha and Kriya' shaktis. Shiva out of his love for the soul, provides it with a subtle body formed with the eight Tatvas of Maya. This enables the soul to have some form of movement. Then Shiva provides it with a suitable gross body and enables it to be born in this world. The state of the soul with the physical body is called 'sakalam'.

On taking birth, the soul starts performing Karma, and also starts experiencing the results of the past Karma until it is exhausted. For it to experience the fruits of further karma, it is bound to be reborn again. This cycle goes on and on until the soul is liberated. In every birth, the soul gains some experience and through it gains knowledge.

As it gains knowledge, the grip of the bond 'Anava' weakens. The soul passes through several stages, before attaining spiritual liberation by the grace of Shiva.

Spiritual Liberation

In order to achieve spiritual development and liberation, Shaiva Sidhanta advocates the development of good qualities by everyone. According to this Sidhanta, 'Spiritual liberation' can be obtained through four paths – Charya, Kriya, Yoga and Jnana. However, these four paths are not considered complementary to each other.

1. ***Charya:*** It involves serving Lord Shiva and devotees in temples and holy places, through such acts like cleaning, cooking, carrying water, gathering flowers, rendering general service, both to Shiva and his devotees. This is known as 'Dasa Marga' – the path of the servant.
2. ***Kriya:*** Worshipping Shiva with body and mind is 'Kriya'. It involves performing devotional acts like worship of the Lord, performing puja, recitation of prayers, singing devotional songs, narration of religious stories, etc. This path is called 'Sat-Putra-Marga' – the path of a good son.
3. ***Yoga:*** Meditating on Shiva and getting united mentally with him is Yoga. It involves practice of yogic methods like asanas, meditation, dhyana, etc. This path is known as 'Sakha-Marga' as through this path one gets an opportunity to act as a spiritual companion with Shiva.
4. ***Jnana:*** It is the path of knowledge by understanding the tenets of Shaiva Sidhanta, practicing them and obtaining Shiva's grace. It is called as 'Sat-marga' (Sat means the Truth). The soul gets closer to the Truth which is – experiencing the true consciousness of the Supreme reality (Shiva). This path is considered as superior to the other three paths.

After liberation, the soul becomes aware of the nature of the Supreme Being. In the liberated state, it enjoys eternal bliss free from all bonds.

It also experiences some kind of duality as it understands that Shiva is Supreme and distinct from itself even though it experiences the Supreme Consciousness of Shiva. In the liberated state, the soul experiences unlimited bliss and freedom from bonds of 'Samsara'.

Guru

Like God, the Guru has an important place in Shaivism. It is the Guru, who decides the suitable path for a disciple based on his inherent ability and inclination. Further, the Guru gives him spiritual guidance at every stage, as he prepares the disciple to receive the grace of Shiva.

Shaiva Practices

Shaiva practices prescribe: Shiva Diksha, Puja of Shiva Linga, recitation of 'Shiva Panchakshari' mantra, and wearing of Shaiva symbols like 'Vibhuti', and 'Rudraksha mala' – as essential parts of 'sadhana' by the followers of the Shaiva Sect, as it helps them in the path of realization of Shiva.

Shaiva Sects and Sub-Sects

There are three prominent Shaiva sects in existence today:

1. Kashmira Shaiva Sect,
2. Dravida Shaiva Sect, and
3. Veerashaiva sect.

There are also other minor Shaiva sects –

1. Dvaita – Pasupata Sect,
2. Dvaita – Advaita Lakulisha Pasupata Sect,
3. Dvaita – Shaiva Sidhanta Sect,
4. Shaiva – Visisthadvaita Sect,
5. Nandikeshvara Shaiva Sect,
6. Raseshvara Shaiva Sect,
7. Kalamukhas,
8. Kapalikas (who worship Shiva in the form of Bhairava and use Tantra Vidya),
9. Maheswara sect.

VEERASHAIVA SIDHANTA

(*Shakti Visisthadvaita*)

Kriya Jnana Samayuktam Veerashaivasya Lakshanam I
Dvaita-advaita Samayuktam Veerashaivasya Lakshanam II

[The characteristic of Veerashaivism is the essential unity of Kriya and Jnana, as well as Dvaita and Advaita]

Veerashaivism is an important off-shoot of Shaiva Sidhanta. But over a period of time it developed its own independent philosophical concepts which are not found in Shaiva Sidhanta and other philosophies. It is also known by many names – Shiva-dvaita, Maheswara mata, Lingayata mata, Shiva Dharma, and Shakti Visisthadvaita.

Veerashaivism is a popular religious tradition which is unique to Karnataka region. The followers of the Veerashaiva sect are also known as 'Lingayats' and have many sub-denominations among them. They are spread all across Karnataka and are also found in border areas of neighbouring states. The term 'Lingayat' is derived from the Kannada word 'Lingavanta' – which means one who wears the 'Linga' on his body.

Origins of Veerashaivism

The 'Pancha-charyas' (Renuka, Marula, Ekorama, Pandita and Viswa) are generally regarded as the founders of Veerashaivism. The 'Pancha-charya Peethas' are in existance at the following places – Balehonnuru, and Ujjini, both in Karnataka; Kedar (Uttranchal); Sri-Shaila (Andhra Pradesh); and Kashi (Uttarapradesh). These Pancha-charyas are considered as custodians of the Veerashaiva faith. Even though these 'Pancha-charya Peethas' are said to be in existence from ancient times, due to lack of historical evidence, Basvanna is widely held as the founder of the Veerashaiva sect.

Basaveswara

(1134 – 1196 CE) (popularly known as Basavanna) was a minister in the court of King Bijjala (of Kalchuryas). Before becoming a minister, Basavanna had accepted Veerashaivism from Jataveda Muni of Saranga

Matha. It is a historical fact that Basavanna rebelled against the caste system prevalent in the society at that time, and eventually propounded a casteless society as the core of his philosophy. He preached humane principles of equality, compassion and dignity of labour. His philosophy began attracting a large number of followers.

Saints like 'Allama Prabhu', 'Akka Mahadevi', 'Siddarama' 'Channabasvanna', 'Adaiah', 'Molige Maraiah' and others played an important role in the spreading of the Veerashaiva movement. Among the Veerashaiva saints, Basavanna gave prominence to Bhakti, Siddarama to Karma, and Allama Prabhu to Jnana and Advaita.

During the early stages, Veerashaivism laid emphasis on social reform, which was unheard of at that time. However there was a strong reaction by the upper classes of the Hindu society, to these social reforms. It resulted in the historic 'Kalyana Kranti' and the followers of Veerashaiva sect moved away to rural parts of North Karnataka from where they got some support.

Later the sect received royal patronage from Vijayanagar Empire and subsequent kingdoms in Karnataka. The religious institutions (Mathas) established over centuries at Gadag, Yedeyuru, Sutturu, Siddaganga, Chitradurga, Sirigere, and other places helped the sect to grow and sustain the Veerashaiva faith and its philosophy.

Unique Features of Veerashaivism

The followers of the sect, believe in Shiva as the Supreme God. He is to be worshipped through 'Shiva Linga' (considered as a symbol of God himself) which is carried by every follower on his body, by means of a 'Shiva-dara'. He could worship this Shiva Linga at his convenience. This eliminated the intervention of a priest.

Even though the faith started as a reform movement in Hinduism, over a period of centuries, Veerashaivism reabsorbed certain aspects of Hinduism, which Basavanna had rejected originally – icon worship in temples, intervention of the priest between God and devotee, certain traditions of ritual purity, giving of gifts to Gurus, stratification of society, etc. Even during Basavanna's time, icon worship was preferred by other saints as the Shiva temples at Sri Shaila, Kudala Sangama and other holy places continued to draw Veerashaiva devotees.

Sources for Veerashaiva Sidhanta

The original ideals of the sect are found in the following sources:

1. Basavanna's 'Vachanas',
2. Allama Prabhu's 'Mantra Gopya',
3. Chennabasavanna's 'Karana Hasuge'
4. 'Shoonya Sampadane' – a collective edited work.
5. Shivayogi Shivacharya's 'Sidhanta Shikamani',
6. Sripati Panditaradhya's 'Srikara Bhashya'.
7. Shivanubhava Sutra, etc.

Later efforts were made to derive Veerashaiva theology from traditional Hindu scriptures like 28 Shaivagamas earlier rejected by Shiva-sharanas. Poets such as Harihara, Raghavanka, Chamarasa, Shadakshari and others composed literary epics in support of Veerashaiva saints.

Essence of Veerashaiva Sidhanta (Shakti Visisthadvaita)

The theological doctrine of Veerashaivism is known as 'Shakti Visisthadvaita'. It is a version of qualified non-dualism, which accepts both difference and non-difference between the Soul and God.

It believes that Shiva is the one and only 'Para Brahman' and advocates the worship of the single God Shiva. *Shiva and his creation are one, yet Shiva is beyond His creation which is real and not illusory.*

God is both efficient and material cause. The soul in its liberated state attains undifferentiated union with Shiva. True Union and Identity of Shiva (Linga) with the soul (Anga), is the goal of life described as Shoonya. This is achieved through a progressive six-stage-path called 'Shat-sthala'.

The Sidhanta also gives primacy to Bhakti which contains the three essential elements of 'Yoga, Jnana and Kriya'. It further tries to synthesize Vedanta 'Tatvas' along with special 'upasana vidhis' which are unique to Veerashaivism. However it rejects the concepts of 'Varnashrama

Dharma', and rituals and sacrifices practiced in Vedic Hindu Religion.

Central to the Veerashaiva Sidhanta are the three unique concepts of:

1. *Pancha-chara* – the five codes of conduct,
2. *Asthavarana* – the eight shields,
3. *Shatsthala* – the six levels of attainment.

A Shiva Bhakta has to practice the above three concepts to obtain Siddhi or 'Shiva Sakshatkara'.

Pancha-chara

They form the religious, social and ethical codes of Veerashaivism and consist of the five codes of conduct to be followed by its followers.

1. *Linga-chara* – It considers the Linga as the image of Shiva. It includes the daily worship of the personal Shiva Linga (also known as Istha-Linga) with all devotion.
2. *Sada-chara* – Following the righteous path according to Dharma in daily life. It includes service of the 'Jangamas' and the poor. It also includes exhibiting good conduct and doing good deeds.
3. *Siva-chara* – Acknowledging that Shiva is the supreme God and there is no god other than Shiva. Siva-chara also includes treating everyone of the followers of the sect as equal without making any distinction between 'Shiva- Bhaktas'.
4. *Gana-chara* – All Shiva Bhaktas are considered as 'Shiva-ganas'. Helping this community and defending its tenets.
5. *Bhrutya-chara* – Showing total devotion to both Shiva and Shiva Bhaktas and showing compassion to all living beings.

Asthavarana

It means the protective shield. It helps a sadhaka in protecting him from evil forces and life's difficulties. It also helps him in the spiritual path towards attaining siddhi. This consists of the following eight elements: Guru, Linga, Jangama, Padodaka, Prasada, Bhasma, Rudraksha, and Mantra. Some explanation is necessary to understand the meaning of each of these concepts.

1. ***Guru:*** Guru is considered as the manifestation of Shiva. Shiva instructs the Bhaktas, through the Guru. Guru gives 'Veerashaiva diksha' to the sadhaka as prescribed in the Shastras and helps him in the spiritual path through proper guidance. Hence, it is important for the sadhaka, to show complete obedience to the Guru.
2. ***Linga:*** is the image of Shiva. The Linga that is given by the Guru is considered sacred and has to be worn by the follower on his body. Performance of daily 'Istha Linga Puja' is considered important and establishes a personal relationship between Shiva and his Bhakta.
3. ***Jangama:*** Jangama is one who has achieved Siddhi or 'Shiva-sakshatkara'. They are considered as 'jivan-muktas'. They are capable of providing guidance to Shiva Bhaktas. Hence they are to be treated with reverence. The Bhakta should not differentiate between Guru, Jangama and Linga and serve all the three with sincerity and devotion.
4. ***Padodaka:*** It is the holy water obtained by washing the feet of Guru, Linga and Jangama. The Bhakta has to daily take this water with reverence as it is considered sacred.
5. ***Prasada:*** The food that is first offered (Shivarpana) to God is called 'Prasada'. The Shiva Bhakta has to daily offer the food first to Linga (or Guru/Jangama) and then take it as prasada.
6. ***Bhasma:*** (holy ash – Vibhuti) is a sign of renunciation. Remembering Shiva while smearing bhasma, provides both internal and external purity to a sadhaka.
7. ***Rudraksha:*** is considered as Shiva's holy eye. Wearing a 'Rudraksha-Mala' helps a sadhaka in securing 'Jnana Dristhi' and move on in the spiritual path towards achievement of Siddhi.
8. ***Mantra:*** The sacred name of Shiva itself is the final 'avarana'. The Panchakshari or the Shadakshari mantra of Shiva is considered the sacred mantra of Shiva. The initiation for recitation of the Mantra has to be done through a guru.

Every follower of the Veerashaiva sect has to compulsorily follow the eight principles enunciated above in his/her daily life. This is also known as 'Ashtavarana Vrata'.

Shat-Sthala Sidhanta

This concept is also considered as central to Veerashaiva Sidhanta. The origins of 'Shat-Sthala Sidhanta' may be traced to the Agamas (especially Parameswara Tantra). It is the concept of six phases/states/paths through which a soul advances in its path of spiritual realization. Each stage brings the soul closer to God, until it attains 'Aikya' (Oneness) with Shiva.

The Shat-Sthala Sidhanta consists of the following stages in Sadhana:

1. *Bhakta Sthala* (stage of devotion),
2. *Maheswara Sthala* (stage of selfless service),
3. *Prasadi Sthala* (stage of earnestly seeking Shiva's grace),
4. *Prana-lingi Sthala* (stage of experiencing all as Shiva),
5. *Sharana Sthala* (Stage of ego-less refuse in Shiva), *and*
6. *Aikya Sthala* (Stage of achieving oneness with Shiva).

The Aikya Sthala is the stage where the soul leaves the physical body and merges with Shiva. Some Veerashaiva saints like 'Channabasavanna' (nephew of Basavanna) held that a soul can reach salvation at any stage in this chain.

Shoonya Sampadane

The life's goal is to attain 'true union of Shiva and the Soul'. This is described as 'Shoonya' or nothingness. This is not an empty void. One merges with Shiva through the path of 'Shat-sthala'. Each stage brings the sadhaka closer to God. The final stage is Aikya – fusing of the Soul with God – a perpetual state of Shiva Consciousness. This is like merging of the rivers with the ocean.

Shiva-Shakti-Yoga

'Sthala' is also interpreted as 'Para-Tatva' or 'Shiva'. The other Hindu faiths also recognize the presence of the six yoga chakras in the human body. Veerashaivism believes that Shiva is present in these six chakras, in 'Linga Rupa' along with the concerned Shakti, which is again a manifestation of Shiva. This is also known as 'Shiva-Shakti Yoga' and represented as shown below:

1. Muladhara – *Achara Linga – Kriya Shakti*
2. Swadhisthana – *Guru Linga – Jnana Shakti*
3. Manipura – *Shiva Linga – Icha Shakti*
4. Anahata – *Jangama Linga – Adi Shakti*
5. Vishudhi Chakra – *Prasada Linga – Para Shakti*
6. Agna Chakra – *Maha Linga – Chit Shakti*

The sadhaka has to obtain the 'sakshtkara' of Shiva in all these six chakras successively starting from Muladhara chakra, in stages. A person who has obtained 'Shiva Sakshatkara' in this way is known as 'Shat-Sthala' Brahmi'. Some consider 'Sahasrara', 'Shikha' and 'Paschima Shikha' as additional chakras.

According to the shastra sentence *'Dvaita-advaita Samayuktam Veerashaivasya Lakshanam'*, Veerashaivism accepts 'Dvaita' (duality between Shiva and the soul) at the Sadhana stage of 'Shat-Sthala-Yoga' and 'Advaita' (oneness of Shiva and the soul), at the stage of attaining 'Siddhi' or becoming one with god.

Veerashaiva Concepts

Veerashaivism developed certain concepts which are considered unique to this faith. Some of them are 'Dasoha' and 'Anubhava Mantapa'.

1. **'Dasoha':** It is an important obligation of the followers of the Veerashaiva community. Dasoha means working hard for a person's livelihood as well as for the maintenance of the society. Dasoha also means selfless service for the benefit of mankind. It also includes the feeding of the poor and hungry without any caste and class distinctions.

2. **'Anubhava Mantapa':** Another unique feature of Veerashaivism was the founding of 'Anubhava Mantapa' at Kalyana, where saints and mystics congregated to participate and debate on issues relating to Veerashaiva religion and philosophy.
   It was presided over by the famous saint 'Allama Prabhu'. Many famous Veerashaiva saints and religious leaders of the time participated in these deliberations – Basavanna, Akka Mahadevi, and Channabasavanna. This also helped in the development of 'Vachana sahitya' literature which is considered unique to Kannada language.

Even among Veerashaiva scholars, some give prominence to Advaita, some to Dvaita and others to Shakti Visisthadvaita. Makutagama and Suprabhedagama are agamas which propound Veerashaivism.

9

Worship of the Mother Goddess

Shivah Shaktya Yukto Yadi Bhavati Shaktah...

[If Shiva is united with Shakti, he is able to create, If he is not, he is incapable even of stirring... (Soundarya Lahari, 1 – Adi Shankara)]

ORIGINS OF THE WORSHIP OF FEMALE DIVINITY

Hinduism is perhaps the only major religion in the world, which emphasizes the worship of God in the form of female divinity. The origins of the worship of the mother goddess, is lost in antiquity and is believed to pre-date the Vedic period. Archeological evidence suggests that the worship of some form of the Goddess was prevalent even during the period of the Indus Valley civilization.

Vedas mention some of the female divinities of the time such as 'Ushas', 'Vak', and 'Saraswati'. Aditi was considered as the mother of all gods. Some of the Vedic Suktas – Sri Sukta, Bhu Sukta, Durga Sukta and Ambhrani Sukta provide important evidence of the worship of female gods during later Vedic times. 'The Gayatri Mantra' is considered as a sacred Mantra to be recited by the devout three times every day.

The Development of the Concept of Devi as the Supreme Goddess

It was during the Puranic period, that the concept of Devi as the Supreme Goddess crystallized and was elaborated further. The most important

Puranic text which is considered central to the worship of Devi as the Supreme Goddess is the 'Devi Mahatmya' – the 700 Slokas (also known as Durga Sapta Shati/Chandi) from Markandeya Purana. Around the same time other Shaakta literature also developed.

Shaakta as a Distinct Sect

The importance given to the worship of Devi, led to the evolution of a wholly distinct religious sect among Hindus called as 'Shaaktas' – who hold the 'Mother Goddess' as the Supreme Deity. Shaaktas believe that the worship of God as the Divine Mother is the easier path to salvation.

Many scholars consider 'Shaaktism' as a dynamic form of Hinduism, as Shakti is considered as the motivating force behind all action and existence in this material Universe. Shakti is also considered as the embodiment of energy and dynamism; whereas Shiva is considered only as her transcendent masculine inactive aspect.

Shaakta Literature

A rich amount of literature for Devi worship and propounding the philosophy of Shaaktism, is available right from Rig Veda (Devi Sukta) to Shaakta Upanishads and Epics, which proclaim the Supreme power of the Divine Mother. Some of the most important sources are:

1. 'Durga Saptashati' (source: Markandeya Purana),
2. Upanishads – 'Tripuropanishad', 'Bhavanopanishad', 'Kaalopanishad', etc.
3. Puranas: Devi Bhagavata Purana and Kalika Purana,
4. Shaakta Agamas/Tantras (28): Kularnava Tantra, Tantraraja, Vamakeswara Tantra, etc.
5. Soundarya-lahari by Adi Shankara,
6. Lalita Sahasranama (considered as the most sacred Sahasranama by the Hindus) and 'Lalita Trishati' both from Brahmanda Purana,
7. Devi Khadgamala Stotra (Vamakeswara Tantra),

8. Several Other Stotras pertaining to worship of different aspects of Devi like 'Shyamala Dandaka', 'Mahishasura Mardini stotra', 'Durga Stotra', etc.

Today, Devi as Shakti is worshipped in both Tantric and Non-Tantric forms. South India and Bengal have developed elaborate and independent rituals in the worship of Devi. Shaaktas worship Devi for both material benefit and liberation. The Shaiva tradition is considered as the male counterpart of the Shaakta tradition as the two sects share some of the common texts, sources and other sacred traditions.

SHAAKTA SIDHANTA

Ya Ekavarno bahudha shaktiyogad varna-anekaan nihitartho dadhati.

[One Varna (colour, meaning the Brahman or Para-Tatva) becomes several varnas because of the influence of Shakti Yoga – Swhetaashwatara Upanishad]

Vedic Interpretation of Shaakta Sidhanta

Shaakta Sidhanta also derives its source and authority from the Vedas. It considers the principles of Shaivism and Shaaktism to be complementary to each other. In this philosophy, Shiva as Nirguna Brahman is inactive, where as Shiva as Saguna Brahman, is dynamic through Shakti and creates the world. The Shakti Yoga also believes in 36 Tatvas and claims unity between Shiva and Shakti. Shiva and Shakti together represent the unitary cosmic principle (described by Vedas as Brahman). Shakti is the cause of all things being seen or experienced.

This unity of concepts is also depicted by the figure of 'Ardha Nariswara' – half Shiva and half Shakti. In this Sidhanta, Brahma (the creator), Vishnu (the preserver) and Shiva (the destroyer) are considered subordinate to Shakti.

Puranic Interpretation of Shaakta Sidhanta

The Puranic and Tantric interpretations of Shaakta Sidhanta are slightly different. They consider Devi as the 'Supreme Brahman' itself (as the one without a second). In this interpretation, she transcends her own primary nature of 'Prakriti'. All other forms of divinity (male and female) are considered merely as her diverse manifestations. In this aspect, Devi is said to combine the power of the Trinity – Brahma, Vishnu and Shiva – for performing the three aspects of Creation, Preservation and Destruction.

In Devi Bhagavata Purana, Devi declares – *I am Manifest divinity, Un-manifest Divinity, and Transcendent Divinity. I am Brahma, Vishnu and Shiva, as well as Saraswati, Lakshmi and Parvati. I am the Sun, I am the Stars, and I am also the Moon, I am all animals and birds,....*

Here, the world itself is thought of as the manifestation of Shakti. As the Universal Mother, Shakti becomes the Supreme Power, by which all of universe is governed. She is also the embodiment of all power which is in the forms of Iccha (will), Jnana (knowledge) and Kriya (Action).

Lalita Sahasranama beautifully and powerfully describes her supremacy over the Universe and other gods by calling her

1. *Pancha-pretaasana-seena* (249),
2. *Pancha-brahmaasana-stitha* (58)

[Lalita is sitting on a cot having Brahma, Vishnu, Shiva and Rudra as legs and Sadashiva as the plank; Brahma, Vishnu, Shiva, Rudra and Sadashiva are called as 'pretas' as they become powerless without the support of Shakti of the divine mother.]

Worship of God as the Divine Mother

One's relationship with one's mother is the dearest and sweetest of all human relations. Hence it is easy for a devotee to worship God as his own mother (maata). From this concept, emerged the philosophy of the supremacy of the 'Divine Mother'– Devi, or the 'Mother Goddess'. In fact the 'Lalita Sahasranama' starts with the divine invocation to Goddess 'Lalita' with the very first name as *'Sri maata (1)'*. SHE is also termed as 'Shakti' or 'The Supreme Power' to which all gods bow in reverence.

SRI VIDYOPASANA

Sri Vidya is considered to be the highest form of worship of the mother goddess. It is a highly systematic discipline, which combines elements of precise knowledge about Sri Vidya, immense devotion to the goddess, and following of precise and systematic steps in the prescribed ritual by the sadhaka. In Shaakta Sidhanta, 'Sri Vidyopasana' is considered the pinnacle of one's spiritual achievement. It is believed that 'Sri Vidyopasana' comes to the sadhaka in his last and final life before salvation.

'Pancha-dasi' mantra is also known as Sri Vidya. It is having 15 syllables. In addition, it has also a secret part which can be taught only by a Guru. This mantra has to be initiated to the Sadhaka by a qualified and enlightened Guru, who is said to appear only when the sadhaka is ready to receive the mantra.

Adi Shankara has composed works like 'Soundarya-lahari' which place greater stress on tantric practices relating to worship of the Divine mother. Works like 'Lalita Sahasranama' also describe the tantric worship of the different forms of the divine mother. 'Sri Chakra Upasana' is considered to be the highest form of 'Tantra Vidya' and is also known as 'Sri-Vidya'. There are 12 methods of Sri-Vidya (methods of worship of Goddess Lalita Tripura-sundari), based on the 12 original 'Upasakas' (See Annexure 5 under Number 12).

Lalita Sahasranama and Other Stotras

'Lalita Sahasranama' is held as the most important and sacred text for the worship of the Divine Mother in 'Dakshinachara'. It describes the various attributes of 'Lalita Tripura-sundari' through enumeration of her one thousand names. Modes of worship of sahasranama include – recitation, archana, and homa. It is also considered as the most beautiful of all the sahasranamas dedicated to the different gods and is held in the highest esteem by Shaaktas.

Along with Lalita sahasranama, other important texts used for the worship of Lalita include – 'Devi Khadgamala Stotra' and 'Lalita Trishati.'

Dasha-Maha-Vidya

There are ten types of Sri-Vidya, which prescribe the worship of the Divine Mother in her 10 different forms as shown below:

1. Kali – the Goddess in the role of Destroyer,
2. Tara – the Goddess as guide, saviour and protector,
3. Lalita-Tripura Sundari – the Beautiful and Supreme (16 year old) Goddess of the three worlds,
4. Bhuvaneswari – the goddess of Earth also known as the Mother of the World,
5. Bhairavi – the goddess who instills fear, destruction and decay,
6. Chinnamasta – manifestation of Parvati and embodiment of sexual energy,
7. Dhumavati – the widow goddess,
8. Bagalamukhi – the goddess who paralyzes enemies,
9. Matangi – the prime minister of Lalita,
10. Kamala – the Goddess of the Lotus (Tantric Lakshmi).

Shaakta Sampradayas in the Worship of Devi

Devi as the divine mother, is usually worshipped as 'Lalita-Tripura Sundari'. In this aspect, the Mother goddess represents the two opposite faces of 'Prakriti' (nature). One is 'Saumya rupa', the calm and beautiful face of nature. The other is the 'Roudra or Ugra rupa', nature in its wild, terrifying and destructive aspect.

Accordingly there are two different sampradayas prevalent in the worship of Devi – 'Samaya mata' and 'Kaula mata'. Both are considered as two different forms of Sri-Vidya.

1. ***Samaya Mata*** *(also known as Dakshinachara as it originated in South India)*: In this Satvic method, Devi is worshipped through Vedic procedures – Recitation of 'Pancha dasi' and 'Lalita Sahasranama'. vegetarian food, fruits and Milk are offered to Devi as 'Naivedya' in this mata. This also includes upasana of 'Sri Chakra yantra (or Maha Meru)' considered as the subtle form of Devi.

'Lalita Sahasranama' describes the procedure of samaya mata as *Samayachara tatpara (98), Samayantastha (97), Samarasya parayana (792), Payasanna priya (480), Haridrannaika rasika (526), etc.*

2. ***Kaula Mata*** *(more prevalent in Northern and Eastern parts of India):* In this Tamasic method, Devi in her 'Ugra' form is worshipped through Tantric procedures. In ancient times, these Tantric rituals seem to have developed as a reaction to the strict Vedic practices and exclusion of people of other varnas (and women) from performing religious rituals and worship. In Kaula mata, there is no restriction on caste or gender for the sadhaka. He/She should be initiated in to the system by a qualified Guru who may be male or female and may belong to any caste.

   'Lalita Sahasranama' describes this kaula mata procedure as *Kaulamarga tatpara sevita(441), Veeragosthi priya (898), Kula sanketa palini (91), Kaulini (925), Kevala (926), Rudhirasamstitha (490), Mamsanishta (500), etc.*

SHAKTI YOGA

The scriptures pertaining to Shakti Yoga stipulate that in order to obtain the blessings of the Divine Mother, one has to worship 'Sri Chakra', meditate on 'Pancha-dashi' mantra, recite the 'Lalita Sahasranama' and practice 'Kundalini Yoga'. This is done through procedures prescribed in 'Tantra Shastra' which are a class of religious manuals.

Shakti Yoga prescribes systematic Sadhana, regular discipline, capacity and evolution of the Sadhaka. It includes 'Spiritual Sadhana' involving Mantra, yantra, nyasa, mudra and the practice of 'Kundalini Yoga'. All this has to be practiced under the guidance of a qualified guru, after due initiation (diksha).

Through Yoga-Sadhana, the Kundalini Shakti residing in Mulaadhara chakra in the sadhaka's body, can be invoked and made to rise through the 6 chakras and the 3 granthis, to enter 'Sahsraara' and rain 'Sudha-rasa' on the sadhaka. Dattatreya Samhita calls the sequence of chakras and granthis as 'Mahat-mangalayathana'.

Shat-Chakra: (The Six Chakras): The various characteristics of these chakras are as follows:

Chakras	Koota	Khanda	Granthis	Shakti	Yogini	Presiding Deity
Mulaadhara	Vagbhava	Agni		Ichaa	Saakini	Maha Kali
Swadhisthaana	-,,-	-,,-			Kaakini	
			Brahma			
Manipoora	Kamaraja	Surya		Jnana	Laakini	Maha Lakshmi
Anahata	-,,-	-,,-			Raakini	
			Vishnu			
Vishudhi	Shakti	Soma		Kriya	Daakini	Maha Saraswati
Agna	-,,-	-,,-			Haakini	
			Rudra			
#	Turiya	Kala			Yaakini	

relates to 'Sahasrara'

Bhaskaracharya (eighteenth century) has written three authoritative works on the worship of Devi: 'Parivasya Rahasya', 'Sethubandha' and 'Lalita Sahasranama Bhashya'. These three works are considered as 'prasthana traya' by upasakas of 'Sri-Vidya'.

Durga Puja

'Durga Puja' is conducted during 'Navaratri' falling in the Hindu month of Ashwayuja (September – October). It is conducted in different parts of India in different styles according to local customs and traditions. However recitation of the holy book 'Devi Mahatmya' (also called Durga Sapta Shati/Chandi) – which is a part of 'Markandeya Purana' – is a common feature during the festival throughout the country. The 700 slokas are recited with great reverence during 'Navaratri' festival by every follower of the sect.

Worship of Different Forms of the Mother Goddess

The Mother Goddess is also worshipped in any of her innumerable forms known to Hinduism. Each form has certain distinguishing characteristics, carries different weapons and worshipped for a definite purpose - power, material wealth, prosperity, warding off evil forces, progeny, destruction of enemies, etc. Some forms of Devi are also worshipped through Tantric methods.

The selection of the form depends on various factors - family tradition, regional tradition, initiation of the Guru in the worship of a particular deity, personal interest in a particular form of Goddess, purpose of worship, etc.

The best known forms of Devi include -

1. *Adi Para-Shakti/Rajarajeswari/Maheswari/Lalita Tripura-Sundari* – The Supreme Divinity as the original Goddess,
2. *Durga/Amba/Ambika/Mahadevi/Kali/Chandi* – Goddess as fighter of demons (in the 'Ugra swarupa'/Roudra posture), destroyer of evil forces, etc.
3. *Maha Saraswati/Maha Lakshmi/Maha Kali* – Devi Mahatmya considers them as three faces of Adi Shakti or Mother Goddess.
4. *Annapurna* – Goddess who provides food and sustenance,
5. *Parvati/Gouri/Uma* – Consort of Shiva and Goddesses of wisdom and Spiritual fulfillment,
6. *Ganga* – Goddess as the Divine river,
7. *Sati* – the goddess of marital relationships,
8. *Kundalini* – the raw cosmic force present in every person.

Besides the above forms, there are other popular manifestations of Devi – Sapta Matrikas (energies of seven different gods), Asta Siddhis, Asta Lakshmis, Nava Durgas, fifteen Nityas, 64 yoginis, etc. These forces assist the Devi in her fight with the 'asuras' in Devi Puranas. (For details refer Annexure 4 and 5).

The worship of the following deities is strictly not part of Shaaktism. However, they are also considered different facets of the same female divinity:

1. *Lakshmi* – Consort of Vishnu and the Goddess of material wealth, prosperity and fulfillment,
2. *Saraswati* – Consort of Brahma and the Goddess of Knowledge/ Learning, music, education. She is also identified with the 'Saraswati' river referred in Rig Veda.
3. *Sita* – as consort of Sri Rama and standing for purity,
4. *Radha* – as consort of Sri Krishna and as the Goddess of Love,
5. *Gayatri* – Goddess as Mother of all Mantras.

Worship of Other Female Deities

Besides, every village also has a 'grama-Devi' temple (which is a predominant feature of rural India since ancient times). Each goddess is known by her traditional local name. These Devi temples are built to protect the village from natural calamities and to ward off evil spirits. All communities participate in the worship and annual festivities of these temples.

Tantric worship and animal sacrifices are also common in some of these Devi temples. There are some documented cases of human sacrifices also.

The Popularity of Goddess as Shakti

Today we find a picture of goddess in some form in every Hindu home throughout India. We also find the images of goddess pasted on vehicles and displayed prominently in shops to ward off evil forces. Let us conclude this chapter with a prayer to the Goddess:

Sarva-mangala mangalye, Shive, Sarvartha Sadhike |
Sharanye Tryambake Gauri, Narayani Namostute ||

This Sloka from Devi Mahatmya (Durga Sapta Shati – 11.10) is repeated by millions of people across India especially during 'Navaratri' and also on special occasions and festivals, to invoke the grace of the Divine mother.

10

Essence of Bhagavad Gita

THE CONTEXT OF THE GITA

Bhagavad Gita (which literally means – the Song of God), is in the form of a dialogue between Sri Krishna and his protégée Arjuna, and placed contextually at the beginning of the Mahabharata war. Arjuna is hesitant to take up the fight, because of doubts that he will have to kill his own relatives, friends and teachers. He throws up his weapons and wishes to abstain from battle. He then turns to his charioteer and guide Krishna for advice.

Krishna considers this act of Arjuna, as the lack of accurate understanding of the nature of things. Arjuna's fear and hesitance have become impediments in doing his duty according to his Dharma. Krishna calls the war about to take place as 'Dharma Yuddha'. He impresses on Arjuna that his duty as a warrior is to uphold Dharma by fighting the war.

Krishna teaches Arjuna, the concepts of Karma, Bhakti and Jnana. He then proceeds to explain the nature of the cosmic order and the paths that lead to true enlightenment. He also preaches different Yogic and Vedantic philosophies. Finally he reveals his identity as the Brahman (Supreme Being) himself through 'Viswva Rupa' – his divine and universal form.

Gita – The Milk Milked by the Divine Cow-heard

It is famously stated that:

Sarvopanishado gaavo dogdhaa gopaala-nandanah I
Paartho vatsah sudheer bhoktaa dughdam geetamritam mahat II

[If all the Upanishads represent cows, Krishna is the milker – the divine cow-heard, who milked these cows for the benefit of all humanity. The milk is *Bhagavad Gita* and Arjuna is the calf who first tasted that milk of wisdom.]

It is said that he who drinks the nectar of Gita, through purification of the heart and regular meditation attains immortality, eternal bliss, everlasting peace and perennial joy.

The Relevance of Gita to the Present Day World

Just like Arjuna, every one of us, finds ourselves in a predicament and a state of confusion at some stage in our lives and Gita is the only source at such times to provide divine guidance in taking our life's decisions. Gita shows us the way to escape this predicament through practice of the paths of Karma, Bhakti and Jnana; and finally attain salvation. Gita is the panacea for all ills of the mind.

We are unable to recognize the Truth (regarding our true nature and purpose, as well as God) because of Maya. Out of ignorance and ego, we bind ourselves to this world, through our desires and actions and remain chained to Samsara and Karma – the cycle of births and deaths. Our true nature is not our body, because it is not permanent. It is like a garment which we change when it gets worn out. It is only our soul which is eternal. We should care for the soul rather than taking care of our impermanent body.

Gita tells us how to live in this world by following the paths of Dharma. We should perform our daily actions with a sense of detachment, and always keep God at the centre of our awareness and activities. Bhakti (Pure devotion) – is also another way of obtaining divine grace. Ultimately it is Jnana (true spiritual knowledge), which helps one to attain salvation.

War as an Allegory

The placement of the Gita, just before the Mahabharata war, in the 'Bhisma Parva' raises some questions. There are many scholars who hold the story of the Gita as an allegory.

1. Swami Nikhilananda considered Arjuna as allegory of Atman, Krishna as an allegory of Brahman and the Chariot as the body.
2. Mahatma Gandhi interpreted the battlefield as the soul and Arjuna, as man's higher impulses struggling against evil.
3. Swami Vivekananda held that the Kurukshetra war is only an allegory; – it is a war constantly going on within man, between the tendencies of good and evil.
4. Some others hold – Ignorance is Dhritarashtra, individual soul is Arjuna, the God within is Krishna the charioteer, body is the chariot, senses are the five horses; anger, jealousy, greed, pride, hypocrisy are our enemies, etc.

However, some others do not accept these views, saying that the message Gita conveys is far beyond these, and is intended to reach the humanity as a whole. The world is like a huge battlefield. Some believe that Gita conveys the message 'that every individual has to fight a war within, in order to gain mastery of the self, if he/she has to emerge victorious from life's-battles'.

Gita, even when taken out of context of the Mahabharata war, stands alone on a higher pedestal, containing the very essence of the 'Hindu Philosophic Thought' and has been a beacon of light and hope for millions of followers of the Hindu faith for the past thousands of years.

The Goal of the Gita

The teaching of the Gita is like a painting on a broad canvas with a universal appeal. Several scholars down the ages hold the view that Gita does not just preach religion. It also shows the path of righteous life leading to salvation. It tries to answer all possible doubts that may arise in the mind of a seeker regarding 'Life', 'Samsara', 'Karma', 'Moksha', etc. The doubts are raised by Arjuna as questions. These are analysed and answered by Sri Krishna.

Just like Upanishads, the goal of the Gita is also to show the path to Moksha/Mukti/salvation. A majority of Upanishads prefer 'Jnana marga' as the right path to Moksha. *Swhetaashwatara Upanishad* preaches Bhakti along with Jnana. Ishopanishad gives importance to 'Karma marga' also. Gita elaborates on these concepts of 'Jnana', 'Karma' and 'Bhakti' and preaches all the three paths.

According to Gita, the goal of life is to free the mind and intellect from complexities and focus on the glory of the Self (Atman), by dedicating one's action to the divine. This goal can be achieved through meditation, action, devotion and knowledge. Gita also describes the virtues, glory and secrets of god.

Every sloka of the Gita is loaded with deep spiritual and multi-layered meaning. That is why it is also termed as 'Gita Rahsya'. This has enabled every Acharya to interpret each sloka of the Gita, to suit his particular philosophy.

Audience of the Gita

Even though Krishna directly addressed Arjuna, in preaching the Gita, the discourse is said to have been heard by the following also:

1. Sanjaya – who had been granted the 'Divya Dristi' by Vyasa, in order to narrate the events of the Mahabharata war to Dhritarashtra,
2. Hanuman – who perched on the flag on top of Arjuna's chariot,
3. Barbarika – an asura and son of Ghatotkacha, who also witnessed the action at Kurukshetra for all the 18 days of the Mahabharata war.
4. Veda-Vyasa – who wrote the epic *Mahabharata* through his 'Divya Dristhi'.

Essence of the Gita

The essence of the Gita, is contained in the Sloka (11.55). It conveys that if one performs his actions with devotion and free from attachment, he attains salvation.

mat-karma-krn mat-paramo mad-bhaktah sanga-varjitah |
Nirvaira sarva-bhuteshu yah sa mam eti pandavah ||

[O Arjuna, he who performs all his duties for my sake, depends on me, is devoted to me, has no attachment, and free from malice to all beings, reaches Me. (Gita 11.55)]

Some scholars quote slokas 8, 9, 10 and 11 of Chapter 10, as conveying the message of the Gita. In these slokas, Krishna states:

I am the source of all creation, everything emanates from Me, Knowing this, the wise, full of devotion, constantly worship Me. They experience fulfillment and bliss. To them I confer the yoga of wisdom, through which they come to Me. Out of compassion for them, dwelling in their heart, I destroy the darkness born of ignorance by shining the lamp of wisdom.

Gita as 'Yogopanishad'

The term yoga covers a wide range of meanings. The function of yoga (taken as a general meaning) is to train the body and mind. Gita can be called as 'Yogopanishad' as each chapter in the Gita is termed as a particular form of 'Yoga.' Through the eighteen chapters, Krishna as 'Yogacharya', pushes Arjuna, through the successive rungs in the ladder of Yoga.

Gita also describes the various forms of Yoga and explains the paths that lead to spiritual knowledge and self-realization, which frees a person from Samsara – the cycle of deaths and rebirths. Krishna describes the best Yogi as one who constantly meditates on Him (meaning the Supreme Brahman).

Gita describes the various types of Yoga relating to meditation, action, devotion and knowledge. A famous commentator – Madhusudanada

Saraswati (b. 1490 CE) divides the eighteen chapters of Gita, into three main sections. According to him –

1. The first six chapters deal with ***Karma Yoga*** *(the path of selfless action)*,
2. The middle six chapters deal with ***Bhakti yoga*** *(the path of devotion)* and
3. The last three chapters deal with ***Jnana Yoga*** *(the path of spiritual knowledge)*.

Another scholar has characterized this system as 'a successive approach' in which *Karma Yoga* leads to *Bhakti Yoga*, which in turn leads to *Jnana Yoga*.

While each path differs, their fundamental goal is the same. It is realization of Brahman – the Ultimate Truth. Jnana yoga is suited for a person of inquiry and rational temperament, Bhakti yoga is suited for a person with emotional temperament, and Karma Yoga suits for a person of action. Each yoga is discussed separately below:

I. ESSENCE OF KARMA YOGA

Karma Yoga deals with 'Action'. It is doing one's duty as per his Dharma. Krishna advocates 'Nishkama Karma' – Karma done without expectations:

> *Karmany-evadhikaraste ma phaleshu kadachana* ।
> *ma-karma-phala-hethur bhur ma te sangoostv akarmani* ॥

[You certainly have the right for prescribed activities but never at any time in their results. You should never be motivated by the results of the actions, nor should there be any attachment in not doing your prescribed activities. (Gita 2.47)]

Performance of selfless action is necessary in order to purify one's existence and proceed on the spiritual path. But action prompted by desire for reward is prohibited by Karma Yoga. Because this reward is independently, pre-ordained by God. Hence it is not correct to imagine that one receives his dues only by his own efforts. This also means that one is not the controller of his own destiny, as it is ultimately ordained by God.

Krishna in the next sloka advises Arjuna that (while doing such Karma), he should be balanced in both victory and defeat. Krishna explains that Karma Yoga is a state of equanimity.

Yoga-stah kuru karmani sangam tyktva dhananjaya |
Siddhi-asiddhyoh samo bhutva sampatvam yoga uchyate ||

[O Dhananjaya, established in the science of Yoga in action, perform your activities giving up attachment and maintain equanimity in both success and failure. (Gita 2.48)]

Here Krishna explains that in Karma Yoga, one should discard mental attachment to one's actions and maintain equanimity in both success and failure. Actions performed with motive are inferior to actions performed as a matter of duty, as the one who is performing such actions is not disturbed either by reward or loss in such actions. He who is disciplined in Karma Yoga, having abandoned the fruit of his actions, progresses in the spiritual path with a steady pace.

Krishna further says:

While concentrating objects of the senses, a person develops attachment to the sense objects; from attachment desires are born and from desire (moha) anger (krodha) arises. Anger leads to delusion and loss of memory (capacity of discrimination), and then to loss of spiritual intelligence (eternal truths of scriptures). Due to defective perceptions, he makes errors leading to sinful actions which ruins him, as he drowns in Samsara leading to endless cycle of births and deaths. (Gita 2.62 and 63)

One who does Nishkama Karma, with utmost faith and reverence, surrendering himself to God, through mind, speech and body, constantly meditating upon God's name, virtues and glory, is really practicing 'Karma Yoga'.

Gandhi preferred Karma Yoga as the path to attain self-realization. He writes: 'This can be achieved by selfless action, by renouncing fruits of action, and by dedicating all activities to God i.e., by surrendering oneself to Him – body and soul'.

2. ESSENCE OF BHAKTI YOGA

Bhakti or devotion is considered as the easiest path to salvation. Various Acharyas have interpreted Bhakti as a method of worship of god, where you show love, remembrance and reverence to god. Ramanuja, Madhva, Chaitanya and several other Acharyas are proponents of Bhakti yoga. Ramanuja advocates pure devotion and sharanagati (surrender) as the only way to salvation. Madhva elaborates on this concept and enunciates the 'Nava-vidha Bhakti' (Chapter 6) to obtain divine grace.

In the Gita, Krishna is categorical in declaring that his devotee is superior even to the greatest yogi:

Yoginam api sarvesham mad-gatenantaratmana |
Shradhavaan bhajate yo mam sa me yuktatamo matah ||

[Amongst all yogis (or those perfected in the science of the individual consciousness attaining communion with the Ultimate Consciousness), one who in full faith is always thinking of me within, deeply dedicated to me, rendering devotional service to me is the most superior of all. (Gita 6.47)]

Krishna further says that these devotees, who have attained Him through Bhakti Yoga, have attained perfection and hence are not subject to Punarjanma – the cycle of births and deaths.

Mam upetya punar janma duhkhalayam asasvatam |
Napnuvanti mahtmanah samsiddhim paramam gatah ||

[The great souls having achieved perfection take refuge in Me, never again assume this transitory birth (Punarjanma) full of misery. (Gita 8.15)]

Sridhara Swami in his commentary on the Gita considers that these devotees, have realized the purpose of human existence and hence attain 'Moksha' or liberation from material existence, as they have been released from Samsara – the perpetual cycle of birth and death. Madhva considers that for a Bhakta, attaining the 'Supreme Lord' is the Ultimate goal of life.

Concluding the Bhakti Yoga, Krishna says *But those who surrender all activities unto Me, meditate on Me with single minded devotion, I become their deliverer without delay from the ocean of death in the material existence.* (Gita 12. 6 and 7). Further in the next sloka, he assures thus:

Mayya eva mana adhatsva mayi buddhim nivesaya I
Nivesisyasi mayy eva ata urdhvam nasamsayah II

[Concentrate the mind upon Me, establish spiritual intelligence in Me, verily you will reside with me, after this existence without doubt. (Gita 12.8)]

Krishna thus assures his devotees that He will quickly redeem them from Samsara, if they focus their minds upon Him exclusively in Bhakti Yoga.

3. ESSENCE OF JNANA YOGA

Jnana means (spiritual) knowledge and through this knowledge, one can attain spiritual realization and attain 'Moksha'. Jnana Yoga teaches the seeker to identify and realize the Ultimate Truth through the power of discrimination. Krishna says that one who has mastered his senses and is full of faith attains such knowledge.

Shraddhaval labhate jnanam tat parah samyatendriyah I
Jnanam labdhva param shantim achirenadhi-gachati II

[One with full faith, attentively focused, who has conquered the senses, attains (transcendental) knowledge, and also quickly attains supreme peace. (Gita 4.39)]

Krishna further says that, if a person is a sinner, he can crossover all these sins, through the boat of such (spiritual) knowledge. Also such knowledge leads to eradication of all sins, just like the way fire burns all wood to ashes.

Api chedasi papebhyah sarvebhyah pap-krt-tamah I
Sarvam Jnana-plavenaiva vrjinam santarisyasi II
yathidhamsi samidognir bhasma sat kurute'rjuna I
Jnanagnih sarva-karmani bhasma-sat kurute tatha II

[Even if you are the most sinful of all sinners, yet you will cross over all sins and miseries, by the boat of transcendental knowledge. O Arjuna, just as a blazing fire turns wood to ashes, similarly, the fire of knowledge turns all reactions from actions to ashes. (Gita 4. 36 and 37)]

Krishna further goes on to describe the various aspects of spiritual knowledge (13. 7–11) as follows:

> *Humility, absence of pride, non-violence, tolerance, honesty, devout service to a Guru, internal and external purity, self-control, steadfastness, renouncing sensual desires, absence of egoism, pondering again and again on the pain and evils of birth, old age, disease and death; absence of attachment towards son, wife and home; maintaining equipoise in all situations, living in secluded and holy places, unflinching devotion to God, always aspiring for self-realization, constantly meditating the Ultimate Truth as the goal of true wisdom, is declared as spiritual knowledge , and whatever contrary to this is termed as ignorance.*

This spiritual knowledge helps a person to discriminate between reality and illusion, Atman and the material body and the final distinction between Atman and Parmatman. This will enable him to attain realization. Krishna says:

> *Kshetra-kshetrajnayor evam antaram jnana-chaksusa* |
> *Bhuta-prakriti-moksham ca ye vidur yanti te param* ||

[Those who perceive by the eye of wisdom, the distinction between the kshetra (the physical body), and kshetrajna (Parmatman) as well as between Atman, and Parmatman, and liberation of living entities from Prakriti (material world), reach the Supreme. (Gita 13.35)]

Philosophical Concepts Propounded by the Gita

Further, Gita explains the following philosophical concepts of the Hindu Dharma, which can be termed as the 'Basic Truths':

Gita (7. 4 and 5) says that God is the source of the entire creation. All beings have evolved from his two fold manifestations of *Prakriti* – the lower material (inanimate) nature consisting of eight elements – Earth, water, fire, air, ether, mind, reason and ego. The higher (animate) nature is in the form of consciousness and also known as Jiva (Atman) which is eternal. The atman takes up residence in the physical body which is part of the inanimate Prakriti. The world is thus created and sustained by God. (7.6)

Prakriti itself is constituted by three qualities (gunas) – Satva (goodness), Rajas (activity) and Tamas (inertia) (7.12). These qualities bind the soul to the body through attachment. They form a veil (Maya), from which the living beings cannot perceive god (7.14).

Synthesis of the Various Paths of Yoga

The three paths described by the Gita, are not mutually exclusive but are certainly complementary in nature. For example, concentration of the mind is needed for a Karma-yogi, to discharge his duties effectively. Similarly to offer the fruits of his actions to God, Bhakti is required. Understanding of the true nature of God is Jnana which is certainly a component of Bhakti. Hence a yogi is one, who discharges his duties through 'Nishkama-Karma', and exhibits pure devotion to god, having acquired the requisite spiritual knowledge. This is the path to salvation and realization of god.

Conclusion

Gita is thus a harmonious blend of Jnana, Karma, Bhakti and Renunciation. According to Gita one should not renounce one's actions or avoid his obligatory duty. But he should conduct his actions with a sense of detachment. He should have a steady and disciplined mind. He should free himself of ego and all the negative qualities. He should not have any desire for the fruits of his actions. He should surrender to god and through complete devotion, and then he will attain Jnana leading to salvation by the grace of God.

Swami Vivekananda says Each soul is potentially divine. The goal is to manifest the divine within, by controlling nature – external or internal. Do this either by work, or worship, or psychic control, or philosophy by one or more, or all of these – and be free. (Raja Yoga – Commentary: Sutra 25, Ch II)

[Apart from these paths taught by the Gita, there are also other types of Yoga by which one can attain salvation:

1. *Raja Yoga*: Also simply termed as 'Yoga' is based on 'Patanjali's Yoga sutras' and deal with concentration of the mind, control of the senses, and meditation, through 'Astanga marga' described in 'Yoga Darshana' (Chapter 5.4)
2. *Hata Yoga:* Gives primary importance to good health and longevity of life,
3. *Japa Yoga or Mantra Yoga:* Attaining salvation through 'Japa' or recitation of a 'Mantra'.
4. *Nada Yoga:* Worshipping and realizing god through 'Nada' – sound (devotional music).
5. *Kundalini Yoga:* Through yoga Sadhana, the 'Kundalini Shakti' present in Muladhara chakra can be invoked and made to rise through the various chakras and enter 'sahasraara'. This is another way of realization of god. (Chapter 9).]

11

Worship of Major Hindu Gods

In this chapter we will discuss the worship of some prominent Hindu gods, who have a universal appeal.

Vishnu, Shiva, Surya, Ganesha, Hanuman and Skanda (who is also popularly known as Subramanya). We will also discuss the 'Panchayatana' form of worship of some of these gods. We will also discuss the role of Tantrism in Hindu religion.

VISHNU

In Rig Veda, Vishnu personifies light and the Sun, and is invoked as a companion of Indra and referred to as the God who separates heaven and earth. 'Aitareya Brahmana' of the Rig Veda extols Vishnu as the greatest and oldest of the gods. The Brahmanas address him repeatedly as 'Yagna-Pati' – the one who accepts the sacrifices and apportions the fruits to the performer.

The Rig Veda says that Vishnu can travel in 3 strides – the first stride is the Earth, the second stride is the visible sky, the third stride cannot be seen by men and is the heaven, where gods and the righteous dead live. This is similar to the story of 'Vamana' which came at a much later stage in the scriptures. The Upanishads also declare the supremacy of Vishnu.

A number of traditions are reflected in the various manifestations of Vishnu – Krishna was seen as a consort of Radha by the followers of Chaitanya (Eastern India); the Ramananda sect associated Vishnu with the life of Rama of Ayodhya, and several Bhakti panthas saw Krishna as an adorable Lord.

The Kathopanishad says: *But he who has understanding for his charioteer (intellect), and who holds the reins of the mind, he reaches the end of his journey, and that is the highest place of Vishnu.* Bharata's 'Natya shastra' cites Vishnu as the presiding deity of 'Sringara rasa'. In the 'Trinity' aspect of the Supreme 'Brahman', Vishnu acts as the 'preserver' and maintains Dharma.

The word Vishnu appears as the second name in 'Vishnu Sahasranama'. Adi Shankara in his commentary, states that 'As he pervades everything he is called Vishnu'. According to Swami Chinmayananda 'That which pervades everything is Vishnu; as he is not limited by space, time and substance'. It is important to note that all the three prominent Acharyas – Adi Shankara, Ramanuja, and Madhva; preferred Vishnu (Brahman) as the personal God for worship.

Characteristics of Vishnu

Vishnu is depicted with an imposing personality which makes the devotee bow his head in reverence. The blue colour of his skin represents his all pervasive nature. The blue also represents the sky, infinite space, as well as the infinite ocean on which he resides. Lakshmi resides on his chest. He wears the 'Kaustubha' mani and a garland of flowers (Vanamala). He rests on 'Ananta or Adi-shesha' the immortal snake. Vishnu's vehicle is 'Garuda' the eagle. Vaikunta is considered his abode.

'Vishnu Sahasranama' declares Vishnu as 'Paramatma' (the Supreme Soul), and 'Parameswara' (the Supreme God). *Bhagavad Gita* declares Vishnu as the Supreme God having 'Viswarupa' – a concept which is beyond the ordinary limits of human perception. In *Bhagavad Gita*, Sri Krishna (an avatar of Vishnu) declares – 'I am the goal, the sustainer, the master, the witness, the abode, the refuge, ... I am the creation and annihilation.... I pervade and support the entire universe'.

Vishnu is attributed with countless auspicious qualities. Among them the following six qualities are considered significant:

1. *Jnana* (Spiritual Knowledge) – the power to know all beings simultaneously,
2. *Aishwarya* (wealth) – because Maha-Lakshmi (the goddess of wealth) is his wife. It also means the supreme power of governance. *(Iswarasya bhavah Aishwaryam)*
3. *Shakti* (Energy/Power) – which makes the universe to perform its functions,
4. *Bala* (Strength) – capacity to support everything at will,
5. *Virya* (heroism/vigour) – Another form of Shakti, which is infinite and indestructible,
6. *Tejas* (halo) – Unmatched spiritual splendour.

To Vaishnavites, Vishnu is the Supreme God. To other sects, Vishnu is one of the 'Trinity of Gods' in his role as the preserver. Vishnu is also worshipped directly as Vishnu or as one of his Dashavatars, most notably as Rama, Narasimha or Krishna. Worship of Venkateswara, another form of Vishnu, is also popular among Hindus of South India.

There are many groups among Vaishnavites. Rudra-Vaishnava Sampradaya *(Vishnu swami)*, Brahma-Vaishnava Sampradaya *(Madhvacharya)*, Sri-Vaishnava Sampradaya *(Ramanujacharya)*, Kumara-Vaishnava Sampradaya *(Nimbaditya)*, Gauda Vaishnava *Sampradaya (Chaitanya)*, and several Vaishnava Bhakti-Panthas (Jnaneswar, Tulsidas, Namdev, Samartha Ramdas, etc.).

SHIVA

Shiva is a major Hindu deity. In the Shaiva tradition, Shiva is considered as the supreme God. Shiva in Sanskrit means 'auspicious'. The name 'Shiva' appears twice (as 27th and 600th names) in 'Vishnu Sahasranama'. Adi Shankara in his commentary on 'Vishnu Sahasranama' has ascribed the following meanings to Shiva: 'the pure-one' and 'one who is not affected by the three gunas – Satva, Rajas and Tamas of Prakriti'. 'Shiva Sahasranama' is found in *Mahabharata* (Anushạsan Parva). 'Rudram and Chamakam' are devotional hymns in praise of Shiva.

The worship of Shiva is believed to date back to the times of Indus Valley Civilization. Rudra was considered a destructive God (father of the Maruths – a group of storm gods) in the early Vedic tradition. But by later Vedic period Rudra rose to prominence, later termed as 'Pashu-Pati' (god of animals) and then became Shiva, the auspicious.

Shiva is often depicted with a third eye (Tryambakam) which burned 'Kama' the god of love to ashes. He is also called 'Neelakantha' as he drank poison churned up from the ocean. Shiva is also depicted in various forms – 'Nataraja' (the Lord of Dance), 'Dakshinamurty', 'Ardha-narishwara' and 'Tripurantaka'. Shiva is usually worshipped in the form of a Shiva-lingam. 'Maha Shivaratri' is a sacred festival day devoted to Shiva. Devotees fast on this day and worship Shiva.

Characteristics of Shiva

Shiva sits on a tiger skin, wears a crescent moon on his head, and a serpent around his neck, holds a trident and damaru, smears his body with ashes (bhasma), and is considered to be residing in cremation grounds (all these aspects symbolize supreme renunciation). The river Ganges flows from his matted hair (Gangadhara – represents spiritual perfection). Nandi, the bull is considered as his 'Vahana' (vehicle). He is attended by a number of 'bhuta-ganas'. Mount Kailas is considered as his abode. Varanasi (Kashi) is considered to be the holiest place for Shiva.

Shiva as Destroyer

A majority of Shaiva sects see Shiva performing the functions of the (Vedic concept of) Brahman in the role of the 'Destroyer' also. In this aspect Shiva represents constructive destruction in the continuous process of Srishthi (Creation), Sthithi (Preservation) and Laya (Destruction) and recreation. This continuous process maintains the Universe. The consort of Shiva is Uma, who represents the perishable Prakriti. The power of destruction (of Shiva), is always associated with the destructible matter.

Lord of Meditation (Dakshinamurty)

Shiva is also known as the eternal 'Lord of Meditation'. He sits in deep meditation on the top of the world – on Mount Kailas in the Himalayas, facing South. His meditative posture symbolizes the ideal of harmony and yogic poise experienced by a realized person. Shiva's eyes are half closed – which means they see the outer world with inner wisdom. This also means he is fully conscious within and without.

The meditating Shiva is seen against the background of the white snow capped Himalayas. The white snow represents absolute purity of mind. A realized person is one who has conquered his ego and kept it under control. Shiva has transcended this ego which is symbolized by the coiled serpent around his neck.

The meditative form of Shiva is also known as 'Dakshinamurty' – the dispenser of Supreme Knowledge. The term 'Dakshina' connotes 'the divine power of subtle perception, generated in a fully integrated and pure intellect'. When the 'Dakshina' power flows towards the 'vasana-conditioned hearts' of the disciples, it is said to turn southward. Shiva in this aspect assumes the form of a Guru, and sitting on the peak of Kailas, turns southward to guide all seekers of knowledge.

The Third Eye

Shiva is said to have a third eye known as 'Jnana chakshu' (eye of wisdom). With this eye, Shiva gets an intuitive vision of the Truth (which is denied to the two eyes of an ordinary mortal). A seeker can get the vision of the 'third eye', only through devotion and contemplation using intellectual discrimination to penetrate into the mysteries of the Truth. This symbolizes the opening of the 'Third Eye of Wisdom'.

The Trident

The three prongs of the Trident represent the three thought textures, three gunas – Satva (pure and noble), Rajas (passionate and agitated), and Tamas (dull and inactive). Combinations of these three thought textures in various permutations yield different individual personalities.

The laying down of the Trident, indicates transcendence of the three gunas and merger of the individual with the supreme Reality.

Nataraja

When Shiva lays down the Trident, he assumes the form of Nataraja – the Lord of Dance. His divine form of dance is an expression of 'Divine Realization'. It represents the finite material world exploding into the infinite universe. It also represents the five-fold activity of Shiva and the concepts of 'Shiva-Shakti' involving the fusion of his static and dynamic states.

Shiva Linga

It is the most popular form through which Shiva is worshipped. As per Shaiva Sidhanta, three of the 'Shiva tatvas' are represented in the Shiva linga. The first 'Shiva Tatva' is represented by a vertical line known as 'Nathan'. Then he acts on the second Tatva called 'Bindu' donated by a dot. Then he acts on the third Tatva called 'Sattakiyam'. It is here he takes on the manifestation of the Shiva Linga.

Shaiva Sects

There are several sects which consider Shiva as their Supreme God. Some of them worship Shiva in 'Soumya Rupa' and others in 'Roudra Rupa'. Some also use 'Vamachara' as the method of worship. (Details are given in Chapter 8)

SURYA (ADITYA)

Tat savitr varenyam bhargo devsya dhimahi dhiyo yonaha prachodayat

[We meditate on the splendour of the Sun, who may enlighten our intellect – Gayatri Mantra]

Surya is one of the five principal deities commonly worshipped by the Hindus in India. Surya (Sun God) also happens to be one of the earliest entities who came to be worshipped as a god. The symbolism of the Sun as a powerful God has influenced all major ancient religions of the world in some form or the other. As the source of heat and light, Sun is considered the source of all wisdom.

In Hindu tradition, Surya is worshipped as the only visible form of god, which can be seen every day. Most Hindus start their day by worshipping the Sun God. It is believed that by worshipping the Sun, one gets energy, health, and prosperity.

Both Shaivites and Vaishnavites, regard Surya as an aspect of their supreme God – Shiva (as Astamurthy) or Vishnu (as Surya-Narayana). Sun is also known as 'Grahapati', as he is the 'Chief of Navagrahas'. According to astrology, Surya represents the soul, intellect, wisdom, will power and a positive force. According to scriptures, the Sun is the dwelling place of our ancestors and is the first of eight 'vasus' (dwelling place of consciousness). The 'Saura' sect worships the Sun God as the supreme deity.

Surya is symbolically represented as a God riding everyday on a golden chariot rising in the east and setting in the west with unending regularity. The chariot has a single wheel, and is driven by seven horses (representing the seven rays or seven colours of light). Sri Rama belonged to Surya vamsha. In *Mahabharata*, the princess Kunti, the mother of Pandavas, gets a son (Karna) from Surya through a mantra given by the sage 'Durvasa'.

A well known Hindu mode of worship of this god is 'Surya-Namaskar'. The famous 'Gayatri mantra' is also associated with Surya, as the ritual of 'Sandhya vandanam' is done using the mantra three times a day at dawn, noon and dusk through offer of water to the Sun.

'Makara Sankranti' (falling around January 15) is a widely celebrated Hindu festival, dedicated to Surya. On this day Sun enters 'Uttarayana' considered as the auspicious period. 'Chhath' is another ancient festival dedicated to Surya and observed in parts of North India. The Sun temple at Konark (Orissa) dedicated to Sun God, is famous for its imposing dimensions, faultless proportions and architectural splendour.

GANESHA

Ganesha, the son of Shiva and Parvati, is easily the most popular god in the pantheon of Hindu gods. His elephant head and big belly makes him also the best known of Hindu gods. 'Ga' symbolises Buddhi (intellect), 'na' symbolises Vignan (wisdom) and 'Isha' stands for 'Lord'. Ganesha is thus the Lord of intellect and wisdom. He is also considered 'Omkara swaroopa' and the 'Lord of fortune'.

He is worshipped by all people regardless of affiliation to any sub-sect in Hinduism, as he is considered as the 'Lord of successes' and 'Destroyer of obstacles' (Vighneswara). Hence, he is invariably invoked at the beginning of every Hindu ritual and ceremony. Even formal occasions and functions begin with a prayer to Ganesha. He is also considered as the God of *Vidya* – Learning, knowledge, intellect and wisdom.

The figure of Ganesha is loaded with multiple meanings and symbolism. He represents the perfect equilibrium between divine force and kindness, as well as between power and beauty. He also symbolizes discrimination which provides the worshipper the power to discriminate between truth (reality) and maya (illusion).

The 'Amarakosha' lists 8 synonyms of Ganesha – Vinayaka, Vighnaraja, Dvaimatura, Ganadhipa, Ekadanta, Heramba, Lambodara, and Gajanana. In sculpture, Ganesha is portrayed in various ways: standing, dancing, playing, etc. Ganesha is also portrayed along with Lakshmi and Saraswati indicating that one has to worship all the three gods to lead a happy and successful life.

Many mythological anecdotes are associated with his birth and his various exploits. Ganesha is also credited with writing the *Mahabharata* to the dictation of sage Veda-Vyasa. There is also a 'Ganapatya' sect, which considers Ganesha, as the supreme God (Brahman). There is also another group which worships Ganesha through rituals associated with 'Tantra Vidya'.

'Vinayaka Chaturthi' is a popular festival celebrated with great enthusiasm and devotion by everyone and especially by students. On this day, an earthen image of Ganesha is worshipped and finally immersed in water. Bal Gangadhar Tilak transformed the once family festival of Ganesha, into a grand public festival in Maharashtra, to imbibe a sense of nationalism among Hindus during the British period.

HANUMAN

Hanuman, the monkey God is also known popularly as Anjaneya, Vayuputra, Maruti and Bajrangbali. He is an ardent devotee of Sri Rama and is renowned for his courage, physical strength, power and selfless service. He is considered as a 'chiranjeevi' (immortal). His presence is said to be felt wherever the sacred *Ramayana* is recited. Arjuna fought the Mahabharata war with a flag displaying Hanuman on his chariot. According to legend, Hanuman is one of the few people to have heard the discourse of *Bhagavad Gita* from Sri Krishna.

Hanuman is worshipped as an important deity in all temples having Vishnu as the principal god. He is worshipped throughout the country to ward off evil spirits and also every village contains a Hanuman temple which acts as a protective boundary guardian. He is also worshipped by wrestlers for strength. It is believed that worshipping Hanuman reduces the malefic effects of 'Shani graha' – one of the 'Navagrahas'.

The followers of Madhva (Dvaita) sampradaya consider Hanuman, Bhima (of *Mahabharata*), and Madhva as incarnations of Vayu (also called Mukhya Prana – the God of Life). Pancha-mukhi Anjaneya is the main deity worshipped by Sri Raghvendra Swamy (of Mantralaya).

The daily recitation of the sacred devotional prayer – 'Hanuman Chalisa' (which forms a part of 'Ramacharita manasa' written by Sant Tulsidas), is said to give people inner strength and deliverance from all troubles. People fast on Tuesdays and Saturdays, recite 'Hanuman Chalisa' and visit Hanuman temples and give special offerings to the god.

SUBRAMANYA (SKANDA)

Subramanya is one of the most revered deities in South India. He is also revered as the 'Supreme Being' by some sects. He is known by many names – Skanda, Kumaraswamy, Kartikeya, Shanmukha, Guha, Velayudha, Murugan, Saravana, etc. Skanda is the eldest son of Shiva and Parvati and brother of Ganesha. Every Shiva temple in South India invariably contains a Murugan shrine. Skanda rides a peacock holding a serpent in its feet. He is considered as the epitome of knowledge.

Skanda Purana extensively deals with his exploits. Skanda is also a principal god praised in ancient Tamil Sangam literature. In Sanskrit epics, Skanda is known as the supreme commander of the gods and as a destroyer of evil forces. Sri Krishna says in *Bhagavad Gita*, 'Among the army generals, I am Skanda'.

Subramanya is worshipped as the Lord of the serpents. The epics relate that Vasuki, the serpent king and other serpents took refuge under Subramanya when threatened by Garuda. The temple at Kukke Subramanya is a famous temple located in the Western Ghats of Karnataka and draws devotees from many parts of India. 'Sarpa Samskara' and 'Ashlesha bali' are the rituals performed in Subramanya temples to get rid of 'sarpa-dosha'.

PANCHAYATANA PUJA

As discussed earlier, each major sect in Hinduism considers the god it worships as the Supreme Being. But this has often led to fanaticism among the different groups. In ancient times, scholars of different sects, wasted much time and energy in arguing as to which god was the supreme god – Shiva or Vishnu or whether both were inferior to Devi – the mother goddess.

History tells us that Tamil Nadu, where the dominant deity has been Shiva, did not tolerate Ramanuja as he was a 'Vishnu' bhakta. He had to flee Tamil Nadu and ultimately find refuge in Melukote in the kingdom of Hoysala Bitti Deva (later named Vishnu-vardhana) in the present day Karnataka.

Hence from the earliest times, there have been continuous efforts to reconcile the worship of different gods without cause for conflict of interests of different groups. The concept of 'Panchayatana Puja' (probably first advocated by Adi Shankara) is thought of as an answer to this vexed issue. In the 'Panchayatana Puja' all the five major deities are worshipped – Vishnu, Shiva, Devi, Surya and Ganesha.

The aim of this concept is to overcome the 'Bheda-bhava' among the different deities of various sects. This practice is followed prominently among many Hindu sub-sects. Note that the placement of deities, change with each 'Panchayatan' and also with each tradition.

In Shiva Panchayatan, Shiva is the central deity and the other 4 deities are worshipped around Shiva – Devi (Ambika) in Ishanya, Vishnu in Agneya, Surya in Niruthya, and Ganesha in Vayavya.

Vishnu		Surya
	Shiva	
Devi		Ganesha

In Vishnu Panchayatan, Vishnu is the central deity and the remaining four gods are worshipped around Vishnu – Devi (Ambika) in Ishanya, Shiva in Agneya, Ganesha in Niruthya, and Surya in Vayavya.

Shiva		Ganesha
	Vishnu	
Devi		Surya

The placement of deities in the case of Devi Panchayatan, Surya Panchayatan and Ganesha Panchayatan is shown below:

Vishnu		Shiva	Shiva		Ganesha	Vishnu		Shiva
	Devi			Surya			Ganesha	
Surya		Ganesha	Devi		Vishnu	Devi		Surya

In Devi Panchayatan, Devi is the central deity and the placement of the other four gods is – Surya in Ishanya, Vishnu in Agneya, Shiva in Niruthya, and Ganesha in Vayavya. In Surya Panchayatan – Devi (Ambika) is in Ishanya, Shiva is in Agneya, Ganesha is in Niruthya, and Vishnu in Vayavya. In Ganesha Panchayatan – Devi (Ambika) is in Ishanya, Vishnu is in Agneya, Shiva is in Niruthya, and Surya is in Vayavya.

These five gods are considered important in the pantheon of Hindu Gods as they represent the 'Pancha-bhutas' too. Ganesha represents the Earth, Vishnu water, Surya represents fire and Ambika represents air. Shiva represents the sky. Adi Shankara is said to have conceptualized and popularized the 'Panchayatan' mode of worship.

A Grihasta (householders) has to worship these five gods to influence his daily life in the following manner –

1. Destroying Obstacles (Ganesha),
2. Providing Health (Surya),
3. Strength and wealth (Ambika),
4. Knowledge (Shiva), and
5. Moksha (Vishnu).

According to Vaidyanathiya ahnikaka kanda –

Aditymambikam Vishnum Gananatham Maheshwaram I
Panchayagnaparo nityam grihasthaha Pancha poojayeth II

In this way the devotee worships his own god (Ishta-devata) as the 'supreme god' but at the same time worships the other gods as different forms of his own god. Temples are also constructed according to this principle. In addition, in Tamil Nadu, Kerala and the western coastal belt, Skanda (Subramanya) is prominently worshipped as the sixth god.

Hindu Temples

Throughout history, art and architecture has developed as a part of religious practices of the people. The places of religious worship have developed into sanctuaries for art and architecture. Royal patronage of religion is also one of the reasons for this development.

Although the same gods are worshipped throughout the country, people of every region portrayed them in sculptures in their own unique way. Hindu gods came to be arranged according to their grades in the hierarchy, in the post Gupta period. Vishnu, Shiva and Durga appeared as supreme gods and put in the centre of the temples where as the other gods were housed in lower positions around these gods. From seventh century onwards, several kings constructed a great many temples to house these gods. Every region evolved its own style in sculpture and temple construction. However, it reached its peak in South India. Stone and bronze were the main media in which the deities were worshipped.

TANTRISM IN HINDU RELIGION

The aim of 'Tantrism' is to enable devotees satisfy their material pleasures and cure them of illnesses. This has led to greater stress on the practice of magic rituals. Tantrism, which probably originated in the early centuries of the Christian era, has influenced all the three religions – Hinduism, Buddhism and Jainism in India to a great extent.

The three words 'Mantra, Tantra and Yantra' relate to an ancient form of Indian tradition, which is considered as different from the Vedic tradition. From the sixth century onwards 'Tantrism' has formed an important component of Hindu religious practices.

Tantrism refers to spiritual practices and rituals associated with the worship of different forms of 'Shakti'. Tantrism exists in Shaiva, Vaishnava, Ganapatya, Saura, and Shaakta traditions. The tantric practices and rituals include both ordinary and secret forms. They include yoga, mudras (gestures), recitation of mantras; mandalas, and yantras (symbolic diagrams); which are used as aids during worship. Through these, the person initiated into Tantrism, is supposed to invoke the divine force for achieving spiritual and magical powers.

The magical rituals and practices, which have come down from ancient times have been systematized and recorded in several tantric texts. These texts exist in the form of Shaiva 'Agamas', Vaishnava 'Pancharatra Samhitas', and 'Shaakta Tantras'. In fact, every region and every sub-sect has its own set of Tantric texts.

12

Punarjanma
(Rebirth/Reincarnation)

Reincarnation in Other Religions

The word 'Punarjanma' means 'Rebirth', popularly known as 'Reincarnation' in English. Several religions like Hinduism, Buddhism, and Jainism, believe in Punarjanma. Some philosophers also call it transmigration (as the soul is supposed to migrate from one body to another body).

Several ancient Greek philosophers like Socrates, Pythagoras and Plato subscribed to this view. Socrates prior to his death said: 'I am confident that truly there is such a thing as living again and that the living spring from the dead'. Plato presented detailed accounts of reincarnation in his major works.

Several scholars believe that the early Christian Church supported the concept of resurrection and after life. Tarot cards are much older than the Christian religion. In the Tarot deck, two cards – 'The Death' and the 'Judgement' cards are said to represent Karma and Reincarnation. In Numerology, the number 20 represents Reincarnation.

Many religions, most notably Hinduism, Buddhism and Jainism, believe that an individual follows the different stages of birth, death, and rebirth; in a continuous cycle. These religions also believe that actions in the present life determine the condition of the next birth. In ancient times, only certain Nastika schools like Charvakas, believed that the life of an individual ends at death and hence they did not believe in the concepts of Punarjanma, Swarga and Naraka.

Reincarnation and Psychology

Reincarnation as a phenomenon has not been explained properly by any of the sciences to date. But during the past century, a significant number of people in the West have come to believe in the 'Reincarnation' theory. In the early twentieth century, William James introduced this principle into the subject of Psychology as part of the critical investigation of 'Para-normal phenomena', which could not otherwise be explained by sciences. Several researchers, notably Professor Ian Stevenson of the University of Virginia, have collected several volumes of case studies in support of this theory.

A Popular Case of Reincarnation

In my book '*Browse Your Future through NUMEROLGY*', I have quoted an extract of a case from a book published in France in 1852 entitled *Research in to the Efficacy of Dates and Names in the Annals of Nations.*

The case relates to two individuals St. Luis (b 1215 CE) and Luis XVI (b 1754 CE), who lived 539 years apart and whose lives followed identical pattern to the exact years but with a difference of 539 years. They both went on to become kings of France and experienced similar events with unerring accuracy.

THE HINDU DOCTRINE OF 'PUNARJANMA'

Punarjanma as Described by the Gita

Punarjanma has been beautifully explained by Krishna in some of the slokas of the Gita:

1. *For one who has taken birth, death is certain and for one who is dead, birth is certain; therefore you ought not to lament for an inevitable situation (2.27)*

2. *Certainly never at any time did I not exist, nor you, nor all these kings, nor in the future shall any of us cease to exist. (2.12)*
3. *As the embodied soul continuously passes, in this body, from childhood to your youth and old age, the soul similarly passes into another body at death. (2.13)*
4. *Just as a man gives up old, worn out garments and wears new ones, in the same way the embodied soul gives up old and worn out bodies and accepts new ones. (2.22)*

Punarjanma Sidhanta

When a person dies, it is believed that death occurs for the body only. Just before death, as all the vital forces of the body get centralized in the inner consciousness (which is present in the mind), the body slowly loses its external functions like the inability to identify people present around the body, inability to hear sounds, inability to talk coherently, etc.

When death occurs, the inner consciousness with all the vital forces leaves the body. This inner consciousness is termed as the 'inner self', also known as the 'Atman' or the 'Soul'. Hinduism believes that the soul is eternal (Gita 2.20) and does not get destroyed at death.

Sage Yagnavalka's Explanation

The earliest reference to Punarjanma Sidhanta is by sage Yagnavalka in Brhadaranyaka Upanishad (4.4). Yagnavalka uses an analogy to elucidate his point:

> *At death the 'Purusha' (the human being) goes back in to breath and is subsequently reborn...*
> *The soul passes from one body to another as a caterpillar comes to the end of a blade of grass and climbs over to another.*
> *The soul is Brahman, it consists of consciousness, mind, breath, sight, hearing, ... desire, non-desire, anger, non-anger, dharma, non-dharma,... everything.*
> *Rebirth takes place through desire, the soul makes itself a new 'rupa'...*
> *He who is without desire, is Brahman and goes to Brahman.*

The Intermediate Stage between Death and Rebirth

There is a time period between birth and death (as we pass through different stages of childhood, youth and old age). Similarly there is a time period between death and rebirth called the 'intermediate stage'. During this stage, after leaving the body, the soul lives on in 'sookshma shareera' and undergoes transformations in forms from 'Preta' to 'Vasu' to 'Rudra' and finally to 'Aditya' Rupa.

Devi Bhagavata further deliberates on what happens in this 'intermediate stage' in the life of the soul. It states (Chapter 4):

> *Poorva deham parityajya jivah karma vashanugah* ।
> *Swargam va Narakam vaapi prapnoti swakrutena vai* ॥
> *Divyam deham cha samprapya yatanadehamarthajam* ।
> *Bhunakti vividhan bhogan swarge va naraketha va* ॥
> *Bhogante cha yadotpatteha smayastasya jayate* ।
> *Tadaiva sanchitebhyascha karmabhyah karmabhih punah* ।
> *Yojataiva tam kalah* ...॥

Depending on the 'Karma Phala', the soul attains Heaven or Hell. Since the soul is still having Kama, it undergoes various experiences in Heaven or Hell. This appears to be a later day concept probably evolved during the 'Puranic Period'. 'Garuda Purana' describes these experiences more elaborately.

After completion of these experiences, the soul gets born again acquiring a new body based on its 'Sanchita Karma'. According to 'Chandogya Upanishad' (5.10.7) a person may get a good rebirth or an evil birth according to the results of one's Karma.

The soul also chooses a family and parents suitable for it to fulfil its desires. The reason for this is 'Avidya' or ignorance and 'Kama' or desire. Until 'Avidya' and 'Kama' are destroyed, the cycle of birth and death continues...

Reasons for Punarjanma as per Hindu Scriptures

Punarjanma is governed by theories of 'Karma', 'Samsara' and 'Moksha'. Under the Karmic theory, *results of good and bad deeds (Karma Phala*

– Punya/Paapa) follow every soul in this and subsequent births. There is no Punarjanma when the soul attains self-realization or Moksha or Mukti or 'Jnana Prapti'. Hindu scriptures describe the cause of 'Punarjanma' in different ways:

1. 'Mundkopanishad' states that one's desire is mainly responsible for one's birth. When desires vanish, Kama gets destroyed. (3.2.2)
2. 'Swhetaashwatara Upanishad' states that the feeling that Jeevatma is different from Paramatma, results in birth. When Jeevatma feels that he is one with Paramatma, it results in Moksha.
3. In order to attain Moksha, the 'Karma Phala' of the Jeevatma should have been destroyed (or reduced to nothing). For this purpose the right path is 'Moksha Sadhana', which may take a life time or several life times also, and this is also a cause for Punarjanma.
4. 'Brahadaranyaka Upanishad' *states that* until all desires are fulfilled, Jeevatma is born again and again. When there are no desires (Nish-kami) such an Atman gets absorbed in the Brahman (4.4.6).
5. 'Adi Shankara's Bhaja Govindam song' describes the concept of Punarjanma as 'Punarapi Jananam, Punarapi Maranam....'

Adi Shankara's Views on Punarjanma

Adi Shankara has further elaborated the concept of Punarjanma as follows: This world is shrouded in Maya. One is trapped in 'Samsara' (cycle of birth and rebirth), due to 'Avidya' (ignorance of the true nature of our existence). This 'Avidya' leads to desire and a perpetual chain of birth and rebirth follows. One is born through desire and the results of Karma.

After many births, one becomes dissatisfied and begins to seek higher forms of happiness through devotion, meditation and other spiritual paths. Through 'Sadhana' he understands that the nature of the soul as eternal. At this stage all desires and pleasures of this world vanish, as they seem insipid compared with the eternal bliss. This is the stage of self-realization. When an individual reaches this stage, he does not wish to be born again. With the liberation from the cycle of births and deaths (Moksha), he becomes one with Brahman the Supreme Being.

At this stage, one should understand the clear distinction between 'Swarga' and Moksha. Swarga is a temporary residence for the soul (which has done good deeds) awaiting rebirth where as there is no return to earthly life in Moksha.

Madhva's Views on Punarjanma

Madhva classifies all souls into three categories – Satvic, Rajasic and Tamasic souls. While there is hope for liberation for Satvic souls, Rajasic by their nature have to undergo Punarjanma for eternity. Tamasic souls are by nature, evil souls and are condemned to hell eternally. That means they are in a perpetual cycle of Punarjanma and Hell. Because of this 'Taratamya' the souls meet their predetermined ends.

Dvaita School differs at the stage of Moksha and emphasizes that the Satvic soul attains eternal bliss as Jeevatma and Parmatman are different entities. The degree of bliss (between souls) also varies according to their 'Karma Phala'.

Buddhist Views on Punarjanma

However, the Buddhist philosophy deals with the theory of 'Karma' in a different manner as it does not believe in the eternity of the soul or the existence of God. All Buddhist traditions accept rebirth, but have different views on events after death. There is no soul but it is consciousness (also called as Vignana) which is continuous birth and death of the mind-states.

There is no consciousness without a living body (Jiva). Some believe that there is an intermediate stage between death and rebirth. In this state, the person does not yet reap the consequences of his Karmic actions, but may still influence his rebirth. Some Buddhist schools believe Karma continues to exist even after death and is carried on to the next birth.

Certain Characteristics of Punarjanma

Here I am making certain hypothesis, which can only be deduced but cannot be proved. According to psychology, heredity and environment play an equally important part in the development of the personality of the individual. But psychology does not explain certain specific phenomena, which are beyond the scope of perception of the human mind.

We see such phenomena in our everyday life. For example, a child whose parents had no knowledge of music, may take to music like a fish taking to water. Psychology classifies them only as geniuses and does not provide an answer. In such cases, Hindu religion provides answers through the concept of Karma and Punarjanma. The child has been able to easily learn music, because probably it had been a musician during its previous birth. Some more examples are given below:

1. Small children (say just 3–6 years of age), becoming highly proficient in professional fields, which will take a normal life time for a person to attain the same degree of proficiency –
   (*i*) Small children reciting 700 slokas of the Gita or such similar text very fluently, even though they may not be able to understand their meanings.
   (*ii*) Small children rendering classical musical ragas or playing musical instruments with great ease.
2. Children with very wide range of differing characteristics are born out of the same parents and brought up in the same environment. But one child may become a scholar and another may become a vagabond. This can be explained by their level of achievements in their previous births.
3. Some people have very short span of life, probably because they have come into this world to fulfil their certain limited Karmic obligations only to that extent.
4. Children remembering certain events from their past life and identifying certain places and persons from past life.
5. Certain people identifying pictures of people/places, even though they had not seen them before.

Methods for Recollection of Punarjanma

Patanjali's 'Yoga sutras' discuss methods by which one can acquire the ability to see his past births. According to Patanjali, our inner consciousness is aware of our previous births and this can be perceived by practicing 'Chitta Vritti Nirodhabhyasa Yoga'.

Certain planetary configurations in a persons' birth chart also gives an indication of a person's past life. But this can be interpreted only by persons who have obtained *Siddhi* in predicting through 'Astrology'.

The early Buddhist texts discuss techniques for recalling previous births by an individual through development of high levels of meditative concentration. Meditative forms like 'Vipassana' (observation of breath and body sensations) leads to awakening the inner consciousness. When once the inner consciousness is awakened, it will take one through different phases of one's past lives.

Modern day Psychologists use 'hypnosis' as a method in taking a person through the journey of past lives. But this appears to be successful in cases of certain individuals only. Probably, hypnosis works on people with weak minds and/or those who have low religious attainments.

Consequences of Remembering Punarjanma

According to some, relationships between persons continue over many lives in some form or the other. Both Astrology and Numerology give indications of such relationships continuing over many births.

In such cases, remembrance of Punarjanma would lead to disastrous consequences. Knowledge of enmity between two individuals would ruin the lives of both the individuals in subsequent births. If a rich person is born poor, then his knowledge of riches in the previous life would make him more miserable in this life. Hence it is good that we are living in a world of Maya and we have no knowledge of our past lives.

Usefulness of Punarjanma Sidhanta

Punarjanma Sidhanta which is unique to Hindu religion (and of course Buddhism and Jainism with variations) has its uses in understanding the nature of life and misery in this world. It explains the consequences of Karma and the necessity of doing good deeds in order to lead a good life. There are some important lessons to be learnt from this Sidhanta:

1. During the period of suffering and misery, an individual can find solace from the 'Punarjanma Sidhanta' that if not in this life at least, he may find happiness in the next life.
2. Since Kama (desire) is one of the main reasons for the rebirth of an individual, it is important that he controls his desires and reaches a stage where all his desires get destroyed and he becomes 'Nish-kami'.
3. Since a feeling of attachment is another reason for rebirth, (as Krishna says in Gita) one should perform his actions without any sense of attachment.
4. The results of good deeds and Sadhana will not go waste when death occurs. The Karma Phala (both good and bad) follows the soul in its subsequent births.
5. The belief that the Karma made in this life will not go waste, helps an individual to lead a good and contented life, as well as hope for a better life in the next birth.
6. It is possible for the Jeevatma to attain Mukti/Moksha/Eternal Bliss (according to the philosophy one believes in) in this life itself, by leading a pious life (free of sins) and performing 'Sadhana' as prescribed by the Shastras.

Moksha is beyond the concepts of Heaven and Hell which are temporary abodes for departed souls. In these abodes the souls enjoy bliss/suffer punishments according to their Karma and then continue into the cycle of births and deaths.

HEAVEN (Swarga)

Most religions believe that heaven is a place of eternal life and the dwelling place of God. Hindus consider this as 'Deva Loka', where the virtuous go. 'Indra' is considered as the King of Heaven. If a soul has done good deeds in its previous life, it enters 'Swarga' remains there for some period of time. Hence Swarga is also considered as an intermediate place where the soul stays waiting for its next birth.

Heaven is also considered as 'Vaikunta' (abode of Vishnu) or 'Kailasa' (abode of Shiva) – these are considered realms higher than the 'Deva Loka' – depending on the sect to which one belongs. Liberation from the cycle of births and deaths leads one to attain Moksha, at which stage, the liberated soul enters Vaikunta/Kailasa (never to return).

Vaikunta

Vaikunta is supposedly located above the 'Satya Loka'. Followers of Vaishnava Sampradaya consider Vaikunta as the ultimate destination of souls who attain Moksha. Rig Veda says *Om tad Vishnoh param padam sada pasyanti surayah* (1.22.20 – 'all the surahs – devas – look towards the feet of Lord Vishnu, as the supreme abode').

Krishna says about Vaikunta in the Gita (15.6) – *The Sun illuminates not that place, nor the moon, nor fire; that is my all illuminating, supreme transcendental abode, having reached from which there is no return.* The various puranas give further description of Vaikunta.

Kailasa (also identified as Mt. Kailas in Tibet) is considered the abode of Shiva. Followers of Shaiva sects believe that the liberated souls reach Kailasa – a place of eternal bliss.

Near Death Experiences

There are several reported cases of people coming close to death (or clinically dead and brought back to life by doctors), reporting certain 'Para-normal' experiences. These are positive experiences of meeting a heavenly light. This is reported as an immense mental feeling of love, peace, and joy which is stated to be beyond human comprehension. Some others have reported negative and distressing experiences as well. Possibly these experiences are directly connected to their respective beliefs and religious practices.

HELL (Naraka)

Many religions hold 'Hell' as a place of suffering and punishment, after life. Early Vedic religion did not have the concept of Hell. Rig Veda mentions only three worlds – Bhu (Earth), Bhuv (antariksha) and Svah (sky). In *Mahabharata*, Dharmaraja passes through Naraka as a punishment for having uttered a lie to Dronacharya in the Mahabharata war.

Naraka is also considered as an intermediate place where the soul stays waiting for its next birth. According to Dharma Shastras, Naraka is a place of punishment for sins. Punishments correspond to sins (or Karma) committed by the soul during its lifetime on earth.

'Yama-Dharma-Raja' as the Judge of Sinners

Naraka is ruled by Yama, the God of Death. He is also the judge of sins committed by individuals. Detailed accounts of all sins committed by individuals are supposedly kept by 'Chitragupta', who is the record keeper in Yama's court. Garuda Purana gives an exhaustive description of hell and punishments meted out to the sinners (just like a modern day penal code). Individuals who finish their quota of punishments are supposedly reborn in accordance with their Karma and to enjoy/suffer their balance of Karmic actions.

> *Probably this was an attempt by Dharma Shastras to persuade people to follow Dharma and dissuade them from committing sins deliberately.*

'Punarjanma' as a concept is unique to the religions of the East and Hindus place a lot of faith in the concept of Punarjanma.

Annexure 1

Jain and Buddhist Philosophies

Jainism and Buddhism (along with Charvaka system which are together classified as Nastika systems of philosophies) came into existence in ancient India, as a reaction to the philosophies and practices which were then prevalent in Hindu religion. As discussed earlier, these systems were in a major way responsible for putting the then Hindu beliefs and philosophical concepts to a very detailed and independent analysis of logic and reasoning.

The Nastika systems rejected those concepts and practices in Hinduism, which they considered as inconsistencies. This helped in refining the Hindu system of beliefs generally. Consequently, every Hindu philosopher started his philosophical treatise by first contradicting the views contained in these systems. These philosophies thus helped in bringing reformation in Hindu beliefs to a large extent.

Comparison of Jainism and Buddhism

Even though Jainism is much older than Buddhism, both religions grew out of the confrontation of 'Shramanic' sects with Vedic Brahmanism. Both were propagated by 'Kshatriyas (warrior class)' and were opposed to Brahmanical orthodoxy. Although they did not call for total abolishment of Varna system, they were opposed to it. At least both the religions did not follow the Varna system, while admitting followers to their respective religions.

Jainism is the most difficult religion to practice because of its uncompromising emphasis on austerity. In spite of this, Jainism has survived and has contributed substantially to the Indian culture and is a part of the rich Indian religious milieu. But unlike Buddhism, Jainism is mostly confined to the Indian sub continent and here too, its influence remains confined to a very small section of the society (merchant communities of western India).

Buddhism almost vanished from the sub continent but eventually spread all over Asia and now as a religion encompasses a variety of traditions and cultures from different countries. Buddhism is a rare world religion in that its followers never used force and violence to spread their beliefs and religion.

Buddha intended his philosophy to be a practical one and hence advocated the Middle Path, in which he offered a balanced and harmonious way of life, steering between two extremes of self-indulgence and total abstinence. Within Buddhism, there are different schools of thought which enlarged and reinterpreted Buddha's teachings. Practice of Buddhism provides insightful solutions to problems like violence, stress and suffering.

Comparison of the Two Darshanas

Both Darshanas do not accept the authority of the Vedas as well as the existence of God – as the Supreme Being. Jaina Darshana is a little closer to Hindu philosophy, as it believes in the existence of the Soul and multiple facets of Truth. It also believes in certain concepts common to Hinduism like Karma, Moksha, results of good and bad deeds, etc., but the interpretation of these concepts vary.

Buddha Darshana is based on the rejection of certain Hindu orthodox philosophical concepts (like existence of Atman, God, etc.). Dharma (termed as Dhamma – in the sense of Truth) is considered as something 'beyond reasoning' or 'transcending logic'. But it accepts certain basic concepts like 'Karma', cycle of birth and rebirth, cause and effect relationships, etc. It also accepts religious tolerance.

A brief description of the two philosophies and their contribution to Indian philosophic thought has been attempted here.

JAIN PHILOSOPHY

Jainism is a unique religion that has lasted for more than 25 centuries, but still has remained within a select group or community of people. Unlike other religions it has not been propagated across the globe. It has often been considered as an ascetic movement as it places strong emphasis on self-control, non-indulgence and renunciation of worldly pleasures. It prescribes a path of non-violence towards all beings in this world.

Throughout history, Jain philosophy remained unified and undivided, though as a religion, it divided into various sects and traditions. The existence of deity was not central to early Jain doctrine. It taught that universe functions according to an eternal law and continually passes through a process of progress and decline. The purification of the soul is the goal of the living. The pure soul is released from the body and then resides in bliss. The purification of the soul required living a balanced life.

A Jain is a follower of Jinas – who have rediscovered the path of Dharma, become fully liberated and taught the spiritual path to others. 'Jina' means a conqueror – one who has conquered all human desires and passions. Followers of Jainism accept the popular Hindu gods but place them below the 'Jinas' in hierarchy.

Tirthankars

Jaina Dharma is considered to be an ancient religion. Yajur Veda mentions the names of the first three 'Tirthankars' – Rishabdev, Ajitnath and Aristanemi. Bhagavata Purana describes Rishabdev as the first Tirthankar who propagated the Jain religion.

'Tirthankar' means a guide who enables one to cross over 'Tirtha' (ford) – the ocean of recurring births in this world. As per Jain tradition, in the current cycle of time, 24 'Tirthankars' (known as enlightened seers) have appeared. 'Mahavira' is the 24th and the last Tirthankar, who lived in sixth century BCE.

Jains follow the teachings of the 'Tirthankars' which are preserved in 'Jainagamas.' Jainism encourages spiritual independence and self-control which is considered essential for one's spiritual development. The goal of Jainism, as is with other Indian religions, is the attainment of 'Moksha'.

Points at which Jainism Differs from Hinduism

Some of the questions raised in Jain philosophy are as follows:

1. If God created this Universe, then who created that God?
2. If God is 'Karunamayi', then why are the majority of the people in this world in poverty, misery and want? Why did he bestow prosperity and happiness only to a few?
3. Why has God given a majority of people a wicked mind that compels them to do wicked deeds?
4. Why does God allow people to do wicked deeds and then punish them for those deeds?
5. If God is in bliss, then all people who are his images should be in bliss. All should be like God, but why is this is not the case?

Essential Features of Jainism

Jainism does not accept the authority of the Vedas. It also rejects the theory that God created this universe. It accepts two sets of proofs 'Pramanas' – 'Pratyaksh' and 'Paroksh'. It deals extensively with problems related to metaphysics, reality, cosmology and divinity. It is a continuation of the earlier 'Shramana' (self-effort) tradition which is believed to have coexisted with the Vedic tradition.

It bases its doctrine on independent existence of soul and matter, denial of the existence of a creative and omnipresent God, strength of Karma, eternal universe, liberation of the soul, and places stress on non-violence, multiple facets of truth, morality and ethics.

The focus is purification of the soul through right conduct, right faith and right knowledge. According to Jain beliefs Moksha can be obtained by following the three important steps:

1. *Right Faith:* Belief in life and teachings of Jain Tirthankars,
2. *Right Knowledge:* Correct knowledge of the system of Beliefs in Jainism,
3. *Right Conduct:* Following of correct behaviour and conduct.

Essence of Jain School of Philosophy

According to Jain beliefs, the Universe is eternal and hence was never created. It is without a beginning and end. The whole universe is a self regulated one. Gods are divine beings that are worthy of worship and emulation. They can be categorized into – Tirthankars, Arihant (one who is liberated from Karmas and is in human form), and Siddhas (the liberated beings). Jainism also believes in demi-gods and goddesses, who dwell in heavens because of their meritorious deeds in their past lives. But they are also considered as un-liberated beings and are subject to further incarnations. Worship of such gods is considered as 'mithyatva' or wrong belief leading to bondage of karmas.

The aim of all Jaina teachings is attainment of salvation or liberation of the soul. According to Jain philosophy, the combination of 'Jiva' (soul) and 'A-Jiva' (matter) causes all diversities in this universe. Jiva is characterized by 'Chetana' (consciousness) and 'upa-yoga' (termed as knowledge and perception). The Jiva is further categorized into liberated and non-liberated souls.

Karmic bondage leads to non-liberated souls having bondage with the body and hence continuously go through the cycles of birth and death. Though the Jiva experiences both birth and death, it is really neither created nor destroyed. When the Jiva is stripped of all its 'Ajiva' bondage, it becomes pure and attains its ultimate Mukti. A liberated soul, is said to have attained its pristine nature of infinite bliss, infinite knowledge and infinite perception. Such a soul is called 'Siddha or Paramatman' (Supreme Soul).

One of the main characteristics of Jain philosophy is the emphasis of the immediate consequences of one's physical and mental behaviour. Every Jiva is potentially divine, independent and is itself the master of its own destiny. Karma plays an important role. Jiva alone chooses its actions and it alone reaps its consequences. Desire is the greatest of all evils.

Every creature living in this world possesses a separate and independent existence and individuality. Every creature has to put forth its efforts to get deliverance from bondage of Karmas and attain salvation, because Dharma is essentially a personal affair.

Ethical Code

All forms of life are considered worthy of respect and even the smallest of creatures, is not to be harmed. 'Ahimsa' (Non-Violence), Kevala Jnana (Right knowledge), and Right conduct are considered to be the core principles of Jain Philosophy. Ethical code in Jainism is taken very seriously:

1. Non-injury (Ahimsa),
2. Non-lying (Satya),
3. Non-stealing (Asteya),
4. Chastity (Brahmacharya), and
5. Non-possession (Aparigrah).

These are almost similar to the five paths of Hindu Dharma enunciated by Manu.

Influence of Jain School of Philosophy on Hindu Thought

The contribution of Jain philosophy in the development of Hindu philosophical thought is quiet significant and substantial. Scholars believe that Jain philosophical concepts like Karma, Ahimsa, Moksha, reincarnation – which had their origins in 'Shramana' school of philosophy, were later assimilated by Hindu religion and philosophy (and also Buddhism) in diverse forms.

The 'Shramanic' view of life – as full of suffering and renunciation of desires – is in stark contrast to the early Brahmanical view of an active life punctuated with rituals and sacrifices. Sages like Yagnavalka tried to incorporate the 'shramanic' ideals into later Vedic thought. It is believed that Jainism influenced Hinduism in a major way in several areas, most notably in the secession of animal sacrifices in Vedic rituals and enunciation of Karmic theory.

Jains consider the following mantra as the most important, most auspicious and most sacred mantra:

Namo Arhantanam, Namo Sidhanam, Namo Ayariyanam,
Namo Upagrhayanam, Namo Loe' sabba sahoonam

['I salute the Arhantas, the Siddhas, the Acharyas, the Upadhyayas, and all the Sadhus in this world'. This mantra is also termed as Jaina -Gayatri mantra and also as 'Pancha-paramesthi Namaskar' mantra.]

BUDDHIST PHILOSOPHY

Buddhist philosophy is based on the teachings of Gautama Buddha. He rejected certain aspects of Indian philosophy prevalent at that time. Buddha cautioned his followers to stay away from intellectual deliberations, saying it as fruitless and useless to speculate on how phenomenal existence started. Because these type of deliberations, totally distracts people from following practices leading to enlightenment.

According to him, the ultimate goal of the religion (Buddhism) is to achieve the liberation of all creatures from pain of existence. He valued only knowledge that could be considered useful for achieving enlightenment. Earliest compilations of Buddha's teachings are known as 'Tripitakas'.

Unlike other philosophies, Buddhist philosophy relies on the direct observation of one's personal experience and on honing certain skills to gain true understanding and wisdom. Buddha intended his philosophy to be a practical one aimed at the happiness of all creatures. It can be summed up as follows:

1. To lead a moral life,
2. To be mindful and aware of thoughts and actions,
3. To develop wisdom and understanding.

Buddhism explains a purpose to life. It explains apparent injustice, inequality and sorrow in this world.

It provides a code or way of life that leads to happiness.

Buddhism views a person as a changing configuration of five factors (skandas) –

1. *Roopa Skanda* (the world of physical form – the body);
2. *Vedana Skanda* (the factor of sensation or feeling – which includes the mind);
3. *Sangna Skanda* (the factor of perception);
4. *Samskara Skanda* (suffering related to birth, death, pride, enmity, etc.);
5. *Vignana Skanda* (Impulses or mental formulations like the faculty of will, and consciousness or awareness). The group of these five Skandas is known as 'Pudgala'.

Three Marks of Existence

The Buddhist teachings refer to the three basic characteristics of the factual and physical world that can be distinguished as the 'Three Marks of excellence'. Each of them is related to humanity in general (other than Nirvana). Each of them goes on to explain the drawbacks or shortcomings of the existing world, which can be averted if one achieves 'Nirvana'.

1. *Anicca* – Impermanence – Buddhist philosophy is based on the law of impermanence. According to this, everything is subject to change, further change and disintegration, although some things may last longer than others. Hence there is never anything like a permanent soul.
2. *Anatta* – no self/no soul – human beings and all of existence is without a soul or self. There is no eternal unchanging part of us (like the Hindu idea of Atman), there is no eternal unchanging

part of the Universe (like the Hindu idea of Brahman). The entire idea of self, is seen as illusion which causes suffering.

3. *Dukkha* – suffering is there in all of existence.

These three marks of existence form the basis of the 'Four Noble Truths' enunciated below:

Four Noble Truths

Buddha's main concern was to eliminate human suffering and to find a cure for the pain of human existence. From this view, follows the four Noble Truths (Arya Satya):

1. **Dukkha Arya Satya** (*Suffering is Universal*): Life includes pain, suffering, sickness and death. We also suffer psychologically from loneliness, fear, jealousy, disappointment, anger, etc.
2. **Dukkha Samudaya** (*Suffering is caused by desire and yearning*): We suffer more if we crave for our wants. Getting what we want does not guarantee happiness. Wanting deprives us of contentment and happiness.
3. **Dukkha Nirodha Arya Satya** (*Suffering can be prevented and overcome*): Suffering can be overcome and happiness can be attained by giving up craving for what we don't have. Then we can be happy and free.
4. **Dukkha Nirodhagamini Pratipada Arya Satya** (*Renunciation of desires can lead to removal of suffering*): Following the eight fold path, will lead us to end of suffering. Conquest of desire leads to attainment of 'Nirvana' or complete enlightenment.

The Eight-fold Path of Sadhana

Buddha advocated the 'Eight fold path' leading to 'Nirvana': *right understanding, right intention, right speech, right action, right livelihood, right effort, right mindedness, and right concentration.* The first two steps constitute wisdom (right understanding and intention), the next three steps ethical conduct (right speech, action and livelihood), the last three steps relate to mental discipline. The combination of these paths was called the 'Middle Path'.

1. **Samyak Drishti** *(Right Views/Understanding)*: Grasping of true reality as per Buddhist teachings (especially about the four Noble truths) and hence, this is not limited to mere intellectual understanding.
2. **Samyak Sankalpa** *(Right Resolve/Intention)*: It is a frame of mind which is selfless, detached and free from malice. It extends loving benevolence to all living beings. In order to obtain good results, right intention should result in good deeds from the individual concerned.
3. **Samyak Vachana** *(Right Speech)*: The speech should always be truthful and pleasant, which means – abstaining from lies, rude and foul language; avoiding gossip, slander, etc. One should speak a gentle, kind and useful truth or not speak at all.
4. **Samyak Karma** *(Right Action/Conduct)*: Abstaining from all vices – killing and violence, stealing, dishonest practices, drinks and improper sexual behaviour. Samyak Karma includes doing good deeds and avoiding bad deeds.
5. **Samyak Jeevana** *(Right Livelihood)*: One should live according to Samyak Karma and abstain from professions which harm others – such as weaponry, butchering animals, selling liquor, deceitful activities, etc. One should take up professions which only take care of basic needs but not to lead life luxuriously.
6. **Samyak Vyayama** *(Right Effort)*: It includes disciplining of the mind by eliminating evil intentions and cultivating a wholesome state of mind. Maintaining alertness, having good intentions, and avoiding negative thoughts, are examples of this path.
7. **Samyak Smriti** *(Right Recollection/Mindedness)*: The process involved in daily existence – body, mind, sensations, experiencing thoughts and ideas – explained in Buddhist forms of meditation like 'Vipassana' (observation of breath and body sensations).This leads to awakening the inner consciousness.
8. **Samyak Samadhi** *(Right Meditation/Concentration)*: This is the final step of the eight fold path. It refers to progressive stages of 'Dhyana' (closer to Hindu idea of meditation) where mind is

gradually cleared of passionate desires, thoughts, even feelings of joy, until only pure awareness remains. And finally the person reaches a state of perfect and permanent calm and equanimity (Nirvana). There are two types of Nirvana – one achieved during the life time of an individual and the second achieved at the time of death (also known as Pari-nirvana).

The Principle of Karma

Karma is considered as the doctrine of cause and effect – actions leading to results. It advocates as the basic principle – the law of causation – according to which nothing occurs by pure chance. All things are cause and are caused by other things, all of existence is conditioned, and nothing exists independently. Besides natural forces, it is the Karma which leads to occurrence of all events. Karma underlines the importance of all individuals being responsible for past and present actions. Good deeds yield good results and bad deeds inevitably yield bad results. The reason for this is considered as 'Avidya'.

Unlike the Brahmanical concept of Karma, the Buddhist notion of Karma was not tied to the regulations or the social ethics attached to the Varna system. (Please refer to the definition of Karma in Chapter 1). The improvement of one's Karma to ensure a better life was dependent on observing the code of social ethics based on the eightfold path unlike the Brahmanical sacred duties drawn up in Smritis.

Buddhist philosophy is an ethical system, which can also be described as a way of life that leads to a very specific goal. The end goal of this philosophy is 'Nirvana' which is an experience beyond all concepts and language and even beyond Buddhist teachings. Starting from a few basic assumptions, Buddhism developed a complex system of philosophic thought, which has stood the test of time for centuries.

Changes in Buddhist Religion and Philosophy down the Centuries

As a result of social and political developments down the centuries, assimilation of many local sects into Buddhism, the splitting of

Buddhism into Mahayana and Hinayana traditions in the early second century CE, Buddhism's interaction with other religions, etc, new ideas came to be accepted and this necessitated changes in Buddhist religion as well as philosophy.

The elevation of Buddha as God, the worship of his image, the concept of 'Bodhisattva', the notion of transferring merit, complicated systems of heavens, fertility cults, etc., – these concepts became part of Buddhism in subsequent centuries. Even though Buddha had opposed deification, the worship of his image carved in stone had started by first century CE.

The 'Bodhisattva' (sometimes in the form of suffering saviour) is another important concept, described as one who works for the good of mankind in an unselfish manner and is willing to forego 'Nirvana' until such time as his work is completed. 'Bodhisattva' was also interpreted as a previous incarnation of Buddha, working towards 'Nirvana' and acquiring merit in successive births.

Another important concept was 'Transfer of Merit'. Merit (similar to 'Punya' in Hinduism) could also be transferred from one person to another through a pious act like offering donations of land, wealth etc. for good causes or to the 'Sangha' to be used for religious activities.

'Nagarjuna' (a Buddhist monk from Deccan, converted from a Brahman family), propagated 'Shoonya-vada' –that we are surrounded by emptiness and what we see is an illusion. 'Shoonya' is 'Nirvana' (or the end of the cycle of birth and death), what every Buddhist is seeking. These ideas were further developed into a variety of philosophical speculations, which Buddha had meticulously avoided.

Tantric beliefs and rituals also influenced Buddhism to a great extent. Vajrayana Buddhism gave female counterparts (termed as Taras) to the existing male figures of the Buddhist pantheon. They are especially popular in Nepal and Tibet.

'Budha', 'Dhamma' and 'Sangha' are considered the three most important aspects of Buddhism and their prayer goes as follows:

Namo Tassa Bhagavato Arahto Sammasambhuddassa
Buddham Sharanam Gatchaami,

Dhammam Sharnam Gatchaami,
Sangham Sharanam Gatchaami

[I salute the one who is the Bhagavant, the Arhant, and the Samyak Sam-Buddha. I salute Budha, Dhamma and Sangha.]

Buddhism registered a decline in India from the seventh century (CE) onwards with the decline of royal patronage, rise in the influence of Shaivism and revival of Sanatana Hindu Dharma by Acharyas like Adi Shankara.

Impact of Buddhism on Hindu Religion and Philosophy

1. How can we be sure of what we are supposed to know?
2. How can we bring our ideas in closer correspondence with reality?

These types of elementary questions raised by Buddhist philosophers led to a churning process in the Hindu philosophic thought and led to an elimination process of the inconsistencies found there in. This helped in refining the Hindu system of beliefs generally.

Consequently, every Hindu philosopher started by first analyzing the important points raised by the 'Nastika' systems, then contradicting these views, and then starting their respective treatises.

Annexure 2

Modern Indian Philosophers

Modern Indian philosophy developed during the British rule in India. The philosophers of this period interpreted traditional philosophy in the present day context. Among them the following philosophers stand out for having made substantial contributions to the Indian Philosophic Thought – Ramakrishna Paramahamsa, Swami Vivekananda, Aurobindo, and Dr. S. Radhakrishnan. Their profiles as well as philosophies are briefly discussed here.

1. SRI RAMAKRISHNA PARAMAHAMSA

Sri Ramakrishna [born as Gadadhar Chattopadhyay (1836–1886)], was a nineteenth century mystic. He achieved world fame by his pursuit of Truth and his realization of the Divine. He was a priest at Kali temple in Dakshineswar. Though (conventionally) uneducated, his teachings attracted a large number of followers.

Ramakrishna was well versed in Advaita Vedanta and 'Shakti Tantra'. He used to convey his messages through short stories and parables. Even though, his teachings were in rustic Bengali they made a powerful impact on the Bengali intellectuals of the time. Swami Vivekananda said of his Master:

> *This great intellect never learnt even to write his own name, but the most brilliant graduates of our University found him to be an intellectual giant.*

Ramakrishna represents the very core of spiritual realization of great seers and ancient sages of India. He reached a depth of 'Nirvikalpa – samadhi' that transcends all time and space; and has a universal appeal. He explains one of his divine visions in his own words thus:

> *When I jumped up like a mad man and seized the sword (to take his life), suddenly the blessed Mother revealed herself. The buildings with different parts, the temple, and everything vanished from my sight, leaving no trace whatsoever, and in their stead I saw a limitless, infinite Ocean of Consciousness, ... I was caught in the rush and collapsed unconscious...within me there was a steady flow of undiluted bliss, altogether new, and I felt the presence of the Divine Mother.* (The Gospel of Ramakrishna – Swami Nikhilanada)

Ramakrishna's Philosophy

Ramakrishna rejected caste distinctions and religious prejudices. He believed that all religions led to the same god. He emphasized 'realization of God' as the supreme goal of all living beings. He coined the phrase 'Kamini - Kanchana' (Women and money – interpreted as lust inside the mind) as an obstacle to god realization.

Ramakrishna looked on the world as *Maya*. He explained that 'avidya-maya' represents dark forces of creation – sensual desire, evil passions, greed, lust and cruelty. These dark forces are responsible for human entrapment in the cycle of birth and death. These forces needed to be fought and vanquished. *Vidya Maya* on the other hand, represents higher forces of creation – spiritual forces, kindness, purity, love and devotion. These forces elevate human beings to higher planes of consciousness.

Ramakrishna believed that all religions are valid and true and led to the same ultimate goal of realization of God. Every religion represents God's diverse aspects to satisfy the manifold demands of various human minds. Different religions give us pictures of one Truth from different standpoints. Their teachings are not contrary but complementary. Harmony of religions is like Unity in Diversity.

His religious school of thought later led to the formation of 'Ramakrishna Mission' by his chief disciple Swami Vivekananda. The Mission has branches worldwide and has been doing yeoman service in propagation of the essence of Hindu religion and Philosophy.

2. SWAMI VIVEKANANDA

Swami Vivekananda [Narendranath Dutta (1863–1902)], was an inspiring personality, and is called the patriot saint of modern India. He was also the most prominent disciple of Sri Ramakrishna Paramahamsa. He is considered a key figure in making the western world become aware of the Hindu Philosophic Thought and also revival of Hinduism in modern India.

As a wandering monk he travelled the length and breadth of India, and also many countries of the world. K. Seshadri Iyer, the then Dewan of Mysore described him as: *a magnetic personality and a divine force which were destined to have their mark on the history of the country.*

With an awe inspiring and powerful speech, he introduced Hinduism to the 'Parliament of World Religions' at Chicago in 1893. His thousands of speeches both in India and abroad made tremendous influence on all classes of people of that time. He is widely considered as having inspired India's freedom movement, by instilling a sense of national pride among a whole generation of freedom fighters including Mahatma Gandhi, Tilak and Subhas Chandra Bose. Sri Aurobindo held him as his spiritual mentor.

He founded the 'Ramakrishna Math' to propagate Hindu religion and 'Ramakrishna Mission' for social service.

Swami Vivekananda's Philosophy

Vivekananda believed that the essence of Hinduism is found in Shankara's Advaita Vedanta. But he interpreted religion as a universal experience of transcendent 'Reality', common to all humanity.

This universal conception, frees religion from dogmas, prejudices, temple priests and intolerance. It makes religion a noble pursuit in search of 'supreme knowledge and happiness'. His concept of 'potential divinity of the soul' gives an ennobling concept of man which is termed as 'spiritual humanism'. He summarized the Vedanta philosophy as follows:

Each soul is potentially divine.
The goal is to manifest this divinity through any of the modes – work, worship, psychic control, philosophy – by one, or more, or all of these.
Arise, Awake and Stop not till the goal is reached.
Serving man is serving God.

Jawaharlal Nehru wrote: *Rooted in the past, full of pride in India's prestige, Vivekananda was yet modern in his approach to life's problems, and was a kind of bridge between the past of India and her present....*

3. SRI AUROBINDO

Sri Aurobindo Ghose (1872–1950), was a poet, yogi, scholar and philosopher, besides being a nationalist and freedom fighter. He participated in the freedom movement as a radical and was imprisoned by the British several times. He is said to have many mystical experiences in Jail. The transformation of Aurobindo from political field to spiritual field was gradual. Later he set up an ashram (Aurovile) in Pondicherry and lived there for the rest of his life.

He documented many of his spiritual experiences. Once he visited a Kali temple on the banks of Narmada. He had no faith in image worship. When he looked at the image he felt a divine presence. He wrote afterwards: *With my Europeanized mind I had no faith in image worship and I hardly believed in the presence of God...but in a moment mysteriously, unexpectedly there is instead a Presence, a Power, a Face that looks into yours, an inner sight in you has regarded the World Mother.*

Another such experience in his own words is reproduced below: *Above my head, a mighty head was seen, A face with the calm of immortality, And an omnipotent gaze that held the scene. In the vast circle of its sovereignty. His hair was mingled with the Sun and breeze;*

The world was in his heart and he was I: I housed in me the Everlasting peace. The strength of one who cannot die.

Aurobindo's Evolutionary Philosophy

His philosophy is based on facts, experiences, and personal revelations. He was a true 'Rishi'. His spirituality was based on reason. The goal of his philosophy was not merely liberation of the individual, but work out the will of the Divine, to effect a spiritual transformation to enable the transformed souls to live a divine life on earth.

His main contribution to Indian philosophy is the introduction of the concept of 'evolution' into Vedantic thought. He rejected the *Maya vada* of 'Advaita Vedanta' and advocated the concept of a 'Super Mind'. He says that it is possible to transcend human nature and also to transform it. Then the individual will live in the world as a free and evolved human being with a new consciousness which would spontaneously perceive truth and act with new inner light.

He argues that human kind is not the last rung in the evolution of life. There is potential for human beings to evolve spiritually beyond current limitations of existence to a 'super mental-spiritual' state. He called this state: 'Divine Life on Earth'. He writes: 'Man is a transitional being. He is not final. The step from man to super man is the next approaching achievement and it is the logic of nature's process.'

He believes that 'Brahman' as the absolute reality, is not limited by any mental conception or duality – in form, time or space. It is the Universe, each individual being, material in the Universe and also transcendent beyond the Universe at the same time. Its nature may be described as 'Sat-chit-Aananda' – infinite existence, infinite consciousness, and infinite bliss. This forms the basis of Aurobindo's system of yoga.

Aurobindo argues that 'Man' is born ignorant, and he does not know the nature of Reality. In addition, man experiences life through division and conflict. To overcome these limitations, man must embark on a process of self discovery in which he uncovers the divine nature. This discovery is done through a three step process –

1. *Psychic Transformation:* A search within to discover his evolving soul. He understands the oneness and unity of Creation, and the harmony of all opposites experienced in life.
2. *Spiritual Transformation:* Then his mind expands and experiences knowledge through light, intuition and revelation, culminating in spiritual transformation.
3. *Supra-mental Transformation:* The first two steps lead to the complete transformation of the mind, heart, emotions as well as the physical body.

This evolution enables the soul to fulfil its human aspirations and realization of god. Aurobindo's philosophy, extends beyond the perfection and transformation of the individual. It includes the evolution and transformation of human society in general.

He also laid down the psychological principles and practices of the integral yoga which he called 'Poorna Yoga'. Its aim is to enable the individual to attain a conscious identity with the Divine and transform the mind and body, to spend a divine life on earth.

Works

Sri Aurobindo synthesized both eastern and western philosophies in his writings. He was the first Indian, to create a major literary corpus in English. He wrote commentaries on Vedas, Upanishads and the Gita. His principal philosophical writings are 'The Life Divine' and the 'The Synthesis of Yoga'. Besides, he wrote a number of literary works, the most noted is *'Savitri: A legend and a symbol'*.

4. DR. S. RADHAKRISHNAN

Dr. Radhakrishnan (1888–1975) was a philosopher and a statesman. He was the first Vice President of India (1952–62) and second President of India (1962–67). He was knighted (by the British government) in 1931 and was awarded 'Bharata Ratna' in 1954. His birthday (September 5) is celebrated as 'Teachers day' throughout the country. His son Sarvapelli Gopal is a noted historian.

Radhakrishnan was also chairman of the 'University Education Commission'. In his report he recommended a university education which aimed to help improve the personality of an individual – as the practical means to the creation of an Indian intellectual society which would build and guide India.

Formative Years

He was influenced to a large extent by Advaita of Adi Shankara. Among his contemporaries, he was influenced by Swami Vivekananda and V.D. Savarkar, as well as to some extent by the ideas of theosophical society.

His experiences as a student in Madras Christian College was important as he later recalled: 'The challenge of Christian critics impelled me to make a study of Hinduism, and find out what is living and what is dead with it… I prepared a thesis (which was later published by the Guardian Press) on the ethics of Vedanta, which was intended to be a reply to the charge that Vedanta system had no room for ethics'.

Radhakrishnan's Philosophy

He was well versed both in Indian as well as Western systems of philosophy. He was a deep thinker and an extensive writer on comparative religion and Indian philosophy. He sought to define and defend Hindu religion and sought to demonstrate that 'Hinduism was philosophically coherent and ethically viable'. He is credited with setting right some of the misconceptions that the western thinkers had about Hindu religion and philosophy. He stated that 'Western philosophers, despite all claims to objectivity, were influenced by theological influences of their own culture'.

He based his philosophy within the basic principles of Adi Shankara's 'Advaita Vedanta' and reinterpreted Advaita Vedanta to suit today's world. His philosophy mainly consisted of 'metaphysical idealism'. For Radhakrishnan, man was essentially a subject not object. He contends that man must be transformed to a higher level of existence so that he can evolve to his potential.

Today, man has lost happiness and peace. Life has become artificial and mechanical. He lives in a period of agonizing strain, grave anxiety and manifold disillusionment. But this suffering of life can be transcended. It is the process of spiritual growth. Death is only a condition. It is a change from one life to another. Death terminates the present life of man in order to substitute a new life for it. Because, it is not possible for man to exhaust all potentialities of life, in a single life.

Liberation is a state of freedom. It means the realization of the self in its pure nature. According to Radhakrishnan, Moksha is not an escape from life, but the realization of life's fullest possibilities – the perfection of his personality.

Philosophical Works

He wrote several books on 'Indian Philosophy' and made all out efforts to make the west understand and respect Indian Philosophy.

He wrote commentaries on the 'Prasthana Traya' – Upanishads (1953), Brahma Sutras (1959), and the Gita (1948). Among his most important works are: *Indian Philosophy* (in 2 volumes, 1923), *The Hindu View of Life* (1926), and *A Source Book on Indian Philosophy* (1957). His most appreciated work is *An Idealist View of Life* (1929).

Annexure 3

Sikhism

We neither are Hindus nor Muslims; Our body and life belong to the One supreme Being, who alone is both Ram and Allah for Us.

[Guru Arjun Dev, *Guru Granth Sahib*, Raga Bhairon pp 1136]

Sikhism is a progressive religion and considered as well ahead of its time in its teachings and beliefs, when it was founded over 500 years ago. It preaches a message of devotion, remembrance of God at all times, truthful living, equality of mankind, and social justice. At the same time it denounces superstitions and conduct of blind rituals.

The word 'Sikh' in Punjabi means a disciple. The followers of Sikh religion are the disciples of God and follow the writings and teachings of the Ten Sikh Gurus. The wisdom of these teachings is enshrined in the holy book *Guru Granth Sahib*. The term 'Sikh' is defined as follows:

'Any human being who believes in:

1. *The Immortal Being,*
2. *Ten Gurus from Guru Nanak to Guru Gobind Singh,*
3. *Guru Granth Sahib,*
4. *The Utterances and Teachings of the Ten Gurus,*
5. *The baptism bequeathed by the Tenth Guru, and*
6. *Who does not owe allegiance to any other religion is a Sikh'.*
   [Reht Maryada – Sikh Code of Conduct]

Influence of Hindu Bhakti Movement on Sikhism

The Vaishnava Bhakti movement (as well as the Sufi movements of Shia Muslims), prevalent in medieval India has influenced the Sikh religion to a considerable extent. The role of the Guru is paramount in Bhakti movements as well as Sikhism.

Sikh Gurus adopted the singing of devotional songs in praise of God, from the singing of Bhajans by the followers of Bhakti movements. Sikhism accepted some of the aspects of Bhakti, and admitted some of its practices into its own ordained sect. It lays down spiritual love as the way to God, but it does not recognize any of the Gods (incarnations) worshipped by Hindu saints belonging to the Bhakti movement.

Sikhism recognizes one and only God. God is real in this world (as He has created it), and hence the world is not *Maya*/Illusory. Sikhism also does not accept renunciation of the world in total pursuit of salvation. Many of the Bhakti and Sufi saints are revered and recognized by *Guru Granth Sahib* – the holy book of Sikhs. It includes select writings of several saints of Bhakti movement of North India – Namdev, Ramdas, Jayadeva and several others.

Origins

Sikhism as a religion (as well as a tradition) is directly connected to the history, society and culture of Punjab. Sikhism was founded in the fifteenth century Punjab, on the teachings of Guru Nanak and ten other successive Sikh gurus, known as enlightened leaders.

Khalsa

The tenth Sikh Guru – Guru Gobind Singh established the 'Khalsa' (meaning pure) order, of soldier saints. Khalsas are Sikhs who have undergone the 'Amrit' ceremony. They are ordained to uphold the highest Sikh virtues of commitment, dedication and social consciousness. They strictly follow the 'Sikh Code of Conduct' and wear the prescribed physical articles of faith – the uncut hair (to be covered by men by a turban), and the kirpan (the ceremonial sword).

Guru Granth Sahib

The religious text of the Sikhs *Guru Granth Sahib* written in 'Gurumukhi' script, is also called the 'Eleventh and final Guru' of the Sikhs. The final version of the Granth was compiled by Guru Govind Singh, in 1678. All text within the Granth is known as 'Gurbani'(the word of the Guru) – according to Nanak was revealed by God directly and the authors wrote it down for the followers.

It contains the writings of six of the ten Sikh gurus and includes select writings of many devotees from different socio economic as well as religious backgrounds – Kabir, Sheik Farid, and several others (apart from the names of Hindu saints mentioned earlier).

Guru Granth Sahib is considered unique in the world of religious scriptures, because it is –

1. Accorded the status of being the head of the Sikh religion,
2. Is a poetry of the gurus and
3. It contains the writings of the saints of other faiths, whose thoughts were consistent with that of the Sikh Gurus.

The language used in the Granth is known as 'Sant Bhasa' – a language related to both Punjabi and Hindi, used extensively by proponents of devotional religion in medieval Northern India. The text contains over 5000 hymns which are poetically constructed and set to classical form of music.

The Granth begins with the 'Mula Mantra' – (translated into English it reads) –

One Universal Creator God, The name is Truth, Creative Being Personified, No fear, No hatred, Image of the Timeless One, Beyond Birth, Self Existent, By Guru's Grace.

Gurdwara

Gurdwara means the gateway through which the Guru could be reached. Any place where *Guru Granth Sahib* is installed and treated with respect is referred to as a Gurdwara. Guru Nanak first started this institution which outlines the basic Sikh principles of service, humility and equality. The most important historical and religious centre for Sikhs is the 'Harmandir Sahib' (The Golden Temple), at Amritsar.

Three main functions are carried out in a Gurdwara:

1. Kirthan – singing of hymns from *Guru Granth Sahib*,
2. Katha – reading of *Guru Granth Sahib* with explanations,
3. Langar – Free Community Kitchen.

Along with these main functions, Gurdwaras around the world, also serve the Sikh community in many other ways – establishment of libraries of Sikh religious literature, schools to teach children Gurumukhi and scriptures, charitable community work, etc. Every Gurdwara has a free community kitchen which serves meals to people of all faiths.

Sikhism does not have priests as in other religions. Sikhs have only custodians of the *Guru Granth Sahib* called as 'Granthi'. Any Sikh is free to read the Granth either in Gurdwara or at home. All people of all religions are welcome to visit the Gurdwara.

ESSENCE OF SIKH PHILOSOPHY

> *Deep within the self is the Light of God. It radiates throughout the expanse of His creation. Through the Guru's teachings, the darkness of spiritual ignorance is dispelled. The hearts lotus flower blossoms forth and eternal peace is obtained, as one's light merges into the Supreme Light. [Guru Amar Das]*

The principle beliefs of Sikhism are faith and justice. They are represented by the phrase: *ik onkar* – meaning one God. Sikhism emphasizes equality among all human beings and rejects discrimination on the basis of caste, creed and gender. It gives prominence to living the life of a house holder rather than an ascetic.

The essence of Sikh Philosophy is summarized as follows:

1. There is only one God and he is the same God for all people of all religions.

2. The soul goes through cycles of births and deaths before it reaches human form. The goal of our life is to lead exemplary existence so that one may merge with God. Sikhs should remember God at all times and practice living a virtuous and truthful life while maintaining a balance between their spiritual obligations and temporal obligations.
3. The true path to achieving salvation and merging with God does not require renunciation or celibacy, but living the life of a householder, earning an honest living and avoiding worldly temptations and sins.
4. Sikhism condemns blind rituals, superstitions, worship of the dead, idol worship, etc.
5. People of all races, religions or sex are all equal in the eyes of God. Women are allowed to participate in any religious function, perform any ceremony, or lead the prayer in any congregation.

Concept of God

Sikhism is a monotheistic and 'revealed' religion. God is omnipresent and infinite. Before creation, all that existed was God and his *hukum* (will or order). The cosmos was created by God's will.

While a full understanding of God is beyond human perception, God is omnipresent and visible everywhere to the spiritually awakened. God must be seen from the inward eye of the devotee, who must meditate to progress towards enlightenment.

The beginning of the first composition in the Sikh scripture is the figure '1' – signifying the universality of God.

There are four stages of spiritual evolution:

1. Manmukh – a self centred person, who lives in the material world and does not think of God.
2. Sikh – who sets out on the path of learning and meets the criteria of a Sikh as laid out in Reht Maryada (Official Code of Conduct),

3. Khalsa – Total dedication to Sikhism. One who has shed his ego and honours the memory of Guru Gobind Singh,
4. Gurumukh – One who has achieved Mukti (Salvation) and is totally God-centred.

Truth: 'Realization of Truth is higher than all else. Higher still is truthful living'. The supreme purpose of human life is to reconnect with Truth. Our ego is the biggest obstacle for re-union with Truth (God), and with Guru's grace, the seeker meditates honestly on 'Word' which leads to the end of ego. Human body is just a means to achieve the reunion with Truth. Truth is a form of matter which lies within human body but is beyond the realm of Time/Death.

Maya: Sikhism teaches devotees to pursue a path to salvation which results in spiritual union with god. The difficulties in pursuing this path is attachment to worldly pursuits (termed as Maya), which commit men and women to endless cycle of rebirths (reincarnation). Maya is defined as illusion or unreality, and is considered as an obstacle in the spiritual path to salvation. People get distracted from worldly attractions which give only illusive satisfaction.

Five Evils: The influence of anger, ego, greed, attachment and lust is known as 'Five Evils' which result in separation of the people from God. It can be remedied only through intense devotion.

Guru: Means the teacher and he is considered as the 'Voice of God'. He is the source and guide for knowledge and salvation. Guru is indistinguishable from God. One gets connected with Guru, only with selfless search for Truth. Ultimately the seeker realizes, that it is the consciousness within the body that is the seeker, and the 'Word' is the true Guru.

Nam: A key practice to be pursued in the remembrance of the 'Divine Name'. It is the total exposure of one's being to the divine name. It is also conforming to Dharma (Divine Order). *Nam Simran,* should lead to 'growing towards and into god' through a gradual process of five stages. The last of these is *sach khand* (The Realm of Truth), the final union of the spirit with God.

Salvation: It can be reached through rigorous and disciplined devotion to God. Devotion must take place through the heart, with the spirit and the soul.

A Sikh should balance work, worship and charity. He should defend the rights of all creatures, especially of fellow human beings. Sikh teachings also stress the concept of sharing – through distribution of free food in Gurdwaras, giving charitable donations and working for the good of the community.

Annexure 4

Hindu Religious Concepts

(Associated with Single Numbers)

Numbers have been used throughout Hindu religion and philosophy as symbolism, as well as to interpret and clarify several concepts. A sloka in *Mahabharata* (extracted from Udyoga Parva) expresses the symbolism of numbers beautifully thus:

> *Ekayaa Dwe vinischitya trimshu chaturbhirvarshe Kuru* |
> *Pancha jitva viditvaa shat saptahitva sukhibhava* ||

[Two (What to do and what not to do) has to be decided by one (The mind). Three (Enemy, Friend, and Udaaseena) has to be controlled by four (Sama, Dana, Bheda, Danda). Ensure victory over five (Panchendriyas), and understand six (Sandhi, vigraha, yaana, aasana, dwaidhee-bhaava and samaashraya). Leave seven (woman, gambling, bête, drink, kathora-vachana, kathina-siksha, earning money through improper means) and be happy.]

There are innumerable Hindu religious concepts which require some explanation. I have categorized them according to their number symbolism in this and the next Annexure. For example, zero represents 'Nothing' or 'Shoonya', it also represents 'Nirguna Brahman' and so on; the number 1 is always accepted as a unit and the beginning of a system. It further represents the planet Sun, the Sun God as well as the first syllable 'Om'. The number 2 stands for 'Dvaita' (dualism), choices as well as pairs of several types of concepts. Number 3 stands for the 'trinity' and so on.

The Sankhya school of philosophy tried to convert some philosophical concepts (of the time) into numbers and on the basis of this, tried to explain the concepts of life and liberation.

However, to my knowledge, categorization of Hindu religious concepts, according to their number symbolism, has not been done before, and such an attempt is made in this book for the first time.

Tarot Cards

This religious symbolism of numbers is also found reflected in the Tarot cards which are believed to be of Egyptian origin. But down the ages, these cards imbibed the culture of many religions – Greeks, Romans, the Catholic Church, the concepts of death and reincarnation from Hinduism, etc. Tarot cards have become a most powerful tool in divining the future.

SYMBOLISM OF SHOONYA '0'

Zero, also known as the cipher, is a universal paradox. The concept of 'Shoonya' is India's gift to the world of Mathematics. According to the Upanishads, Zero (Bindu or Shoonya) represents God (as **Nirguna Brahman**) and absence of creation, also called the inactive sublime state of Godhood. 'Shoonya' is also the foundation of Advaita Vedanta as well as Buddhist philosophy.

According to Veerashaiva Sidhanta, when Atman the Soul merges in Shiva, it is described as 'Shoonya' or nothingness. It is also a perpetual state of Shiva Consciousness. In this context, zero also stands for **'Ananta'** – eternity, the infinite, and the Universe. Its mystic nature helps us to understand eternity. Although the value of zero is nil or nothing, in association with other numbers, its value is greatly enhanced as it follows the repetitive principle. For example: 10, 100, 1000, etc.

In numerology the occurrence of a zero represents a pause, a turning point in life, a wait before a new adventure. Again, the combination of zero with any other number metaphysically reduces the power of that number, even though mathematically it may increase its value. In the Tarot deck, zero is represented by a card having the fool (or a jester) represented by a youth who is generally unaware of life's dangers as his life is ruled by fate.

In India, while presenting gifts, one does not give Rs. 10 or Rs. 100, but adds one to make it Rs. 11 or Rs. 101 to make it auspicious and nullify the effect of zero.

SYMBOLISM OF NUMBER 1

Saguna Brahman and 'Om' the First Sound: Number 1 is the first number in the number system. This number represents 'The Creator' also known as 'Saguna Brahman'. 'Om' is considered as the first sound, which emanated in the universe. The number 'One' also symbolizes 'Atman' the Soul. It is said that *the knowledge of the 'Brahman' is to be obtained through 'Omkara' (symbolized as the bow) by using Atman (as the arrow) to reach the target (Brahman) with devotion.*

The Advaita Vedanta depicts the number 1, as one which has no parallel: like the Sun – who lights the entire world, Agni who has the power to burn as no one else can, Indra, the only king of Gods, and 'Iswara' who is omnipotent and omnipresent.

Infinity: Number 1 also represents **'Ananta'** or the infinite, when an infinite number of zeros are added to it, to denote 'infinity'.

The Sun: The number 1 represents 'The Beginning' and also symbolizes the planet Sun. After death, the soul is said to undergo transformation in form from *Vasu* to *Rudra* and finally unite with *Aditya* the Sun God. In Hindu mythology, the Sun is represented by a King riding a chariot drawn by seven horses. These seven horses represent the seven rays of light and the seven days of the week too.

The Sun, as we know, is the centre of the Solar system around which all other planets revolve. It has an assertive, individualistic and proud nature. It influences the intellect. As the Sun is the source of heat and light, the number 1 is considered to be the source of all wisdom and the basis of all numbers. All other numbers are followers of 1 and hence it is the leader of the house. Its symbolic representation is a circle with a point at the centre. It represents all that is creative, individual and positive and stands for force, boldness and creativity.

Characteristics of Number I

While interpreting the characteristics of a person, the number 1 is associated with the mind and indicates good intellectual capacity. Hence, it represents mental pursuits such as knowledge, education, teaching, learning, writing, and literary work. The colours of this number are the colours of the Sun – all shades from the palest yellow to deep orange and golden colours.

SYMBOLISM OF NUMBER 2

Number 2 is the second number in the number system. It is considered to be the female counterpart of 1, as the two together create the third number (1 + 2 = 3). Number 2 stands for balance as well as contrast. It maintains equilibrium through a mixture of positive and negative qualities. It is a symbol of relativity and change.

Prakriti and Purusha: The number two represents the two faces of Nature: *Prakriti* and 'Purusha'. When these two are joined together in *Srishthi* (creation), then male and female (Shiva and Shakti) forms are born.

The Dvaita philosophy is based on 'dualism' – 'Atman' and 'Paramatman' are considered two separate and distinct entities. There is also a very popular question representing dualism – Which came first – 'the egg or the chicken'?

Duality of Concepts: The number two also represents several twin (dual) opposing concepts: 'Jeevatma-Paramatma', 'Chetana- Jada', 'Chara-achara', 'Murtha-amurtha', 'dharma-adharma', 'birth-death', 'day-night', 'light-darkness', 'good-bad', 'sukh-dukh', 'victory-defeat', 'profit-loss', 'heaven-hell', 'Jnan-ajnan', 'Vidya-Avidya', 'Sun-Moon', 'Earth-Sky', 'Cause-Effect', etc.

Gita says that a person's mind should be perfectly serene in the midst of pairs of opposites – cold and heat, joy and sorrow, honour and ignominy, friends and foes, the virtuous and the sinful.

Ayanas: The Hindu year consists of two 'ayanas' (six monthly periods) – 'Uttarayana' and 'Dakshinayana'.

1. *Uttarayana* – A period of 6 months when the Sun seems to move northwards from the Tropic of Capricorn to the Tropic of Cancer – considered as the daytime of the Gods. It starts from the Makara Sankranti festival.
2. *Dakshinayana* – A period of 6 months when the Sun is seen moving to the south of the Tropic of Cancer towards the Tropic of Capricorn – considered as the night time of the Gods.

The period of 'Uttarayana' is considered auspicious. Mahabharata war is said to have taken place in 'Dakshinayana' and hence Bhishma waited till the commencement of 'Uttarayana' to leave his body.

Paksha: There are two pakshas in a month (Shukla – Krishna). Shukla Paksha is the bright half of the Lunar month from new moon to full moon. On the other hand the Krishna Paksha is the second half of Lunar month from full moon to new moon.

Twins: The Hindu philosophy recognizes the importance of several twins (or couple) – the two wheels of a cart for example. Lava and Kusha, Nakula and Sahadeva, and Ashwini devatas are twins. When we utter one name, the other name comes to us automatically. The conversation between 'Astawakra' and 'Vandi' in *Mahabharata*, equates 'Agni with Indra' and 'Narada with Parvata' to indicate that they are inseparable like twins.

Couple: The husband and wife, as a couple are indispensable for running a family. In the same way, the following couples are always thought of together – Rama and Sita, Dushyanta and Shakuntala, Nala and Damayanti, Satyavaan and Savithri; etc.

Similarly there are also other instances, when we think of one person, we also think of the other automatically. When we read *Ramayana*, we find that where there was Rama, we would always find Lakshmana with him. Their relationship has been an ideal model for others to emulate:

Similarly we speak of Rama and Anjaneya, Bharata and Shatrugna, Krishna and Arjuna, Bhima and Arjuna, etc.

Number 2 is symbolized by the Moon. All ancient religions gave importance to the Moon and related it to growth and decline of plant, animal and human life. The rays of the Moon are considered to have the power to cure diseases and prolong life. The Moon is also equated with wisdom and justice. The Moon is related to two numbers (2 and 7) of which 2 gives negative vibration. This is interpreted as the position when the moon is in conjunction with the Sun (New Moon). During this phase, the Moon does not throw reflected light upon the Earth.

In the Tarot deck, the second card is the highest card and is represented by a highly spiritual card showing the 'High Priestess' grasping a scroll containing all the secrets of life. Being very powerful, it is considered especially lucky in Tarot reading. The colours of number 2 are all shades of green, creams and whites.

SYMBOLISM OF NUMBER 3

The number three, stands for comprehension, understanding and judgement. From ancient times, the number 3 was considered the fruit of the union of the first two numbers 1 and 2. The colours of number 3 are all shades of mauve, violet and purple.

It is symbolized by the powerful planet Jupiter, which plays an important role both in astrology and numerology. While Jupiter represents the 'Supreme God' in Roman mythology, the Hindus consider it as 'Guru' from whom all knowledge flows to the disciples. In the Tarot deck, the number 3 card represents the 'Empress' or the 'Mother Earth' and fertility. The card also indicates growth in all things.

As in other religions, in Hindu mythology, religion and philosophy; the number 3 represents several 'Trinity of concepts':

1. Brahma, Vishnu and Maheswara;
2. Lakshmi, Saraswati, and Parvati;
3. The three Vedas (Trayi) – Rig, Yajur, and Sama;
4. The Three Jyotis – Agni, Surya and Chandra,

5. The three gunas – Satva, Rajas, Tamas;
6. The three kalas: (periods of time) – bhoot (past), varthaman (present) and bhavishyat (future);
7. The three states of mind: Jagrat (awake), swapna(dream), and sushupti (deep sleep);
8. The three types of pitru-devatas – pitru, pitamaha, and pra-pitamaha representing the three types of Gods: Vasu, Rudra and Aditya;
9. 'Om Tat Sat' are the three words which describe the universal Brahman,
10. The three 'maatras' (a-u-m) in the sacred sound 'OM';
11. The three karanas – 'Kaya (action), Vacha (speech), and Manasa (mind)'.
12. 'Tri-Sandhya kalas' – the three periods of a day – morning, afternoon and evening, when the 'Gayatri Japa' is performed,
13. The three forms of Shakti – Iccha, Jnana, Kriya;
14. The three states of being: Srishthi (birth), Sthithi (being), and Laya (death);
15. The three steps taken by Vishnu as Vamana to end Bali's reign;
16. The three worlds – Swarga (Heaven), Matsya (Earth), and Patala (Nether world);
17. The three Agnis: Garhapatya, Dakshina, Ahavaniya;

Shiva is also known as '*Trinetra*'. Sun, Moon and Agni are also interpreted as the three eyes of Shiva. *The yagnopavita has three threads.* All animals are classified into three types as those belonging to land, water and sky – Bhuchar, Jalchar, and Khechar; The Hell is supposed to have only three entrances – Kama, Krodha and Lobha (Gita 16.21).

Other examples of trinity of concepts: The three phases of the Moon; the three dimensions of Space (length, breadth and height); the three states of matter (Solid, Liquid and Gas), the three sides of a triangle. Force, Matter and Consciousness is also treated as a trinity.

Dattatreya (who has 3 Avatars) is considered to be the combined incarnation of the Trinity of Gods – Brahma, Vishnu and Shiva and signifies the unity of the three aspects of Creation, Preservation and Destruction of the Supreme Brahman. He has 4 dogs which symbolise the four Vedas and a cow which symbolizes the Mother Earth.

Trivarga Sidhanta: Manu-smriti advocates a harmonious balance between Dharma (code of conduct), Artha (acquisition of wealth) and Kama (fulfillment of desires). Acquirement of wealth and fulfillment of desires must conform to Dharma. Artha and Kama become 'Purusharthas' only when they conform to Dharma. (Chapter 3)

The 'Madhu Parka' which was used to welcome a guest in ancient times had three ingredients – Ghee, Curd and Honey – the mixture was served to the guest in a brass vessel.

'Prayag' is the meeting point (Triveni- sangam) of the three sacred rivers: Ganga, Yamuna and the mythical Saraswati. Here Saraswati is also known as 'Gupta-gamini'. Hence 'Prayag' is also known as 'Teertha-Raj'.

Characteristics of Vishnu, Shiva and Surya: Among the three most important Gods, Vishnu is known as 'Alankara-priya', Shiva is known as 'Abhisheka-priya' and Surya is known as 'Namaskara-priya'.

Trivaram Satyam: It is believed that which is said thrice becomes true. For emphasizing a point we repeat a word or a sentence thrice. In the Court of Law, also one who takes the witness stand, has to say: 'I will speak the truth, the whole truth and nothing but the truth'.

The third time happening of any event is considered to be lucky; as the popular saying goes – 'third time lucky'. In an auction room, it is natural to call the last bid three times before the fall of the hammer. Vows are repeated by couples three times.

'Om Shanti, Shanti, Shanti-hi': We chant 'shanti' thrice to emphasize our intense desire for peace. It is chanted aloud the first time addressing the unseen forces. It is chanted softer and milder the second time directed to our immediate surroundings and those who are in our proximity. It is chanted as a whisper the last time as it is directed to one-self.

Tapatrayas: All obstacles and problems originate from three sources:

1. *Adi-daivika:* The unseen divine forces over which we have no control – natural calamities like floods, earthquakes, tsunami, etc.
2. *Adi-bhoutika:* The physical factors around us which happen daily – accidents, crime, pollution, etc.
3. *Aadhyatmika:* Problems which arise from our bodies and minds – diseases, jealousy, anger, frustration, etc.

Achamana

Achamana is a ritual (performed as a part of Sandhya-Vandana or any other ritual) in which the person performing it takes spoonfuls of water three times chanting the names of (Keshava, Narayana, Madhava or Rig, Yajur and Sama Vedas) and sips water chanting God's name.

SYMBOLISM OF NUMBER 4

Even though number 4 is considered the twin to number 1, it has a distinct character of its own. It is the first square number (as $2 \times 2 = 4$) in the number series of perfect squares. Its solidity is represented by the geometrical figure 'Square'. It represents the four concepts of 'Reality, Concentration, Thought and Perception.

4 is represented by the Sun in its negative aspect in the Western System and by 'Rahu' in the Indian System of astrology and numerology. Hence it is not considered a fortunate number. It is written as '4 – 1'. The fourth house in astrological birth chart of a person indicates happiness. It is also an indicator of the person possessing innate capacities and a proper balance of mind.

In the Tarot deck, the number is represented by 'The Emperor' card and represents stability, protection and success through discipline. But the Emperor also represents an authority to be feared and respected. It also means a number 4 person is not easy to influence as he follows his own judgement. The colours of number 4 are all shades of grey fawn, and electric shades.

Dharma: Four is the number of Hindu 'Sanatana Dharma'. Dharma is supposed to walk on four legs. Yagna, Adhyayana, Dana, and Tapas are the four important aspects of Dharma. Vedas which constitute Hindu Dharma are also four in number (This includes Atharva Veda which was not originally considered as a part of 'Trayi'). The 4 Vedas are also described as the entrances to the 'Chintamani griha' of 'Devi Lalita Tripura-sundari'. Most of the Hindu gods are shown with four hands because they enforce 'Dharma'.

'Ashramas' The four Ashramas are – Brahmacharyashrama, Grihasthashrama, Vanaprasthashrama and Sanyasashrama. These are explained in Chapter 3 (Dharma).

Neeti Sutra (Code of Ethics)

According to Code of Ethics, 'Sama (Concilation), Dana (Liberality), Bheda (creating dissention), and Danda (punishment)' are the suggested four ways of bringing round a man. The last one is resorted, when the first three fail. These are also the four essential qualities for a king for ruling his kingdom justly.

The Four Yugas

The Hindu Scriptures divide Earth's time into 4 periods – known as the Yugas – Krita, Treta, Dwapara and Kali. Krita Yuga (also known as Satya Yuga) is considered to be period of truth and righteousness. Each Yuga lasts for several thousands of years and we are now in Kali Yuga. However, there is difference opinion as to their extent. One estimate puts Krita at 17,28,000 years, Treta at 12,96,000 years, Dwapara at 86,400 years and Kali at 43,200 years.

Chaturmasya Vrata

This is mainly followed by 'Sanyasis' for four months from 'Ashadha Pournima'. This period corresponds to the rainy season and ancients believed that it was not wise for people to travel in this season due to swollen rivers and swamps. Hence the Sanyasis and followers of this Vrata, stayed in a place and conducted this Vrata.

In this Vrata, consumption of the following is prohibited – Vegetables in the first month, Curds in the second month, Milk in the third month, and Pulses in the fourth month. This is supposed to enable them to meditate with more concentration.

Dhanur-Vidya

It is also known as 'Dhanur-Veda'. It has four parts called 'padas': Sutra, Shiksha, Prayoga and Rahasya. There are also four types of Dhanur-Vidya:

1. *Pani-Mukta:* Basic Dhanur-Vidya relating to 'Bana-prayoga'.
2. *Amukta:* Using only 'Mantra-Shakti' relating to prayoga of Khadga, Dhwaja, etc. and creating fear among opponents.
3. *Muktaa-mukta:* Dhanur-Vidya relating to maha-astra-prayoga which can be controlled with 'Upa-samhara'.
4. *Mantra-mukta:* Astra-prayoga along with maha-mantra, which has no upa-samhara.

Number 4 has deep religious associations all over the world. The number 4 also represents several practical concepts in Hinduism:

1. The four *Purusharthas* (human ends) are – Dharma (following the religious path), Artha (wealth), Kama (desire) and Moksha (freedom from rebirth);
2. Gayatri Mantra is divided into *four padas* – A oum, tatsavitur-varenyam, bhargodevasya dhimahi, dhiyoyonaha prachodayat.
3. According to 'Shaakta mata', Para, Pashyanti, Madyamaa, and Vaikhari are the *four stages of speech ('Vaak').*
4. The *chatur-mukha-Brahma* has four faces.
5. The four components of army (foot soldiers, horses, elephants and chariots) are known as *chaturanga bala* in ancient Indian military parlance; (For details see Annexure 8)
6. *The four elements – Earth, Air, Fire and Water* were considered necessary for human life.
7. We also have the Four Seasons *(Spring, Summer, Autumn, and Winter).*

SYMBOLISM OF NUMBER 5

The number 5 is a versatile and mercurial number and is symbolized by the planet Mercury. 5 is associated with quick silver, with its well known volatile qualities. It is a number of variety and adaptability. It deals with the material factors of life. 5 was held in great veneration by the ancients and was considered a magical number. It is said to stand for humanity and human relations.

In the Tarot deck, the number is represented by the 'High Priest' who sits before the keys of the Vatican to unlock the knowledge of God. The colours of number 5 are all shades of silver grey and glistening white and glittering materials.

Meaning of the Word 'Pancha'

In Sanskrit, 'Pancha' is attributed with two different meanings - one represents the number five, and the other means vastness. For example lion is known as *Pancha-sya* as its face is wider than its other body parts. According to Madhva, the Universe is called 'Pra-Pancha' because of the existence of five fundamental differences (Pancha Bheda).

Death is also known as *Panchatvam gataha,* as after death, the body becomes one with the five elements: earth, water, fire, air and sky. Bhagavata Purana interprets 'Bramhanda' as belonging to the number 5: *Pancha-bhihi, Pancha-bihi Brahma...*

SHIVA

Five is the sacred number of Shiva. 'Panchakshari' (Namah Shivaya) is the sacred mantra of Shiva. Shiva's body is said to contain five mantras called 'Pancha brahma'. As forms of Shiva, each form has its own name and distinct iconography: Sadyojata, Vamadeva, Aghora, Tatpurusha, Ishana. These forms are represented as five faces of Shiva and are associated with the five elements (Pancha-bhutas), five senses, five organs of perception, and five organs of action.

'Pancha-Brahma Upanishad'says: *One should know all things of the phenomenal world as of a fivefold character, for the reason that the eternal verity of Shiva is of the character of the fivefold Brahman.*

In South India, the following five temples of Shiva are considered to be particularly important, as manifestations of Shiva as the five elements:

	Form of Shiva	Manifestation	Location	State
1	Jambukeshwar	Water	Trichy	Tamil Nadu
2	Arunachaleswar	Fire	Tiruvannamalai	Tamil Nadu
3	Kalahastheeswara	Air	Sri Kalahasti	Andhra Pradesh
4	Ekambareswar	Earth	Kanchi	Tamil Nadu
5	Nataraja	Sky	Chidambaram	Tamil Nadu

Pancha-Brahma: Lalita Sahasranama calls the following 5 Gods as Pancha-Brahma – Brahma, Vishnu, Rudra, Iswara and Sadashiva. Goddess Lalita is said to sit on a cot with Brahma, Vishnu, Rudra, and Iswara as its 4 legs; and Sadashiva as its plank. These Pancha-Brahmas are also known as 'Pancha-pretas' as they get the 'Kriya-Shakti' only by the grace of Goddess Lalita - Brahma for creation, Vishnu for preservation, Rudra for death, Iswara for total destruction and Sadashiva for giving Anugraha.

The 'Pancha-Krityas' are also described as Srishthi (creation), Sthithi (preservation), Samhara (destruction), Tirodhana (total destruction) and Anugraha (back to original state).

PANCHA NARAYANA TATAVAS

Representation of God	Five Elements	Pancha Tanmatras	Pancha Jnanendriyas	Pancha Karmendriyas	Pancha Pranas	Pancha Angulis
Narayana	Akash	Sound	Ear	Vak	Prana	Angustha
Vasudeva	Vayu	Touch	Skin	Pani	Apana	Tarjani
Sankarshana	Agni	Roopa	Eye	Pada	Vyana	Madhyama
Pradyumna	Apah	Rasa	Tongue	Payu	Udana	Anamika
Anirudha	Prithvi	Gandha	Nose	Upastha	Samana	Kanistha

Pancha-Bhutas

This is an important doctrine that took shape in Rig-Veda and early Upanishads – 'Pancha-bhutas' – Earth, Water, Air, Sky and Fire. The human body is regarded as the combination of the Pancha-bhutas and the soul. In 'Susruta Samhita', there is an integrated exposition of the way in which the Pancha-bhutas shape the human body from its very conception:

1. *Earth (Prithvi):* The Earth sustains all beings and nourishes them. The mountains, the rivers, the trees and vegetation – all give themselves for the welfare of all beings that reside on the Earth.
2. *Air (Vayu): Vayu* is verily the Brahman (Pratyaksha Brahma) – the source of life for all beings, without which we cannot live. Air absorbs as well as purifies everything. It remains unseen, quiet, and unobtrusive. Though it roams everywhere, it never gets attached to anything. Scriptures point out that we must move in the world unattached like the wind. Dvaita calls *Vayu* as 'Jivottama (the Lord of Life)'.
3. *Sky/Space (Akash):* It accommodates everybody and everything as it is vast and unlimited (just like the true nature of the self).
4. *Water (Aap):* Water is cool and refreshing. When we drink, it gives us energy and when we bath, it purifies as well as refreshes us.
5. *Fire (Agni):* Fire is bright, brilliant and is always ever moving upward. It consumes everything and purifies them by burning. It also remains unaffected by whatever it touches.

The characteristics of Pancha-bhutas are:

	Bhuta (Element)	**Characteristic (Guna)**
1.	*Akash* (Sky)	*Shabd* (Sound)
2.	*Vayu* (Air)	*Shabdh and Sparsh* (Touch)
3.	*Agni* (Fire)	*Shabdh, Sparsh and Rupa* (Form)
4.	*Aap* (Water)	*Shabdh, Sparsh, Rupa and Rasa* (Liquid)
5.	*Prithvi* (Earth)	*Shabdh, Sparsh, Rupa and Rasa and Gandha* (Smell)

(Kaala, Dikku, Atma, Manas are considered as additional bhutas + additional Tatvas according to Tarkika mata)

Sri Krishna says that there are only five reasons for an event to happen in this world: body, earth, Atman, Indriyas and God. *Adhisthanam tatha karta....panchamam* (Gita 18.14).

Pancha Pandavas: In *Mahabharata*, we are familiar with the Pancha Pandavas – Dharmaraja, Bhima, Arjuna, Nakula and Sahadeva. Incidentally 'Draupadi' is also known as 'Panchali'. Upa-Pandavas are also five in number. They are the sons of Pandavas born out of Draupadi – Prati-vindhya (from Dharmaraja), Suta-Soma (from Bhima), Sruta-Karma (from Arjuna), Sataa-neeka (from Nakula), Sruta-sena (from Sahadeva).

Pancha-Yagnas: The Shastras divide the daily obligatory yagnas (sacrifices) into five types:

1. *Brahma yagna* - relates to Veda-adyahana and adhyapana – study of Vedas, performance of Sandhya, and Gayatri Japa, etc.
2. *Deva yagna* – relates to performing 'Agnihotra' and offering of 'havis' to Gods through, yaga, homa and Havana.
3. *Pitru yagna* – relates to offering of tarpana, shraadha, pinda-pradana, etc. to ancestors,
4. *Bhuta yagna* – relates to looking after and offering food to the aged and sick people, animals/birds, Bali-vaisvadeva, etc.
5. *Manushya yagna* – showing love and respect to fellow human beings and help them when in need, entertainment and feeding of guests, poor people, etc.

The following are also considered Pancha-yagnas: Agnihotra, Darshpoorna, Chaturmasya, Pashu, Soma-yagna.

In Hindu mythology and religion, the number 5 represents several other concepts as well:

1. The human body contains the 'Pancha-koshas' – Annamaya, Pranamaya, Manomaya, Vignanamaya, and Anandamaya.
2. Scriptures relate five Gurus as: Father, Mother, Agni, Atman and Guru who gives knowledge.
3. *Pancha Pativratas:* A pativrata is a holy woman who is faithful to her husband in thought, word and deed. The five 'pativratas'

are – Ahalya, Draupadi, Sita, Tara and Mandodari. Reciting their names every day is supposed to bring 'Punya' to the concerned person.

4. 'Manmatha' the god of love carries five arrows.
5. The five mathras are – gandha, rasa, rupa, sparsha and sound;
6. 'Panchamruta' consists of the five types of pure food items – Milk, Curd, Ghee, Sugar (Jaggery) and Honey, which is used in anointing ('abhishekha') of the deities.
7. *Panchagavya* – This relates to the five things given by the sacred cow in the Hindu religion – *Gomutra, Gomaya, Milk, Curd,* and *Ghee – are* used to purify the human body.
8. According to Hindu Dharma, the following five things help a person gain respect in his community: wealth, age, relations, achievements and Jnana (knowledge).
9. The five essential characteristics of a married woman: Sindhoor, Mangalya Sutra, Bangles, Nose ring and Silver ring on the second finger of the right foot.
10. The Pancha pranas (*vayus*) are– prana, apana, vyana, udana, and samana;
11. The five sacred things required in worship are – Gandha, Pushpa, Dhoopa, Deepa and Naivedya.
12. *The Hindu panchanga* has five essential elements – 'Vara, tithi, nakshatra, yoga and karana'. The kala nirnaya – the decision on time, in Hindu system is also based on these five elements.
13. *Jnanendriyas* and *Karmendriyas:* The Manu-Smriti calls the five sensory organs – ears, skin, eyes, tongue, and nose as Jnanendriyas. The other five organs (which are organs of action) – the anus, generative organ, mouth, hands and feet are called 'Karmendriyas'.
14. *The Pancha Mudras:* The followers of Madhvacharya and certain Vaishnava sects wear the following five mudras on their body: Shankha, Chakra, Gada, Padma, and Narayana.
15. Pancha Sarovar: Manasa Sarovar (Himalayas), Pushkar, Bindu Sarovar, Pampa Sarovar (Karnataka), Narayan Sarovar (Kutch);

16. The sacred River Saraswati is formed by the meeting of the 5 rivers: Suprabha, Kanchana, Prachi, Nanda, Vishalika.
17. *Panchagnis:* Garhpatya, Dakshinagni, Ahavaniya, Sabhya, Avatathya;
18. The five rivers which flow west (Paschima Vahini) – Vipasha (Biyas), Airavati (Ravi), Vitasta (Jhelum), Chandra-bhaga (Chinab), and Shatadru (Sutluj);

Evolution

The Hindu mythology interprets the evolution of human beings in five stages. The first five 'avatars' of Lord Vishnu pertains to these five stages:

1. *Matsya* (Fish) – indicates the evolution of beings living in water (Jalachar).
2. *Koorma* (Tortoise) – indicates the evolution of beings which could travel over both land and water (Ubhayachar).
3. *Varaha* (Boar) – indicates the evolution of land beings (bhuchar).
4. *Narasimha* – indicates the evolution of beings which were half human and half animal.
5. *Vamana* – indicates the evolution of man in complete form.

Pancha Teerthas: Pushkar, Kurukshetra, Gaya, Ganga, and Prabhas; There are 3 Pushkar Sarovars – Jestha Pushkar (Presiding Deity – Brahma), Madhya Pushkar (Presiding Deity – Maha Vishnu), Kanistha Pushkar (Presiding Deity: Rudra);

Classification of Slaves

The 'Artha Shastra' classifies slaves (Gulams) into 5 categories:

1. Dhwajahruta (slave captured in war)
2. Atma-vikrayi (a person who sells himself to raise funds – ex. Harish-Chandra)
3. Garbha-dasa (child born to a dasi)

4. Ahitaka (Person who cannot repay loans and hence becomes a slave)
5. Danda-Praneeta (Person who becomes a slave, as a result of punishment imposed by a King).

Narada Smriti adds one more classification – slave obtained through Dyuta (Gambling). These slaves could be sold, mortgaged, played as wealth in gambling, etc.

SYMBOLISM OF NUMBER 6

The mathematical characteristic of 6 is that it contains the basic three numbers 1, 2 and 3 ($1 + 2 + 3 = 6$ and $1 \times 2 \times 3 = 6$). 6 is the symbol of dependability. It is in harmony with nature and considered a perfect number because it is divisible both by an even number (2) as well as by an odd number (3). It is the middle number in the trinity of numbers (3, 6, and 9). Six is also associated with the study of the occult: telepathy, divination, fortune telling, etc.

In the Tarot deck, the number 6 card represents the 'Lovers' card. It stands for love affairs and also relationships involving friends and relatives. The colours of the number 6 are all shades of blue.

Venus is the ruling planet of this number. It is commonly known as the 'morning star' and is seen as a radiant planet in the eastern morning sky before sunrise. It can also be seen by the naked eye just after sunset. The planet has two interpretations in Hindu mythology–

1. One denotes a fair complexioned youth representing love and sensuality,
2. The other denotes an elderly sage 'Shukracharya' the teacher of the 'Asuras'.

Venus is also known as 'Shukra' (meaning semen) in Sanskrit, and hence represents the sensuous side of human nature. Its attributes are romance, beauty, sexual pleasure and pursuit of the arts such as Music, Poetry, Dance, Fine Arts, etc. In Roman mythology, Venus represents the Goddess of love.

Arishadvargas (Six Cardinal Sins)

The 'Manu-smriti' advocates control of the senses (Indriya-nigraha) as a charioteer controls his horses. The control of the human instincts leads to controlling the six cardinal sins (durgunas) also known as 'arishad-vargas' which impede the spiritual progress of man: Kama (desire), Krodha (anger), Lobha (greed), Moha (passion), Mada (pride), and Matsarya (enmity). These six enemies within oneself need to be conquered through 'Indriya-nigraha'.

Gayatri Mantra: For the purpose of performing 'anga-nyasa and kara-nyasa' the mantra is divided into six words – Om tasavituhu, varenyam, bhargodevasya, dhimahi, dhiyoyonaha, prachodayat.

Shaastanga Namaskar: Prostrating fully with all the six organs of the body – the feet, knees, stomach, chest, forehead and arms touching the ground in front of the Gods or the elders.

Athathaiyis are those people who commit the following 6 sins –

1. Taking away others wealth by unfair means,
2. Burning others to death,
3. Killing unarmed people,
4. Taking away wealth and wives of others,
5. Taking others' lands/property by force,
6. Putting chaste women to shame.

Other Concepts associated with the number 6 are:

1. The number six symbolizes the human mind. The mind is the sixth sense organ with six faculties – reason, emotion, thought, awareness, knowledge, and intelligence.
2. Skanda is known to have six faces (Shanmukha).
3. The Shadakshari mantra of Lord Shiva *Om Namah Shivaya* has six characters.
4. There are six Hindu Schools of Philosophy (Shad-Darshanas – See Chapter 5).
5. Shat Darshanas are also interpreted as – Shaiva, Vaishnava, Shaakta, Soura, Ganapatya, and Skanda. The followers of these cults worship their respective gods prominently.

6. A king in ancient India was entitled to one-sixth of the produce from the farmers as his share.
7. An ideal Indian woman is supposed to have six qualities: Dasi (in work), Manthri (in advice), Mata (in feeding), Rambha (in bed), Dharitri (in excusing lapses), and Laksmi (in beauty);
8. The six seasons (ruthus) are; Vasantha, Greeshma, Varsha, Sharat, Hemant, and Sishira;
9. *Shadguna*: The six gunas: Samagra Jnana (complete knowledge), Aishwarya (wealth), Vairagya (Renunciation), Bala (Strength), Yashas (renown), dharma (religious path),
10. Kalika purana describes the six characteristics of 'Bhaga' as Aishwarya, Dharma, Yashas, Shri, Jnana and Vignan.
11. The six auxiliaries of Vedas are Shiksha (accent, pronunciation), Vyakarana (grammar), Chandas (prosody), Nirukta (etymology), Jyotisha (astrology), and Kalpa (sacrificial and social rules).
12. These six give happiness to an individual - Artha (wealth), Aarogya (health), Priya Bhaarya (good wife), Vashyascha putra (obedient son), Arthakari-cha-Vidya (suitable Vidya which helps in acquiring wealth).

SYMBOLISM OF NUMBER 7

The number 7 is considered a spiritual and sacred number in the Hindu tradition. Ancient man believed in the magical influence of 7 and the seven planets on human life. History is replete with examples showing the importance of 7 in the scheme of things. In every religion and culture, 7 stands for the manifestation of the mysterious force of nature. Through the study of the mysterious, it explores the unknown. *Saptamam Daiva Chintanam* is one of the popular sayings in Hindu scriptures.

It is symbolized by the full Moon in its positive aspect. In this position, it is exactly opposite to the Sun and reflects the full light of the Sun on the Earth. However, in the Hindu tradition, Kethu (the southern node of the Moon) is considered as the ruling planet of 7. Kethu is depicted as a headless torso with the body of a fish. It is also considered as 'Moksha-karak' (Brahma-manasa putra) in the Hindu tradition. This aspect helps a person to detach himself from worldly affairs and move towards spirituality.

Number 7 is also represented by the crescent moon (as in Tarot Cards), as each phase of the moon is completed in 7 days and 7 is considered as the number that governs the underlying rhythm of the universe. In the Tarot deck, it represents the 'Chariot' which stands for movement and progress, and gives the charioteer a choice to choose between paths of good and evil. The colours of the number 7 are all shades of green and pale shades.

When any number is divided by seven, the result is an infinite series. Hence seven is considered to have a close relationship with 'Anantatva' (eternity). Ancients believed that 7 was the only number capable of dividing the number of eternity. If for example, 1,000,000 is divided by 7, we get 142857. If more zeros are added to1 and divided by 7, the number 142857 keeps recurring which from time immemorial has been considered a 'sacred number'. If the digits in this number are added we get 27, which by further addition yield a 9.

Surya, the Sun God rides on a chariot drawn by seven horses, each one corresponding to a particular colour (Varna) , energy (Shakti) and day of the Hindu week. Surya or Aditya also represents 'Paratatva' or the supreme Brahman. The seven horses also represent the Sapta Jivas or Sapta pranahs.

The lotus which cannot be crossed with other plants and flowers has seven petals. Buddha, Goddess Lakshmi and several other Gods in Hindu Mythology are always seen sitting on the lotus as it is considered pure.

Seven is represented in nature in several ways –

1. The seven days of the week,
2. There are seven original notes in the Classical Indian musical scale: Sa (Shadja), Ri (Rishabha), Ga (Gandhara), Ma (Madhyama) , Pa (Panchama), Da (Daiwata), and Ni (Nishada);
3. The seven colours (VIBGYOR) merging to form the colour white,

4. The seven continents,
5. The seven wonders of the ancient world,

The number 7 appears very frequently in Hindu scriptures –Sapta Jivas, Sapta dhatus, Sapta dwipas, Sapta sagaras, Sapta lokas, The genealogy in Hindus is calculated for seven generations.

Other Important religious concepts relating to 7 are:

1. The seven steps (sapta-padi) the bride and bridegroom undertake during a Hindu marriage, each one owing allegiance to the other in this life.
2. Sapta Puris' (the seven holy places) are – Ayodhya, Mathura, Maya (Haridwar), Kashi, Kanchi, Avantika-Puri, Dwaravati, – by visiting these places one is supposed to obtain 'Moksha'.
3. The 'Shakti-Chakras' are also seven in number: Muladhara, Swadhisthana, Manipura, Anahata, Vishudhi, Agna and Sahsrara;
4. The sacred rivers are seven: Ganga, Yamuna, Saraswati, Godavari, Narmada, Sindhu and Kaveri;
5. In ancient days the guests were treated with seven kinds of 'satkaras' – Gandha, Pushpa, Dhoopa, Deepa, Naivedya, Achamana, and Tambula.
6. The Veena has seven strings.
7. The ancients had classified seven types of animals that could be domesticated and seven other types that belonged to the forest.
8. *Ratha Saptami* is a festival celebrated on Magha Shukla Saptami. On that day Narayana is worshipped in 'Suryamandala': *Dheyassada Savitrumandala madhyavarthi...*

Sapta Lokas

According to scriptures, the cosmos is divided into 14 parts called Lokas, 7 above the earth and 7 below. The 7 lokas above the earth are – Bhuh, Bhuvah, Suvah, Mahah, Janah, Tapah, and Satya. These seven worlds are said to correspond to seven planes of consciousness in our bodies.

They also correspond to the 7 chakras in the human body as also the seven planets in the Solar System. The seven Lokas below the earth are – Atala, Vitala, Sutala, Talatala, Rasatala, Mahatala and Patala.

Sapta-Shati /Sapta Matrukas

The 'Durga Sapta Shati' (which consists of 700 slokas) refers to Sapta matrukas, the seven manifestations of Durga – Bramhani, Maheswari, Kaumari, Vaishnavi, Varahi, Chamundi (Narasimhi) and Indri. As their names suggest they are the shaktis (energies) of Brahma, Shiva, Kumara (Skanda), Vishnu, Varaha, Narasimha, and Indra respectively.

Chiranjivis

The 'chiranjivis' (immortals – who have no death) are seven in number – Aswathama, Bali, Vyasa, Anjaneya, Vibhishana, Krupa and Parasurama.

Aswathama Balirvyaso Hanumamscha Vibhishanah |
Kripah Parasuramashcha Saptaite Chirjeevinah ||

Sapta-Rishis

There are also 'Sapta-Rishis' sages: Kashyapa, Atri, Vasistha, Viswamitra, Gautama, Jamdagni, Bhardwaja. Some scriptures name Marichi, Atri, Angiras, Pulastya, Pulah, Kratu and Vasistha as the Sapta-rishis – symbolized by a 'Sapta-rishi Mandala' (constellation of stars known as 'Ursa Major'). They are also known as 'Brahma's manasa putras'.

Ramayana

Ramavatar is the seventh avatar among 'Dashavatara (incarnations) of Lord Vishnu. The sacred work *Ramayana* is divided into seven chapters called 'Kandas'. Rama is said to have been born in 'punarvasu' the seventh star. The war between Rama and Ravana was fought for seven days, according to some scholars.

[Valmiki's story gives us a wonderful lesson. It is the responsibility of the head of the family to earn and take care of his family. But if

he earns through unlawful or wicked means, the sins committed by him are his alone and are not shared by his family.]

SYMBOLISM OF NUMBER 8

8 is the first cube ($2 \times 2 \times 2 = 8$) in the series of cubes. 8 stands for solidity and perfection. It is represented by a double square. When halved its parts are equal (4 and 4). When halved again, its parts are still equal {(2, 2); (2, 2)}. Hence, it shows a four-fold balance.

The number 8 also represents two worlds – the material and the spiritual. It is also a number associated with fate and signifies completion, old age, decadence and death. 8 is symbolized by the malefic planet Saturn and consequently with unhappy characteristics. Saturn is a slow moving planet as it takes 30 months to cross each house of the zodiac, and hence causes things to happen very slowly. Its effects are felt for a longer period of time than the effects of any other planet.

In the Tarot deck, the card number 8 is named 'Strength' and represents man's domination of the animal kingdom. From ancient times, 8 is symbolized by irrevocable fate both in the lives of individuals and nations. The colours of the number 8 are all dark shades.

Asta-Vasus

The number eight symbolizes the division of space and divinities into constituent parts. In the earliest Vedic texts we find reference to eight 'Adityas' (Asta-vasus) – Mitra, Varuna, Aryaman, Amia, Bhaga, Dhatar, Indra and Vivasvat. In the Vedas we also find reference to eight 'Rudras' – Bhava, Sarva, Ishana, Pasupathi, Bhima, Ugra, Mahadeva and Rudra – who were the monsoon gods of thunder and rain and who were much feared by the Vedic people as the monsoon rains brought all sorts of problems – diseases, sickness, death, destruction of properties and agricultural crops, etc.

Krishna is considered the eighth 'avathar' among the 'Dashavatars' of Lord Vishnu. He was also the eighth child born to his mother Devaki. He was also born on the eighth day (asthami) of 'krishna paksha.' The sacred

'Narayana manthra' is also an asthakshari: *Om Namo Narayanaya.*

Ashta Siddhis: The sacred 'Ashta Siddhis' are also eight in number: These also represent the eight different aspects of God – the Supreme –Being:

> *Anima Garima chaiva Laghima Mahima tatha* |
> *Praptihi Prakamyam-ishitvam vashitvam chastha siddhyaha* ||

1. *Anima*: Ability to become smaller than an atom,
2. *Garima*: Ability to become bigger and heavier than a mountain,
3. *Laghima*: Ability to become lighter than air,
4. *Mahima*: Ability to show 'bruhat swaroop' – become bigger than the sky,
5. *Prapthi*: Ability to reach 'Chandra-mandala' as also obtain objects,
6. *Prakamya*: Ability to obtain any desired object through sankalpa,
7. *Ishitva*: Ability to acquire control over all physical entities,
8. *Vashitva*: Ability to take control of desired entities including animals and human beings.

By maintaining purity in thought and action, and by dedication, it is possible for a person to obtain one or two of the above siddhis. However, it is extremely rare for any one person to acquire all the eight siddhis. Only Anjaneya and a few Rishis are said to have acquired all the eight siddhis.

Ashta Lakshmis: The different forms of Lakshmi are also eight in number – *Adi-Lakshmi, Dhanya-Lakshmi, Dhairya-Lakshmi, Gaja-Lakshmi, Santana-Lakshmi, Vijaya-Lakshmi, Vidya-Lakshmi, Dhana-Lakshmi.* Vishnu is also known to have eight shaktis.

Ashta Dikpalakas

The directions are also eight in number. The presiding deities of these directions are known as 'Ashta-dikpalakas': They are:

1. East – Indra,
2. South-East –Agneya (Agni),

3. South – Dakshina (Yama),
4. South-West: Niruthya (Niruthi),
5. West – Paschima (Varuna),
6. North-West: Vayuvya (Vayu),
7. North – Uttara (Kubera),
8. North-East – Ishanya (Ishana).

These deities play an important role in Hindu 'Vastu-shastra' and temple construction.

Eight Types of Marriages

The ancient Hindu religion recognized eight types of marriages (Vivahs) – Bramha, Daiva, Arsha, Prajapatya, Asura, Gandharva, Rakshas, and Paishacha.

1. *Brahma Vivah* – The father of the girl searching for a suitable groom and arranging the marriage of the girl with the groom,
2. *Daiva Vivah* – A girl given away to a priest at the end of a yaga or a yagna as 'Dakshina'.
3. *Arsha Vivah* – The girl's father takes a pair of oxen or some such valuable gift and gives the girl to the groom,
4. *Prajapatya Vivah* – Marriage made between the boy and the girl, with the intention that the couple will lead religious lives,
5. *Asura Vivah* – The bridegroom collecting a mutually agreed fixed amount from the bride's father and marrying,
6. *Gandharva Vivah* – The boy and the girl marrying by mutual consent,
7. *Rakshas Vivah* – The groom fighting a battle and then carrying off the girl and marrying without the girl's consent,
8. *Paishacha Vivah* – When everybody at the girl's home is sleeping, kidnapping the girl and marrying.

Swayamvara: Apart from the above 8 types of marriages, there was also a system of marriage – prevalent among the then royal families and also (kshatriyas – warrior class) – in which the princess chose (by garlanding) her husband, from among the young princes invited for the purpose. It was also customary to hold a sport among the princes to determine their prowess in the use of weapons.

Ashta Mathas – Madhvacharya gave sanyas diksha to 8 disciples who in turn founded the following 8 mathas for the purpose of worship of Sri Krishna of Udupi:

1. *Vishnu Tirtha* – Sode Matha
2. *Janardana Tirtha* – Krishnapura Matha,
3. *Vamana Tirtha* – Kanuru Matha,
4. *Narasimha Tirtha* – Adamaru Matha,
5. *Upendra Tirtha* – Puttige Matha,
6. *Rama Tirtha* – Shiroor Matha,
7. *Hrishikesha Tirtha* – Phalimaru Matha,
8. *Akshobhya Tirtha* – Pejavar Matha.

Some more religious concepts concerning the number 8:

1. Eight Gunas, according to Vidura Neeti, which bring name and fame to an individual:
   Pragnaa, Kaulyam, Dama, shruta, parakrama, mita-bhashita, Daana, Krutagnata.
2. The eight important aspects of Dharma are – Yagna, Adyayana, Dana, Tapas, Satya (honesty), Kshama (excuse), Dama (controlling the senses) and Alobha.

SYMBOLISM OF NUMBER 9

9 is a unique number and is regarded as a number whose positive aspect is constructive and negative aspect destructive. It also represents matter which cannot be destroyed. It is the only number when multiplied by any other number always reproduces itself. For example: $9 \times 5 = 45$ $(4 + 5 = 9)$, $9 \times 7 = 63$ $(6 + 3 = 9)$, etc. In the Tarot deck, it represents the 'Hermit' which is a guiding card of wisdom and truth. The colours of the number 9 are all shades of crimson or red.

All ancient races encouraged a fear of the number 9 and all its multiples. The Hindu astrology recognizes 'Nava-grahas' which include the 7 creative planets along with 'Rahu' and 'Ketu'. The number 9 represents man and physical force in every form. It also denotes energy, destruction and war. In ordinary life, it represents activity, energy, ambition, leadership and courage. It represents strife, quarrels and accidents, particularly from fire and explosion.

It is symbolized by the planet Mars. It is a planet of heat, energy, war and destruction. Mars is the God of War in Roman mythology. (Mars is also known as 'Mangal or Kuja' in Sanskrit and considered malefic in nature). The number nine is also considered a sacred number. It is customary to place navaratnas and navadhanyas, below the idol, while installation in a temple.

Some important concepts relating to Number 9:

1. Nine months represent the pre-natal life of a child.
2. The Bhagavatha purana mentions nine forms of devotion.
3. There are also 'Nava grahas', 'Nava rathnas', 'Nava dhanyas', 'Nava Durgas', 'Nava rasas', 'Nava Rathri's (the nine – nights of Durga festival, also known as Dasara),
4. Lord Kubera is described as the lord of nine types of treasures.
5. *Bala:* the nine year old form (or up to nine years) of goddess Lalita Tripura-sundari.
6. The 'Nava Rasas' in Indian literature are described as Sringar, Veera, Karuna, Adbhuta, Hasya, Bhayanak, Bhibhats, Roudra and Shanta.
7. The nine aksharas in one pada is called 'Bruhati Chandas'.

Navavidha Bhaktis: Shravana, Keertana, Vandana, Smarana, Sakhya, Archana, Padaseva, Dasya (relationship between Sri Krishna –Kuchela, Sri Rama – Guha), and Atma nivedana.

Shravanam Keerthanam Vishnoh Smaranam Paadasevanam |
Archanam Vandanam Daasyam Sakhyam Aatmanivedanam ||

Navarathna's: Ruby (Manikya), Pearl (Mouktika), Cats eye (Vaidhurya), Emerald (Marakata), Topaz (Pushyaraga), diamond (Vajra), Sapphire (Neela, Indra Neela), Gomedhaka (Hessonite) and

Coral (Pravala), These precious stones have been worn by people from times immemorial. They are said to ward off evil spirits, improve one's personality, cure certain illnesses, etc.

Sri Rama Navami is celebrated on the ninth day of Chaitra Shukla Navami, when Sri Rama was said to have been born in 'Punarvasu' nakshatra.

Navaratri as a festival, is celebrated by the followers of all Hindu cults. The tenth day is known as Vijaya Dashami (Dasara). The festival celebrated for nine days in the month of Chaitra, is called 'Vasanta Navaratra'. The festival celebrated for nine days in the month of Ashwayaja is called 'Sharan-navaratra' as it also falls in 'Sharat Rutu'. The Sharan-navaratri is the more famous of the two, as Durga is worshipped in her three forms – Maha Kali, Maha Lakshmi, and Maha Saraswathi, During this period, people worship their respective deities too.

Sacred works like Vedas, *Ramayana*, Narayana Hridaya, Lakshmi Hridaya, and Saptashati parayana is also done by the devout during this period. This period is also considered auspicious for conducting all auspicious functions by the Hindus.

Dhanyas Related to Navagrahas

The following 'Navadhanyas' are used in the worship of Navagrahas: Sun – wheat; Moon – rice; Mars – tor; Mercury – Green gram, Jupiter – chana; Venus – avare; Saturn – black till; Rahu – Uruddal; Kethu – horsegram; Mrintyunjaya – Cube Jaggery;

Nava-Bhaya (Fears): There are nine types of fears:

1. Bhoga-bhaya: Always fearing that whatever one is enjoying, may leave him/her,
2. Roga-bhaya: Fearing that one may be afflicted with some disease,
3. Kula-bhaya: Fearing that he may commit some mistake, which will bring bad name to his Kula.
4. Vitta-bhaya: Fearing loss of money, wealth, etc.
5. Maryada-bhaya: Constant fear of insult before others,

6. Guna-bhaya: Fear of getting a bad name through some deed,
7. Rupa-bhaya: Fear of getting his/her beauty spoiled through accident, old age, etc.
8. Shastra-bhaya: Fear of losing to a more learned/intelligent person,
9. Bhale-bhaya: Fear of physically losing to a person who is stronger than him.

Even though these are common fears that any person may face, the fear of death (Marana-bhaya) is a fear which over-rides all these fears.

Annexure 5

Hindu Religious Concepts

(Associated with Compound Numbers)

Numbers starting from 10 onwards are called Compound Numbers in Numerology. They play quiet a significant role in Hindu religion and philosophy through their symbolism and interpretation of several religious and metaphysical concepts.

SYMBOLISM OF NUMBER TEN

The number 10, shows the transition from units to double numbers and therefore denotes a change. The ancients considered it to be a perfect number. In fact, even today, in several sports events, a perfect 'ten' is awarded for a flawless performance. This number also represents the 'Wheel of Fortune' which denotes regular rise and fall in one's fortunes.

Concept of Brahman

10 is considered as the number of completion in Hindu religion. One represents 'Saguna Brahman' and zero represents 'Nirguna Brahman'. These two forms of Brahman fuse in the number 10, representing the incarnation of the Supreme God, in all his splendor. This also, in a way symbolizes the self- realized Yogi (For example – Nachiketa), who has experienced the 'Brahman' or the 'Supreme God'.

DASHAVATARA *(10 Incarnations of Vishnu)*

Sri Krishna in *Bhagavad Gita* says that he takes birth in every age to establish Dharma whenever it is threatened. Each such birth is considered as an incarnation (avatar) of God. Lord Vishnu has 10 incarnations in the forms of 'Dashavatara' – Matsya, Koorma, Varaha, Narasimha, Vamana, Parasurama, Rama, Krishna, Buddha and Kalki.

1. *Matsya* – the fish, appears in Satya Yuga. (represents the beginning of life), He saves saint Vaivasvata.
2. *Koorma* – the tortoise appears in Satya Yuga (represents growth of life), He offers his back as pivot for Mandara parvata used in the churning of the ocean.
3. *Varaha* – the boar appeared in Satya Yuga (represents a thinking animal). He kills the demon 'Hiranyaksha' recovers the stolen Vedas, and releases the earth from the bottom of the ocean.
4. *Narasimha* – Man-Lion appeared in Satya Yuga (almost in human form). He kills the demon 'Hiranyakashipu' who had gained immunity from death by man, beast or god.
5. *Vamana* – the Dwarf appeared in Treta Yuga (represents a young man). By measuring the earth and sky by his giant steps, he claims the kingdom of Bali and sends him to 'patala loka' by placing the third step on Bali's head.
6. *Parasurama* – Rama with an axe, appears in Treta Yuga representing an angry man. He goes round the earth 21 times killing all the Kshatriya princes.
7. *Rama* – Sri Rama appears in Treta Yuga and represents a perfect man in an ideological world. He is the main character in the epic *Ramayana.*
8. *Krishna* – Sri Krishna appears in human form in Dwapara Yuga and teaches Jnana to the world through *Bhagavad Gita.*
9. *Buddha* – (here is considered from the Hindu perspective) taught knowledge and the right path of salvation to the masses.
10. *Kalki* – is expected to appear at the end of Kali Yuga and propound the true Dharma again.

Incarnations of Other Gods: Dakshinamurty is considered an incarnation of Lord Shiva. Vidura of *Mahabharat* is said to be an incarnation of Yama Dharmaraja. Hanuman, Bhima and Madhva are considered incarnations of Vayu (the God of life). Dattatreya is considered incarnation of the 'Trinity' of Gods – Brahma, Vishnu and Maheswara. Sita, the wife of Rama is considered an incarnation of Lakshmi the consort of Vishnu.

Dasha Pranah: The ten pranas in our human body are: Prana, Apaana, Vyana, Udaana, and Samana (Vayus); Naaga, Kurma, Krikara, Devadatta and Dhanjaya (Upa Vayus).

Some of the other religious concepts relating to the number 10 are:

1. The human body is said to undergo ten 'avasthas' – Garbhavasa, birth, Baalya, Kumara, Powganda, Kishora, Youvana, Proudha, Vardhakya and mrityu (death).
2. The major Upanishads are ten in number: Isha, Kena, Katha, Munduka, Prashna, Mandookya, Aitareya, Taithiriya, Chandogya, and Brhadaranyaka.
3. *Dasha-mudras*: (arrangements of fingers during archana) are ten in number: Sanskhobhini-mudra, Shanmukhi-mudra, Khechari-mudra, Jalandara-mudra, Odyana-mudra, Maha-mudra, Shambhavi-mudra, Yoni-mudra, Jnana-mudra, and Trikhanda-mudra;
4. The ten people who should be respected: Guru, father, elder brother, king, uncle (mother's brother), father-in-law, grand-father (both mother's father and father's father), eldest among relatives and father's brothers.
5. According to *Ramayana*, Ravana was called 'Dasha-greeva' because he had 10 heads. Rama killed the ten headed Ravana, the demon king in the battle.
6. In some vratas, the 'kartru' wears a holy cotton thread on the wrist, having ten threads.
7. 'Danas' are auspicious and ten in number – cow, earth, gold, silver, vastra, till, grains, ghee, jaggery and salt.

8. In ancient times, it was customary for kings to start conquests on 'Vijaya Dashami' the tenth day after celebrating nine days of Dasara. Even today, 'Vijaya Dashami' is considered an auspicious day for starting all new ventures.

SYMBOLISM OF NUMBER ELEVEN

The number 11 operates through the higher emotional side of nature. In the Tarot deck, it is represented by the figure of 'Justice'. It is considered a mystic and ominous number in numerology. In the scriptures of several religions, it represents bad omens, sin and penance. It is also a number of spiritual advancement.

Some of the concepts related to the number 11 are:

1. Manusmriti calls 'Mind' (Manas) as the eleventh organ of the human body which controls the five Jnanendriyas and the five Karmendriyas.
2. There are 11 incarnations of 'Rudra', the God of destruction and also 'Rudrani'.
3. The 11 Rudras are – Mrugavyadha, Sarpa, Niruthi, Ajaika pada, Ahirbudnya, Pinaki, Dahana, Iswara, Kapali, Sthanu, and Bhava.
4. There are 11 Karanas in the Hindu Panchanga.
5. 'Ekadashi' the eleventh day is considered sacred. People fast on this day to purify their sins.

According to Narada Bhakti Sutra, there are **eleven types of Bhaktis**:

1. *Gunamahatma-sakti:* Worshipping God as an embodiment of all virtues (ex: all saints belonging to Bhakti panthas),
2. *Rupa-sakti*: Worshipping God through any of his forms,
3. *Puja-sakti:* Worshipping God as though God has come to our home as a guest,
4. *Smarana-sakti*: Always remembering God through, swarupa-smarana, rupa-smarana, or nama-smarana,

5. *Dasya-sakti*: Serving God as though one is a servant of God (ex: Anjaneya),
6. *Sakhya-sakti*: Worshipping God as though he is one's friend (ex: Arjuna),
7. *Vatsalya-sakti*: Treating God as though he is one's child (ex: Yashoda),
8. *Kanta-sakti:* Treating God as though he is one's spouse (ex: Radha),
9. *Atmanivedana-sakti:* Worshipping God by offering one's Atman, Heart, Mind, etc.
10. *Tanmaya-sakti*: Becoming one with God – nothing else matters,
11. *Parama-virahasakti*: Forgetting everything and pine for God as though one has lost his/her spouse. (ex: Meera, Akkamahadevi).

SYMBOLISM OF NUMBER TWELVE

The number 12 has several symbolic representations –the 12 zodiacal signs (Sun signs – Rashis), the 12 hour day/night, the 12 months in a year, the 12 men and women who form a jury, etc. In the British System, 12 is still the standard of measurement – a foot consists of 12 inches.

'Dwadasha Suryas': Dhatru, Mitra, Aryama, Indra, Varuna, Amsha, Bhaga, Vivaswanta, Pusha, Savitru, Twastru and Vishnu – each Surya rules over a particular month of a solar year.

Dwadasha Jyotirlinga: Shiva Mahapurana describes the 12 Jyotirlingas in India. Shiva is said to reside in these 12 places as 'Linga-swarupi' and blesses the devout.

Saurashtre Somanatham cha
Srishaile Mallikarjunam |
Ujjayanyam Mahakalam
Oumkare Parameshwaram ||

Keadaram Himavathrusthe
Dakinyam Bhimashankaram |
Varanyasam tu Vishwesham
Trayambakam Gautamitate ||

Vaidyanatham Chitaabhoomou
Nagesham Darukaavane |
Setubandhe tu Ramesham
Ghushmesham cha Shivalaye ||

Dwadshaitani Namani
Prataruthaya yah pateth |
Sarvapapavinrmuktah
Sarvasidhi phalam labheth ||

This is akin to Dashavataras of Lord Vishnu.

Some of the concepts relating to number 12 are:

1. There are 12 'Rashis' each one corresponding to a sign of the Zodiac.
2. The Hindu calendar (both solar and lunar) has normally 12 months in a year.
3. There are 12 different procedures of Sri Vidya (12 methods of worship of Goddess Lalita Tripura-sundari), based on the original 12 'Upasakas' – Manu, Chandra, Kubera, Lopamudra, Manmatha, Agastya, Agni, Surya, Indra, Skanda, Shiva and Durvasa (also known as Krodha-bhattaraka).
4. The Vasudeva mantra *Om Namo Bhagavate Vasudevaiah* has 12 characters.
5. Lord Vishnu is worshipped through 12 names (Dwadasha nama stotra) starting from 'Keshava'.
6. Certain religious festivities are performed once in 12 years. Kumbabhisheka, Mahamastabhisekha, etc.

Twelve Methods of Obtaining Children

In ancient times, obtaining children was the paramount objective for a person for propagating his lineage (Vamshodhara) as also for 'pitruruna-parihara'. The Hindu scriptures permitted obtaining children through 12 methods. When a person was not able to get children from the first method, then the next and subsequent methods were to be used for obtaining children.

1. *Swayamjata (Owrasa)*: is the son obtained through the 'Dharma-patni' married according to scriptures.
2. *Praneeta*: is the son obtained through the wife by the grace of a 'Maha-purusha'.
3. *Parikreeta*: is the son obtained through the wife but paying money to a 'taponistha'.
4. *Pownarbhava*: is the son born to a wife through a second marriage.
5. *Kaaneena*: son born to a couple even before marriage – is considered a legal son of the same couple when they marry,
6. *Kunda*: son born to a wife even when the wife has an extra-marital relationship,
7. *Datta*: son given by parents for adoption,
8. *Kreeta*: son bought through payment of money,
9. *Kritrima*: son received for some reason even though his parentage is unknown,
10. *Apavidha*: accepted as a son by a third person even though he is rejected by his parents,
11. *Sahoodha*: son born to a woman after her marriage (but being pregnant from another person before her marriage)
12. *Gnataretasa*: son born to a woman of low caste.

Out of these 12 types of children, the first six were considered 'gnatis' and were entitled for property rights and positions as the wife considered as 'kshetra' was the biological mother of these children.

Obtaining a son from the husband's brother (*devar*) was also a permitted method for a woman. However, the last 6 types of children were not entitled for property rights and positions. Further with the change in times, several of these methods have been considered by the society as 'irreligious'.

Thirteen

The number 13 is a peculiar number with unique characteristics. Even though 13 is considered an inauspicious number in the West, in India 13 was considered auspicious. The 'Shukla-paksha-Trayodashi' (the thirteenth day after the new-moon) is considered to be extremely auspicious. The demon named 'Keshi' is said to have battled with Vishnu for 13 days.

Fourteen: In ancient India, distances were measured in 'Yojanas'. A yojana measures approximately 14 kms.

Fifteen: Each Hindu month consists of two parts – Shukla Paksha and Krishna Paksha. Each Paksha is divided in to 15 tithis (days). The 'Pancha-dashakshari' mantra of goddess 'Lalitha Tripurasundari' has 15 characters.

SYMBOLISM OF NUMBER SIXTEEN

Shodhasha Samskara: Man from birth is supposed to undergo **16 'samskaras'** (sanctifying rites enjoined on a Hindu) beginning with Garbhadana and ending with Uttarakriya – the funeral rites.

(*i*) Garbhadana – Making wife pregnant through Dharmic rituals,

(*ii*) Pumsavana – Ritual performed at the third month of pregnancy,

(*iii*) Seemantonnayana – Ritual usually performed in the seventh month,

(*iv*) Jatakarma – Welcoming the child at birth,

(*v*) Namakarana – Naming ceremony,

(*vi*) Nishkramana – Taking the child out of the house for the first time (the child is usually taken to a temple),

(*vii*) Annaprashana – First feeding of solid food (rice),

(*viii*) Chuda Karma (*Chowla*) – Tonsure of the child before the family deity,

(*ix*) Karna Vedha – Piercing the ears for the first time,
(*x*) Vidyarambha – Akshara-bhyasa,
(*xi*) Upanayana – Sacred thread ceremony – it is also a ceremony which intiates a person into learning,
(*xii*) Vedadhyayana – Learning of Veda and other scriptures,
(*xiii*) Godana samskara (also called Keshanta) – At the end of education at 'Gurukula', the parents have to give a gift to the Guru and remove the hair of the child.
(*xiv*) Samavartana – The ritual of send off at Gurukula.
(*xv*) Vivaha – The person entering 'Grihastashrama'.
(*xvi*) Antyesthi – Uttarakriya performed after death.

Examples of Number 16 Symbolism:

1. The Goddess 'Lalitha' is also known as 'Shodashi'. She is also worshipped through the most sacred 'Shodashakshari' mantra which has 16 characters. In some vratas, the 'kartru' wears a holy cotton thread on the wrist, having sixteen threads.
2. Moon is usually called 'Shodashkala Prapoorna' – because Moon goes through 16 tithis , from new moon to full moon;
3. There are 16 Kalas: Prana, Shradha, Akash, Vayuh, Agni, Jala, Prithvi, Indriya, Manas, Anna, Veeryah, Tapas, Mantra, Karma, Loka and Nama.
4. **'Shodashopachara Puja':** According to scriptures, Gods/ Goddesses are to be worshipped with 64 types of 'Upacharas'. Since it is not possible to do it every day, the shodashopachara puja is done in worshipping each God or Goddess. Here idols made of Gold, Silver, Brass, Copper or Pancha-loha are usually used in this form of worship. The shodashopachara consists of offering:
   (*i*) Avahana – A form of welcome,
   (*ii*) Asana – Providing seat,
   (*iii*) Padya – Washing of feet,
   (*iv*) Arghya – Offering water,
   (*v*) Aachamaneeya – Sipping water,

(*vi*) Snana – Giving bath (including panchamruta abhisheka)
(*vii*) Vastra – Offering clothes,
(*viii*) Upavita – Offering 'Yagnopavita' the sacred thread,
(*ix*) Gandha/Akshata – Offering sandalwood paste and akshata
(*x*) Patra/Pushpa – Offering leaves and flowers,
(*xi*) Dhoopa – Offering dhoopa through incense sticks,
(*xii*) Deepa – Lighting of sacred lamps,
(*xiii*) Madhuparka /Naivedya – Offering of food, fruits, milk, etc.
(*xiv*) Tamboola – Offering of Beatle nuts/leaves
(*xv*) Neerajana – Offering Neerajana/arati
(*xvi*) Visarjana – This is usually not done in nitya puja, but done on special occasions when worshipping deities made of earth, sand, wood and other materials (Ex. Ganesha/ Durga). Instead of 'Visarjana', 'Namaskar' is offered to the God/Goddess every day.

5. Tantra-raja describes the 16 'Nityas' of Devi present in Sri Chakra as – Kameshwari, Bhagamalini, Nitya-klinna, Bherunda, Vahni-vasini, Maha-vajreswari, Shiva-dooti, Twarita, Kulasundari, Nitye, Neela-pataake, Vijaya, Sarvamangala, Jwalamalini, Chitra, and Tripurasundari.

Eighteen

18 is the most important number in Hindu mythology (as well as Hindu philosophy), as 1+8 yields a nine which is considered another number of perfection. The number also signifies victory as well as eternity.

As we have already seen in Chapter 1, the number 18 especially belongs to the epic *Mahabharata*. The epic has 18 parts called 'Parvas'. The Mahabharata war was fought for 18 days. The total units of army participating in the war were 18 'akshohinis'. The famous *Bhagavad Gita* has 18 chapters. The 'maha puranas' and Upa puranas are also 18 in number.

Nineteen and Twenty Three

Two favourite numbers of numerologists are 19 and 23, which are regarded as extremely favourable. 19, symbolized by the Sun, is called the 'Prince of Heaven' and 23 is called the 'Royal Star of Lion'. These are considered extremely fortunate numbers and promise success if they appear in connection with future events

Twenty One: It is a number related to Lord Ganesha. He is the twenty first God in the Indian pantheon of Gods. He likes to be worshipped by all things which are 21 in number – garike, modaka, flowers, leaves, fruits, etc.

Twenty Two: Varaha Mihira classified the various types of jewels available then, into 22 categories.

Twenty Four is another important as well as sacred number as the *maatras* in the 'Gayatri' chandas are 24 in number. Each *maatra* is also associated with a Varna and a Rupa of Lord Sri. Krishna. The Gayatri mantra reflects all the four yogas – Jnana yoga, Karma yoga, Bhakti yoga and Raja yoga. A day consists of 24 hours.

The adhyatma Tatvas are 24 in number. They consist of the Pancha Karmendriyas, Pancha Jnanendriyas, Pancha bhutas, Pancha pranas, Mind, Avidya, Kama and Karma – the human being is bound by these 24 Tatvas. Only when he attains 'Jnana' he is released by these 24 Tatvas.

Twenty Seven

The Lunar month is governed by 27 stars (nakshatras) – each star roughly ruling over a day. They start from Ashwini and end with Revati. A person has to be born under one of these birth stars. These stars are further classified under the twelve 'rashis'. There are also 27 yogas.

Thirty is another important number as a Hindu month is divided into 30 *thithis* each representing a day.

Thirty Two: According to 'Mudgala Purana' 32 different forms of Vinayaka (Ganapti) are worshipped: Bala, Taruna, Bhakta, Veera, Shakti, Dwija, (Vara) Sidhi, Uchistha, Vighna, Kshipra, Herambha, Lakshmi, Maha, Vijaya, Nrutya, Oordhwa, Ekakshara, Vara, Tryakshara, Kshipra- prasada, Haridra, Ekadanta, Srishthi, Uddanda, Runamochaka,

Dhundhi, Dwimukha, Trimukha, Simha, Yoga, Durga and Sankshtahara Ganapati. However, on Ganesha Chaturthi day 'Vara Sidhi Vinayaka' is most prominently worshipped.

Thirty Three: There are 33 prominent devatas headed by Indra: Astha Vasus, Ekadasha Rudras, Dwadsha Adityas, Indra and Prajapati.

Thirty Six: Shaiva Sidhanta recognizes 36 Tatvas that govern this world.

Fifty One (51): The 'Tantra Chudamani' enumerates 51 Devi 'Shakti Peethas'.

Fifty Five (55): When we add the numbers 1 + 2 + 3 + 4 + 5 + 6 + 7 + 8 + 9 + 10 we get 55. This 55 is also taken to represent a complete Man, as the fingers in each of his hand number 5.

Sixty is another important number which represents a cycle of Hindu astrological years, which repeat once every sixty years:

1	Prabhava	21	Sarvajit	41	Plavanga
2	Vibhava	22	Sarvadhaari	42	Keelaka
3	Shukla	23	Virodhi	43	Soumya
4	Pramoda	24	Vikruti	44	Sadharana
5	Prajapati	25	Khara	45	Virodhikrut
6	Angirasa	26	Nandana	46	Paridhavi
7	Sri Mukha	27	Vijaya	47	Pramadicha
8	Bhava	28	Jaya	48	Ananda
9	Yuva	29	Manmatha	49	Rakshasa
10	Dhatru	30	Durmukha	50	Nala
11	Iswara	31	Hevilambi	51	Paingala
12	Bahudhanya	32	Vilambi	52	Kalayukti
13	Pramathi	33	Vikari	53	Sidharthi
14	Vikrama	34	Shaarvari	54	Raudri
15	Vishu	35	Plava	55	Durmati
16	Chitrabhanu	36	Shubhakrutu	56	Dundubhi
17	Swabhanu	37	Shobhakrutu	57	Rudhirodgari
18	Tarana	38	Krodhi	58	Raktakshi
19	Parthiva	39	Viswavasu	59	Krodhana
20	Vyaya	40	Parabhava	60	Akshaya

SYMBOLISM OF NUMBER SIXTY FOUR

1. Chatushasthi: There are 64 vidyas (disciplines of study) that a person has to master.
2. The 'tantras' are also considered to be 64 in number.
3. The yoginis (Bramhi, Lopamudra, etc.) are said to be 64 in number.
4. Lalita Sahasranama describes 64 kalas of Goddess Lalita Tripura Sundari.
5. There are also 64 types of 'upacharas' (corresponding to 64 kalas) as a part of worship of the Goddess. These upacharas are described in 'Parasurama-kalpa-sutra'.
6. As already discussed Moon has 16 Kalas. Since, every tithi has 4 sandhya kalas (Udaya-sandhya, Madhya-sandhya, Sayan-sandhya and Madhya-ratri-sandhya) the total kalas are 16 × 6 = 64 in number.
7. The 64 Kalas of Goddess Sri. Lalita Tripura-sundari are –

1.	Geeta	33.	Pattikaavetra-baanavikalpa
2.	Vaadya	34.	Taksha-karma
3.	Nrutya	35.	Takshana
4.	Alekhya	36.	Vaastu-vidya
5.	Visheshaka-Bhedya	37.	Rooparatna-pariksha
6.	Tandula-Bali	38.	Dhaatu-vaada
7.	Kusuma-Vikara	39.	Maniragaakara-gnana
8.	Pushpaastarana	40.	Vruksha-ayurveda
9.	Darshana	41.	Mesha-kakkuta-laavaka-yudhavidhi
10.	Vasnaanga-Raaga	42.	Shuka-saarika-pralapana
11.	Manibhumika-Karma	43.	Utsaadana
12.	Shayana Rachana	44.	Samvahana
13.	Udaka Vaadya	45.	Keshamardana Kaushalya
14.	Udakaghaata	46.	Akshara-mustikaa-kathana

15.	Chitraashva yoga	47.	Mlechitaka-vikalpa
16.	Maalyagrathanavikalpa	48.	Deshabashaa-vignana
17.	Sekharapeedayojana	49.	Pushpa-shakataka
18.	Nepathya-samyoga	50.	Nimitta-gnana
19.	Karnapatrabhanga-gandhayuktabhooshana yojana	51.	Yantra-maatruka-dhaarana
20.	Indrajaala	52.	Maatruka-sampatya
21.	Kanchapoorayoga	53.	Maanasi-kavyakriya
22.	Hastalaaghva	54.	Abhidaana-kosha
23.	Chitrashakhapuja-bhakta-vikara-kriya	55.	Chando-vignana
24.	Paanaka-rasaasava-raagayojana	56.	Kriyaa-vikalpa
25.	Soochivaanakarma	57.	Chalitaka-yoga
26.	Sootra-Kreeda	58.	Vastra-gopana
27.	Veenaa-damaruka-naada-prahelikaa	59.	Dyuuta-vishesha
28.	Pratimaala	60.	Akarsha-kreeda
29.	Doorvaachaka-yoga,	61.	Baala-kreedanaka
30.	Pustaka-vaachana	62.	Vainayaka
31.	Naatakaakyayikaa-darshana	63.	Vaijayaka
32.	Kaavya-samasya-poorna	64.	Vyayamika

One Hundred (Shata mana) is considered to be a complete number as a man's maximum life span is considered to be normally 100 years. While conducting blessings, the elders bless the younger ones with the mantra: *Shatamanam bhavati....* (May you live to be a hundred years...)

One hundred is also associated with Kauravas – the 100 sons of Dhritarashtra and Gandhari.

101 kalashas containing sacred water are used for 'Kumbabhishekha' and *purification of temples/gopurams.*

SYMBOLISM OF ONE HUNDRED AND EIGHT (108)

The number 108 is considered the most sacred number in Hindu tradition. Some explanations are given below:

1. **Number of Beads in a Rosary:** *Sharada Tilak* – an ancient Sanskrit text dealing with 'Tantrik Yoga' – has given the number of beads that should be used in a rosary (Japa-Mala) for different purposes –
    1. For destroying an enemy – 15 beads,
    2. For salvation – 25 beads,
    3. For general purpose – 27 beads,
    4. For wealth – 30 beads,
    5. Fulfillment of desires (children, rise in position, etc,) – 54 beads
    6. For all occasions, the perfect rosary – 108 beads.
2. 108 is a sacred number in Hindu tradition. It is a number which is considered a highly spiritual number: 108, which is by addition of its digits 1 + 0 + 8 yields again a 9. That is why, the standard Hindu rosary which is used for the purpose of meditation has 108 beads in it. Another explanation is given below.
3. A circle has 360 degrees. There are 60 ghatis in a day. When 360 is multiplied by 60 we get 21,600 time divisions of 24 hours of a day called viphalas, and half of this amounts to 10800 representing 12 hours of a day or night. The number 108 is arrived at by dropping the end zeros. Thus the number 108 is said to coordinate the rhythm of time and space so that it is in harmony with nature as well as God.
4. Hence, every prominent god/goddess is worshipped through their 108 names known as 'Astothara'.

One thousand (1000) is another sacred number.

1. In Hindu religion and philosophy, 'Sahasra' is also taken to mean 'Ananta' meaning infinity.
2. The Supreme Being known as 'Purusha' is also described as 'Sahasra shirsha', 'sahasraksa' and 'sahasrapath'.
3. Every prominent Hindu God/Godess is worshipped through his/her 'sahasranama stotra' which is considered very sacred.

One thousand Eight (1008) is another number which the Hindu tradition recognizes as a sacred number. This number is used in meditation, yagas and yagnas to propitiate the Gods.

One lakh is another important number. For obtaining 'Mantra-Siddhi' one is supposed to recite a mantra as per laid down procedures, in lakhs. For example if a mantra has 7 characters, then one should recite it for seven lakh times for obtaining 'mantra-Siddhi'.

The Vedic Form of Counting

The Vedic Mathematicians adapted 10 as the basis of numeration and based their calculations on the decimal scale. The decimal place value system had been developed as early as the fourth century C E.

1. Below is given the names of numbers as they are called, where each term stands for a number which is greater by unity than the preceding term:
   1 (Eka), 2 (Dvi), 3 (Tri), 4 (Chatur), 5 (Pancha), 6 (Shat), 7 (Sapta), 8 (Astha), and 9 (Nava),
2. Next they named the multiples of ten in an order where each term stands for a number greater by 10 than the preceding term:
   10 (Dasha), 20 (Vimshati), 30 (Trimshat), 40 (Chaturvimshat), 50 (Panchashat), 60 (Shasti), 70 (Saptati), 80 (Asthat), 90 (Navati),
3. The other numbers were written using the principles of addition and subtraction. For ex. 19 was called 'ekanna-vimshati'.

4. Then they gave names to numbers where each term was ten times greater than the preceding term:
   100 (Shata), 1000 (Sahasra), 10,000 (Ayuta), 1,00,000 (Niyuta), 10,00,000 (Prayuta),
5. In ancient system, no other system reached this state of perfection in counting and finally the world adapted the Indian system of counting as the best system.

In praise of the contribution of Indians to the development of the number system, the great French Mathematician P.S. Laplace (1749–1827) wrote:

> *It is India that gave us the ingenious method of expressing all numbers by the means of ten symbols, each symbol receiving a value position, as well as an absolute value; a profound and important idea which appears so simple to us that we ignore its true merit, but its very simplicity, the great ease which it has lent to all computations, puts our arithmetic in the front rank of useful inventions, and we shall appreciate the grandeur of this achievement when we consider that it escaped the genius of Archimedes and Apollonius, two of the great minds produced by antiquity....*

It is again Hindus who discovered the precession of the Equinoxes and the calculation that such an occurrence takes place every 25,827 years.

Annexure 6

Symbolism of Numbers in Astrology and Numerology

Now we come to the wonder world of occult studies also known as 'Predictive Sciences'. These are Astrology, Numerology, Palmistry, Divination, Physiognomy, etc. All these branches of knowledge use the symbolism of numbers extensively, especially in predicting events in the lives of individuals. From the dawn of civilization, Man has been fascinated by these occult subjects. However, during the Middle Ages, these subjects captured the fascination of people to such a great extent, that one of the first books ever printed (after the invention of the printing press) was a work on palmistry, *Die Kunst Ciromantia* printed in Augsburg in 1475.

IMPACT OF NUMBERS ON HUMAN LIFE

Numbers play an important role in the lives of individuals. In fact they dominate our whole life. We are born on a particular date, important events in our lives take place on particular dates and finally we die on a particular date. As we carefully analyze, we can see the interplay of specific numbers in our lives. Experience tells us that if two persons have the same number, they quite often exhibit similar qualities and lead similar course of life.

In Numerology, number symbolism as well as, the well established relationship between numbers and planets, are used as a key to interpretation of human behaviour. Numerology considers odd numbers male, solar, dynamic and powerful; and even numbers as female, lunar, static and weak.

Numerology interprets the life of an individual through the study of the following five parameters: Birth Number, Secondary Number, Name Number, Year Number, and Destiny (Fadic) Number. An analysis of these five parameters helps us to interpret the personality and characteristics of a person and further predict future events in his life. If a person has all his numbers in perfect harmony, then he is bound to lead a good and fruitful life.

Navagrahas

Both Astrology and Numerology developed simultaneously in ancient India along with development of Geometry, Astronomy and Mathematics. Astrology came to be developed as the study of the Sun, Moon and Planets and their effect on human beings. Ancient Man considered only the seven planets (as was then known to him) – Sun, Moon, Jupiter, Mercury, Venus, Mars and Saturn, as creative planets. He also named the days of the week after these seven planets.

In Hindu Religion, along with these seven planets, Rahu and Ketu (the north and South Nodes of the Moon) were included and these nine planets were termed as 'Navagrahas'. These nine planets were also considered as the different facets of the same divinity and worshipped. Hence almost every ancient temple in India, had an identified place for worshipping the 'Navagrahas'.

Relationship between Numbers and Planets

Symbolically each number is also identified with a planet and a day of the week. The relationship between numbers and planets is common to both Indian and western systems with the following exceptions. The ruling planet of the number 4 in the Hindu system is Rahu (the northern node of the Moon), whereas in the western system the ruling planets of number 4 are the Sun (in its negative aspect) and Uranus. Similarly, the ruling planet of number 7 is Ketu (the southern node of the Moon) in the Hindu system, whereas in the western system, it is the Moon (in its positive aspect) and Neptune.

Table A6.1 Days of the Week, Ruling Planets and Numbers

Day	Associated Number*	Day of The Week	Ruling Planet
1	1 – 4**	Sunday	Sun
2	2 – 7**	Monday	Moon
3	9	Tuesday	Mars
4	5	Wednesday	Mercury
5	3	Thursday	Jupiter
6	6	Friday	Venus
7	8	Saturday	Saturn

* *According to Numerology, the Sun and the Moon are the only two planets having double numbers.*

Numbers and Human Behaviour

Human behaviour is usually interpreted according to their, birth or secondary numbers and persons with the same birth/secondary numbers exhibit similar qualities which are taken after their ruling planets. Broadly the qualities pertaining to these numbers are as shown in the Table below:

Table A6.2 Numbers, Planets and Human Behaviour

Number	Related Planet	Associated Symbolism in terms of Human Qualities
1	Sun	Royal, Authoritative, Strong, Disciplined, Thinker, Proud
2	Moon	Queenly Attributes, Change, Delicate, Artistic, Friendly
3	Jupiter	Spiritual, Friendly, Disciplined, Self-centered, Ambitious
4	Rahu	Impulsive, Secretive, Short tempered. Unconventional, Rebellious
5	Mercury	Intelligent, Sensitive, Fragile, Dual nature, Good judgement
6	Venus	Romantic, Sensual, Diplomatic, Manipulative, Magnetic, Sociable

7	Ketu	Mystical, Spiritual, Intuitive, Philosophical, Indecisive, Moody
8	Saturn	Wise, Malefic, Suffering, Determined, Sincere, Indiscipline
9	Mars	Strong, Rustic, Warlike, Ambitious, Short tempered, Unstable

Numbers and Music

Numbers and music show very close affinity. Number 1, 3 and 9 people like martial, inspiring and full-blooded music, while number 2 and 7 people like string and wind instruments like the violin, pipe, tabla, drums, etc. If number 6 people like romantic and sweet, lilting, rhythmic music of all kinds, those with number 5 like extremely original or unusual music. Number 4 and 8 people have a special leaning for the organ and make good choir groups. They always like music tinged with melancholy or a religious fervour, bhajans, etc.

Numbers and the Zodiac

It was astrology, which divided all mankind into 12 different groups and assigned each of them a zodiacal sign (called in Astrology as 'Rashis'), according to the month (represented by a number called in Numerology as the Secondary Number) in which each individual is born. If we randomly select 100 people, from different parts of the world, but born in the same month, we are sure to see many similar characteristics and qualities which are common to all of them, even though they belong to different social and cultural backgrounds, have differing levels of education, are brought up in different environments and speak different languages.

The future of individuals, are also predicted on the basis of the positions of the planets in the 'Rashi Kundali'.

Table A6.3 Numbers and the Zodiac

Sl. No.	Zodiacal Sign	Indian Names (Rashis)	Secondary Number (Numerology)	Periods of Birth
1	Aries	Mesha	9 (+ve)	21 March – 19 April
2	Taurus	Vrishabha	6 (+ve)	20 April – 20 May
3	Gemini	Mithuna	5 (+ve)	21 May – 20 June
4	Cancer	Karka	2 – 7 *	21 June – 20 July
5	Leo	Simha	1 – 4 *	21 July – 20 August
6	Virgo	Kanya	5 (–ve)	21 August – 20 September
7	Libra	Tula	6 (–ve)	21 September – 20 October
8	Scorpio	Vrishchika	9 (–ve)	21 October – 20 November
9	Sagittarius	Dhanu	3 (+ve)	21 November – 20 December
10	Capricorn	Makara	8 (+ve)	21 December – 20 January
11	Aquarius	Kumbha	8 (–ve)	21 January – 19 February
12	Pisces	Meena	3 (–ve)	19 February – 20 March

People born in the same month or with a common secondary number share several common qualities.

Numbers and Names

A person is always known by his name rather than by any of his numbers. Hence the name number plays a key role in one's professional and social life as well as marriage. The name number has a distinct potency of its own and hence plays a major role in a person's life and career. Since the birth number cannot be altered, the name by which a person becomes popularly known should be carefully chosen so that the name number vibrates harmoniously with his birth and other numbers. In case of people whose birth number is 4 or 8, it is better to choose a name which yields a 1, 3 or 6.

There are several systems – Chaldean, Hebrew (Kabala), Hindu, Chinese, etc – which are used to interpret the alphabet. In the Chaldean-Hebrew – Kabala system, a number is assigned to each of the 22 Hebrew alphabets. In my view, the Chaldean system advocated by Cheiro, is the best. As the English language has 26 letters, Cheiro assigned more than one letter to each number as shown below: In this system no letter has been assigned the number 9 as it represented the 9-letter name of God in Hebrew.

Table A6.4 Association of Numbers and the English Alphabet (Chaldean System)

1	**2**	**3**	**4**	**5**	**6**	**7**	**8**	**9**
A	B	C	D	E	-	-	F	-
-	-	G	-	H	-	-	-	-
I	-	-	-	-	-	-	-	-
J	K	L	M	N	-	O	P	-
Q	R	S	T	-	U	-	-	-
-	-	-	-	-	V	-	-	-
Y	-	-	-	X	W	Z	-	-

The meaning of a name can be interpreted by adding together numbers that correspond to each letter in that name. The compound number (also known as the name number) so obtained will indicate and interpret the peculiar characteristics and often the destiny of the person having that name.

While generating and interpreting the name number, *the most commonly used name of the person* is taken into consideration. For ex. if a person's name is 'K. Ramakrishna Srinivasan' and he is known only by the name 'Ramakrishna' then only 'Ramakrishna' should be taken for generating the name number.

Let us generate a compound number for the name: 'Ramakrishna':

Table A6.5 Generation of Name Number

R	**A**	**M**	**A**	**K**	**R**	**I**	**S**	**H**	**N**	**A**	**Total**
2	1	4	1	2	2	1	3	5	5	1	27

As can be seen, the numbers when added together yield the compound number 27. This number symbolizes the 'Sceptre' and is considered a good number, promising authority, power and command. Hence this person will lead a successful life with a good career.

It is always lucky for a person to have complete harmony between his/her birth and name numbers. The vibrations of both would then be harmonious and that would promise greater success. For instance, if the birth number is 1 and the name number yields a 19 (which is a part of Number 1 series i.e., 1, 10, 19, 28), then we say that the birth and name numbers are in harmony. Hence, the person is indeed fortunate and has a greater promise of success.

Suppose a person's birth number is 2 and his name number makes a 17 (which is an 8), then both the numbers would not be in vibration with each other. In fact the birth and name numbers clash with each other. In this case, there would always be a mix-up in his affairs apart from encountering delays and failures on the personal and professional fronts. It would be a daunting task to decide which number to use as his most important number and on which date he has to undertake his most important work. Since he cannot alter his birth number, the alternative is to alter her/his name number suitably, to get a name number which will be in harmony with the birth number. She/he can do so by adding or dropping some letters from his/her name.

Suppose a person's birth number is 6 and his name is 'RAMARAO' The name yields the compound number 18 (which in itself is not a good number) and does not vibrate favourably with 6. Hence it would be advisable for the person to change his name to 'SRI RAMARAO' which yields the favourable name number 24 (which is also a 6).

Harmony, Attraction and Repulsion between Numbers According to Numerology

Just like people, numbers also exhibit certain individuality and characteristics. They exhibit forces of vibration, attraction and repulsion between themselves. These may be described as of the following types:

(a) Two numbers vibrating with each other representing complete harmony between them.
(b) Two numbers attracting each other representing a good amount of friendship between them.
(c) Two numbers repulsing each other representing total disagreement between them.
(d) Two numbers behaving passively with each other representing no outstanding influence between them.
(e) Two numbers vibrating *with* or attracting *each other*, but *negatively*, representing that even though the numbers vibrate or get attracted, the result is always an unhappy one for those who use these numbers together.

The table given below gives us an idea of how numbers behave in relation to one another:

Table A6.6 Relationship between Numbers

Number	Vibrates with	Attracts	Repulses	Passive
1	9	4*, 8*	6, 7	2, 3, 5
2	8*	7, 9*	5	1, 3, 4*, 6
3	7	5, 6, 9	4, 8	1, 2
4	6*	1* 8*	3, 5, 9	2*, 7
5	5	3, 9	2, 4	1, 6, 7, 8
6	4*	3, 9	1, 8	2, 5, 7
7	3	2, 6	1, 9	4, 5, 8
8	2*	1*, 4*	3, 6	5, 7, 9*
9	1	2*, 3, 6	7	4*, 5, 8*

* *The attractions/vibrations indicated for these numbers are negative in nature and may not be lucky for the individuals coming under these particular combinations. However, these attractions will be beneficial to numbers 4 and 8, and between 4 and 8, the number 8 is the beneficiary.*

The above relationships between numbers are important when considering long term friendships/partnerships/unions/marriages between people having respective birth numbers.

ASTROLOGICAL SIGNIFICANCE OF PLANETS

The Sun

The Sun is the ruling planet of Number 1 and also those people whose birth dates fall on 1, 10, 19, and 28 in any month. The sun is also ruler of those people having secondary number 1 – those born under the zodiacal sign of Leo (21 July – 20 August). The number 1 people are usually considered authoritative, strong, intelligent, extroverts and helpful to their friends. Those people who are born on nineteenth of any month are considered most fortunate.

All religions and cultures originally gave the prime of place to the Sun in their pantheon of Gods. Since the Sun is the source of heat and light, all living beings depend on the Sun for the life force. It is considered as the source of consciousness also. Hence the Sun influences the intellect. According to Hindu mythology, the Sun God is a warrior king, who rides on a chariot with a single wheel and drawn by seven horses. The Sun passes through one of the twelve signs of the zodiac each month.

According to Hindu scriptures, the Sun is the dwelling place of our ancestors and also the first of eight *vasus.* Associated with Lord Vishnu, the Sun is characterized as having a stable, selfless, strong, royal and authoritative nature. He is the Lord of the East. The Moon, Mars and Jupiter are his friends. Saturn, Venus, Rahu and Ketu are considered his enemies. Mercury has a neutral relationship with the sun.

The Moon

The Moon is the ruling planet of people with 'Birth Number 2' (those people born on 2, 11, 20 and 29 in any month), or 'Secondary Number 2' – those born in the zodiacal sign of Cancer (21 June – 20 July). The irregular movement of the Moon gives the number 2 people a fluctuating nature. The Moon also plays a major role on their emotional life too. The number 2 people are peaceful, sensual, artistic and love privacy.

The Moon reflects the light of the Sun through the special gem present on its surface known as the moonstone (Chandra shile). This light is said to contain creative energy which is magnetic and positive. This light also has a special medicinal effect on plants, human beings and animals. The word 'Soma' (which means nectar) is another name of the Moon. The Sun, Mars and Jupiter are its friends where as Mercury, Venus, Saturn, Rahu and Ketu are considered its enemies.

From the dawn of history, the Moon has played an important part in the life of human beings. The phases of the Moon has served as 'time measures' and as the calendar of Nature. It is a proven fact that at the full moon – nature, animals as well as humans, are much more active than during any other period. The ancients used to take up all activities involving new ventures, expansion and growth (like planting, travel, conception, investment, etc.) during the period of waxing of the moon – Shukla paksha. Similarly, they used to take up negative activities (like reaping of crops, extermination of pests, tantric acts, etc) during the period of waning of the moon – Krishna Paksha.

Jupiter

Jupiter is the ruling planet of people with 'Birth Number' 3 (those born on 3, 12, 21 and 30 in any month) or secondary number 3 – those born in the zodiacal signs of Sagittarius (Dhanu: 21 November – 20 December) and Pisces (Meena: 19 February – 20 March). The number 3 people are bold, courageous, learned, ambitious, disciplined and hardworking.

Jupiter is the largest planet in the Solar System. It is known by the name of 'Guru' (teacher) in Hindu mythology. Hence Jupiter helps expansion of consciousness and knowledge. He is also known as *vachaspati* (Lord of speech). Jupiter is considered important for progeny, education and marriage. He is friendly towards Sun, Moon and Mars. He feels enmity with Venus and Mercury. He is neutral towards Saturn.

Mercury

Mercury is the ruler of number 5 people – those with birth number 5 (those born on 5, 14, and 23 in any month) or secondary number 5 – those born in the zodiacal signs of Gemini (Mithuna: 21 May – 20

June) and Virgo (Kanya: 21 August – 20 September). Those born on twenty third of any month are considered very fortunate.

Mercury is the smallest planet in our Solar system and associated with a dual nature. It gives a rational, analytical and materialistic attitude to people. Number 5 people are associated with quick response, changeable character and restlessness. They also take interest in the study of the occult sciences. They remain youthful and attractive into their old age.

Mercury is friendly to Sun, Venus, Rahu and Ketu. He is neutral to Saturn, Mars and Jupiter. He feels enmity towards the Moon.

Venus

Commonly known as the morning star, Venus governs the adolescent stage of human life and is associated with passion and love. Venus is the ruler of number 6 people – those with Birth Number 6 (those born on 6, 15 and 24 in any month) or secondary number 6 – those born in the zodiacal signs of Taurus (Vrishabha: 20 April – 20 May) and Libra (Tula: 21 September – 20 October). The number 6 people are commonly known to be active, artistic, sensuous and passionate. Though number 6 is considered a weak number, those born on 24th of any month are considered as very fortunate.

In Hindu mythology, Venus is associated with two different images – one is a fair complexioned youth, who is an embodiment of love and sensuality. The other image is that of a bearded and aged 'teacher of asuras' (known popularly as Shukracharya). Venus is friendly towards Mercury and Saturn. He feels enmity towards Sun and Moon. He is neutral towards Jupiter and Mars.

Saturn

Saturn is the ruler of number 8 people – those with birth number 8 (those born on 8, 17 and 26 in any month) or secondary number 8 – those born in the zodiacal signs of Capricorn (Makara: 21 December – 20 January) and Aquarius (Kumbha: 21 January – 20 February). Saturn rules over old age. Hence number 8 people always appear older (than their chronological ages) and behave like old men.

Known in Sanskrit as 'Shanaishchara', it is the farthest of the seven planets, and takes approximately 30 years to complete one revolution round the Sun. Saturn is a planet of darkness and rules over the darker side of human nature. Since it takes 2 ½ years to transit a sidereal zodiacal sign, its effects are felt for a longer duration than any other planet.

Saturn is the most malefic of all planets. When Saturn is well positioned in a natal chart, it gives wisdom, sincerity, love of justice, long life and authority. When Saturn is badly aspected in a natal chart, it brings obstruction, delay, humiliation, enmity, premature ageing, and gives them suicidal tendencies.

Mercury, Venus, Rahu and Kethu are friends of Saturn. It has enmity with the Sun, Moon and Mars. Its relationship with Jupiter is neutral in nature.

Mars

Mars considered as a malefic planet, is the ruler of number 9 people – people whose birth number is 9 (those born on 9, 18 and 27 in any month) or secondary number 9 – those born in the zodiacal signs of Aries (Mesha: 21 March – 19 April) and Scorpio (Vrishchika: 21 October – 20 November).

In all cultures, Mars is associated with war and destruction. Mars is the Commander-in-Chief, to the assembly of Gods. Hence Mars signifies courage, bravery and self-confidence. Because of the malefic effect of Mars, the Number 9 people are usually restless, egoistic, short-tempered, impulsive, insensitive, quarrelsome, lovers of destructive weapons, cruel and often violent. Mars is friendly with Sun, Moon and Jupiter, where as it has enmity towards only Mercury. Saturn, Venus, Rahu and Ketu are neutral to it.

Rahu and Ketu

These are the two nodes of the Moon, which reflect the bipolar nature of man. These two (placed 180 degrees apart) are considered as half-planets in Hindu astrology, do not exist as material entities like the other seven planets. They are the points at which the path of the Moon, intersects with the path of the other planets. In ancient times, astrologers used to determine the exact dates and timings of Solar and Lunar eclipses, with the help of these nodes and hence they were considered important and gradually they were given the status of half-planets. Rahu is known as the dragon's head and Ketu is known as the dragon's tail. They have retrograde motions.

Rahu, the north node of the Moon, is the ruling planet of number 4 people – people whose birth number is number 4 (those born on 4, 13, 22, and 31 in any month). Rahu also rules the zodiacal sign of Virgo, which is also ruled by Mercury. Number 4 people are energetic, artistic, intelligent, bold but secretive. Number 4 people also help the downtrodden and are always ready to challenge the high and the mighty. Rahu, is a malefic planet and acts as an active and disruptive force, which works mainly at the mental level. It makes people lethargic, pleasure seeking, confused, and ignorant. It deliberately forces people to perform bad deeds. Venus and Saturn are his friends. He is neutral towards Mercury and Jupiter. He has enmity towards Sun, Moon and Mars.

Ketu, the south node of the Moon, is the ruling planet of number 7 people – people whose birth number is 7 (those born on 7, 16, and 25 in any month). Since number 7 is considered a spiritual number, many number 7 people try to forego worldly pleasures and work towards spiritual enlightenment. Number 7 people are also naturally attracted towards the study of predictive sciences. Some also acquire the power of healing those possessed by evil spirits.

In Hindu mythology, Ketu – the dragon's tail, is depicted as a headless torso with the body of a fish. Ketu though considered less malefic, is also known as 'Moksha-karak' (liberation from worldly bondage/cycle of life and death). In its favourable aspect, it bestows non-attachment towards worldly desires as also gives spiritual tendencies. It also gives intuition, wisdom and power of discrimination. When it is not in astrologically favourable position, it can make people highly sensitive, emotional and lose power of discrimination.

Ketu is friendly with Mercury, Venus, Rahu and Saturn. It has a neutral relationship with Jupiter and has enmity with Sun, Moon and Mars.

For further details please refer to my book Browse Your Future through Numerology.

Annexure 7

Pancha Tantra

The 'Pancha tantra' stories – teaching the five abilities of intelligent living – in the form of moral parables, are another significant contribution of Indians to the mankind. The aim of these Pancha tantra tales is to convey knowledge and wisdom to the ordinary people through the fascinating medium of fables, in which a large majority of actors are animals.

The central theme of Pancha tantra is the harmonious development of the powers of man – a life in which security, prosperity, resolute action, friendship, and good learning are so combined so as to bring eternal joy.

The original collection of Pancha tantra fables in Sanskrit contained 84 (this number varies from version to version) wise and witty stories, spread over five books. These five books are called:

1. *The Loss of Friends,*
2. *The Winning of Friends,*
3. *Crows and Owls,*
4. *Loss of Gains,*
5. *Ill – considered Action.*

These are the most widely known and best collection of charming stories in the world and are current in India for the past several thousand years. From North India, these stories travelled through Persia, Arabia, Syria and to all most all countries of the then civilized world. From South India these stories travelled to the South-east Asia, Japan and beyond. These stories also inspired many similar stories in several languages.

The only comparison to the Pancha tantra tales is perhaps the 'Jataka Tales' of Gautama Buddha, which too travelled from India to other countries along with Buddhism.

The Pancha tantra stories have been told and retold (probably with hundreds of changes in form, content, structure, and setting) among various peoples of the world and have fascinated generations of young minds beyond one's imagination.

These stories were translated into Persian and Syrian languages for the first time in the sixth century and by fifteenth century some version of these tales became available in almost all modern languages of the world. Over the centuries, these stories became so popular that some of the earliest books ever printed in English, German and other European languages contained some versions of these stories.

Annexure 8

How Many Fought the Mahabharata War?

Mahabharata describes the formation of one akshohini (unit of an army as part of Chaturanga - Bala):

1. 1 Patti = 1 Chariot, 1 Elephant, 5 Foot soldiers and 3 Horses;
2. 3 Pattis = 1 Senamukha;
3. 3 Senamukhas = 1 Gulma;
4. 3 Gulmas = 1 Gana;
5. 3 Ganas = 1 Vahini;
6. 3 Vahinis = 1 Prutana;
7. 3 Prutanas = 1 Chamu;
8. 3 Chamus = 1 Anikini;
9. 10 Anikinis = 1 Akshohini.

According to this, 1 akshohini sainya contains 21,870 chariots, 21,870 Elephants, 1,09,350 foot soldiers, and 65,610 horses. The 18 akshohinis who fought the Mahabharata war in Kurukshetra contained a total of:

1. 3,93,660 chariots,
2. 19,68,300 foot soldiers,
3. 3,93,660 elephants and
4. 11,80,980 horses.

Taking in to account, the number of people who fought using chariots, on elephants and on horseback, the total number of people (as well as animals) who fought the Mahabharata war runs into millions. Could the war field in Kurukshetra really accommodate this huge army of several millions? We have only to imagine the number of (additional millions of) people who serviced this huge army.

Considering the population of the country at that time (about 3,500 years ago), these figures seem to be rather too unrealistic.

Or if we consider that poetic freedom has given us this huge figure and if we drop the last two digits from the numbers who fought the Mahabharata war, I think we are closer to a realistic figure:

1. 3,936 Chariots,
2. 19,683 foot soldiers,
3. 3,936 elephants and
4. 11,809 horses.

These figures seem to be reasonable enough and we can safely approximate the number of people who fought the Mahabharata war at a little less than a lakh which seems to be reasonable enough.

We can compare these figures with the strength of the Magadha army (a thousand years later) which was estimated by the Greek writers in the fourth Century BCE as 20,000 cavalry, 2,00,000 infantry, 2,000 chariots and 3000 elephants. These estimates led to the Greek soldiers to refuse to campaign further and Alexander had to turn back. Historians consider even these figures to be exaggerated.

Annexure 9

Information Relating to Vedas

	RIG VEDA	KRISHNA YAJURVEDA	SHUKLA YAJURVEDA	SAMA VEDA	ATHARVA VEDA
Revelation	Agni	Vayu	Surya	Surya	Angirasa
Upa Veda	Artha Veda	Dhanur Veda	————	Gandharva	Ayurveda
Samhitas	Shakala- Bhasala (10 Mandalas)	Katha Maitrayini	Kanva Madhyandina	Archika Uttara- Archika	(20 Kandas)
Brahmanas	Aitareya Kaushitaki	Taitariya Brahmanaka	Shathapatha, Kanva/ Madhyandina	Chandogya Arsheya (Total 13)	----------
Aranyakas	Aitareya Sankhyayana	Taitariya Aranyaka	Brhadaran- yaka Aranyaka	Chandogya- Aranyaka	----------
Kalpa Sutras	Deva Daivata	Manusha	--------------	Paitya	-----------
Shrauta Sutras	Aswalayana Sankyhayana	Apastamba Bhodayana Hiranya kesi Katha Laugakshi	Bharadwaja Vaikhanasa Vadhula Manava Vasaha Paskara	Anupada Samatantra Panchavi Anusutra Kshudra- Sutra (Total 10)	Vaitana Nakshatra Angirasa Shanti
Grihya Sutras	Aswalayana Sankyhayana	Manava Laugakshi	Katyayana Salva	Badira Arsheya Mashika Gautama	Kaushika
Dharma Sutras	Vasista	------	------	Gautama	------
Veda Mantras	10,552 (1028 Suktas in 10 Mandalas)	1,10,296 (4 Kandas)	1,975 (40 Adhyaya)	Archika (585) Uttara- Archika (964)	5038 Sutras in 731 Suktas

Upanishads	10	32	19	16	31
Important Upanishads	Aitareya Kaushitaki, Tripura Nada-bindu Prabhoda Mudgala	Taitariya Katha Swhetaash-watara Shuka Aksha Narayana	Ishavasya Brhadaran-yaka Yagnavalka Katyayani Hamsa Subala	Kena Chandogya Maitrayana Jabala Vaṣudeva Sanyasa	Prashna Manduka Mandukya Atma Maha-na-rayana
Upanishad Maha Vakya	'Prajnanam Brahma'	'Aham Brah-masmi'	'Aham Brah-masmi'	'Tatvamasi'	'Ayamatma-Brahma'

Source: Extracted from Sadbodha Chandrike *(Vol. 103–11).*

Epilogue

LET US HAVE OUR OWN PHILOSOPHY!

A Pilgrimage through Life...

Hinduism is like a vast ocean. Through this book, we have gone through a religious pilgrimage, as well as a philosophical journey...

A journey which has taken us on a visit to various important points of pilgrimage – Concepts which are central to Hinduism... Dharma, Artha, Kama, Moksha... Karma... Punarjanma, ...

An ocean of religious literature – the holy scriptures – the Vedas, the Upanishads, the Epics – Ramayana and Mahabharata, the Brahma sutras, ... the Puranas...

And the various philosophies which are as mighty as the Indian rivers – the Shad-Darshanas... the Vedanta – Advaita, Visisthadvaita, Dvaita, Bheda-abheda, Shaiva, Veerashaiva, Shaakta,... the various gods – Brahma, Vishnu, Shiva, Devi – the Mother Goddess, Ganesha, Hanuman, Skanda...

And finally the sacred paths preached by Sri Krishna in the Bhagavad Gita – Karma Yoga, Bhakti Yoga and Jnana Yoga, ...

This list is almost endless...

We have visited many places... We have waded through many rivers... We are now at the very end of this pilgrimage. This is a journey through life, rediscovering ourselves... rediscovering our beliefs and values and our very own religion...

It is quite possible that many of us might have got a sense of getting lost in this ocean of Hinduism.

However this Hindu Sanatana Dharma is quite a unique religion. There is never a cause for any doubt. Within the broad spectrum of Hindu religion, every one of us is free to follow a simple philosophy of our very own, worship a god – *whom we may like* and follow a path of Swa-Dharma – *which we may create.*

Our Very Own Philosophy

Just like the learned Acharyas, who propounded their own schools of philosophy, Hindu religion basically gives us a right to propound our very own brand of philosophy and the right to believe and worship a God of our choice. This is not possible in any other religion (where it would be considered as sacrilegious).

Freedom of –
Thought, philosophy, faith as well as worship – are in fact, the very essence, greatness and strength of the Hindu religion.

Readers are invited to go through a simple philosophy enunciated below. They are at complete liberty to add, remove and modify and create their own brand of Hindu religion and philosophy.

OUR OWN RELIGION... OUR OWN PHILOSOPHY!

Ethics

1. *Let us live a simple, happy, moral and contended life, free from prejudices.*
2. *Let us respect the opinion of others, as we wish others to respect our opinion.*
3. *Let us be truthful, honest and sincere in our intentions and actions.*
4. *Let us develop wisdom and the capacity to discriminate between right and wrong.*
5. *Let us have our own rules of Dharma. But it should not come into conflict with Dharma followed by those around us.*

6. *We are going to enjoy the fruits of our actions (good deeds/bad deeds resulting either in 'Punya or Paapa') in this life itself, as we do not know whether there is another life after death.*
7. *Even if we do have another life, the good deeds done in this life, will certainly help us to lead a good life in our next life also.*
8. *Hence let us behave properly and live in all humility.*
9. *Let us help others as much as possible, without expecting any returns. If we cannot help a person, at least let us not harass or harm him at any cost.*

Belief in the Existence of God

All of us have to recognize a unitary cosmic force, which acts as an underlying order in Nature. This Force is responsible for our very existence and the existence of this world. Let us respect this force as Brahman, the Supreme Being, which controls this universe. To all of us He is God, who is worshipped by different names in different religions.

Let us worship this God, whose divine grace is necessary for us to lead happy lives.

Let us have our own philosophical basis, because we may get doubts at some point of time in our life, and then we will need to find answers. Many consider Gita as the best guide in this respect. We may choose any other scripture also to guide us.

Religion and Form of Worship

1. *Our ultimate goal in Life is 'Realization of God'.*
2. *Let us believe that all deities are manifestations of this same god.*
3. *Hence let us choose a god (Ista Devata) whom we like and worship him with all devotion. When we reach a particular stage, we will see our 'Ista Devata' in every god.*
4. *Let us not showcase our 'worship of god'. Others need not even know whether we are religious or not.*
5. *Let us choose a mantra or a method of worship, in which we can conveniently worship god.*
6. *As Ramanuja says, let us show total sharanagati to our god.*

7. *At the same time, we should not condemn other religions/ philosophies/gods worshipped by others.*
8. *As Ramakrishna Paramahamsa states: 'All religions are valid and true and lead to the same ultimate goal of realization of God.*

Bibliography

Books

1. Arthur W. Ryder – *Panchatantra*
2. Arvind Sharma – *Classical Hindu Thought*
3. Aurobindo – *Life divine*
4. Bapat P.V. – *2500 years of Buddhism*
5. Basham A.L. – *The Wonder That was India*,
6. Bose A.C. – *The Call of the Vedas*
7. Dasgupta (Dr.) – *A History of Indian Philosophy*
8. Harish Johari – *Numerology – A Key to Human Behavior*,
9. Hanumanta Rao G. – *A Set of 28 books on Indian Philosophy (Kannada)*
10. Hiriyanna – *Essentials of Indian Philosophy*
11. Jagannatha Rao D. – *Browse Your Future through Numerology*,
12. Jaini J.L. – *Outlines of Jainism*,
13. Justice M. Rama Jois – *Peep into Eternal Values of Manusmriti*,
14. Justice M. Rama Jois – *Dharma*,
15. Kane P.V. – *History of Dharmasastra*
16. Mahadevan T.M.P. – *Outlines of Hinduism*,
17. Nandimath S.C. – *A Hand Book of Veerashaivism* (1942)
18. Nilakanta Shastri K.A. – *A History of South India*
19. Padmanabhachar C.M. – *Life and Teachings of Sri. Madhvacharya*
20. Radhakrishnan (Dr.) – *The Hindu View of Life*,
21. Radhakrishnan (Dr.) – *Indian Philosophy* (Volumes I and II)

22. Rig Veda Samhita – *Manmath Nath Dutta*
23. Romila Thapar – *History of Early India* (2002),
24. Sharma D.S. – *Hinduism through the Ages*
25. Sharma B.N.K – *Madhwa's Teachings*,
26. Shivapada Sundaram – *The Shaiva School of Hinduism*
27. Shankaranarayana Bhat A.K. – *Hindu Dharmada Parichaya* (Kannada)
28. Swami Nikhilananda – *Atma Bodha of Sri Shankaracharya*
29. Swami Nirvedananda – *Hinduism at a Glance*,
30. Swami Shivananda – *Sadhana*,
31. Swami Tattvananda – *The Quintessence of Vedanta of Sri Shankaracharya*
32. Swami Vivekanada – *Complete Works*,
33. Tilak – *Gita Rahsya*
34. Yamunacharya (Prof.) – *Ramanuja's Teachings*,
35. Warder A.K. – *A Course in Indian Philosophy.*

Puranas/Shastras/Scriptures

1. Bhagavata Purana
2. Garuda Purana
3. Kalika Purana
4. Devi Bhagavata
5. Markandeya Purana
6. Brahmanda Purana
7. Shiva Purana
8. Tantra Raja
9. Tantra Chudamani
10. Dattatreya Samhita
11. Parashurama-kalpa-sutra
12. Yagnavalka Smriti
13. *Ramayana*
14. *Mahabharata*
15. *Bhagavad Gita*
16. Mudgala Purana

17. Sharada Tilak
18. Vishnu Yamala Tantra
19. Vamakeswara Tantra
20. Padma Purana
21. Skanda Purana
22. Chandogya Upanishad
23. Ishopanishad
24. Swetaaswatara Upanishad
25. Taittiriya Upanishad
26. Brhadaranyaka Upanishad
27. Kathopanishad
28. Pancha-Brahma Upanishad
29. Kautilya's Artha Shastra
30. Susruta Samhita
31. Narada Bhakti sutra
32. Patanjali – Yoga Sutra

List of Websites: www

1. wikipedia.org
2. Internet Encyclopedia of Philosophy (iep.utm.edu)
3. shivallibrahmins.com
4. saivaworld.org
5. bhagavad-gita.org
6. asitis.com
7. dishq.org
8. hinduwebsite.com
9. hindunet.org
10. liveindia.com
11. bu.edu
12. om.guru
13. ramakrishna.org
14. indianetzone.com
15. jainism.org
16. veerashaiva.inf

17. classicalkannada.org
18. exoticindiaart.com
19. hinduism.about.com
20. sikhs.org
21. allaboutsikhs.com